LOSING MY
RELIGION

LOSING MY RELIGION

HOW I LOST MY FAITH REPORTING

ON RELIGION IN AMERICA—AND

FOUND UNEXPECTED PEACE

WILLIAM LOBDELL

COLLINS
An Imprint of HarperCollins Publishers

HarperCollins books may be purchased for educational, business, or sales promotional use. For information, please write: Special Markets Department, Harper-Collins Publishers, 10 East 53rd Street, New York, NY 10022.

Designed by Mary Austin Speaker

Library of Congress Cataloging-in-Publication Data is available upon request.

ISBN 978-0-06-162681-4

09 10 11 12 13   OV/RRD   10 9 8 7 6 5 4 3 2

To my wife, Greer, and my four boys, Taylor, Tristan, Matthew and Oliver
and
To those wounded by the church

ACKNOWLEDGMENTS

WHERE TO START is easy. I'm deeply grateful for my wife, Greer, who has hung with me—in good times and in bad—for more than 20 years, and my four wonderful boys: Taylor, Tristan, Matthew and Oliver.

I owe a special debt to Hugh Hewitt, who never stopped being my best friend even after our spiritual paths diverged. My little brother Jim, his wife, Colleen, and my old friend Will Swaim were especially supportive of this book and offered quick and invaluable feedback. And thanks to my parents, Robert and Nancy Lobdell, who have always been the biggest fans of my career.

Several of my colleagues at the *Los Angeles Times* deserve special praise, especially Roger Smith, who so expertly edited the article that provided the seed for this book, and Christopher Goffard, Dana Parsons, Steve Marble and Stuart Pfeifer, who provided spot-on critiques and unwavering support.

Tricia Davey, my agent and former Mater Dei High School homecoming queen, was an enthusiastic backer of this book from the start, giving me a major confidence boost. Bruce Nichols, my editor at HarperCollins, used gentle suggestions, encouraging words and an amazing editing touch to keep my story heading in a straight line.

Thanks to Julia Sweeney and David Price for generously allowing me to excerpt their works.

I owe my sanity to Judith Van Dixhorn, a woman of deep insight and charity, and Howard Stern, who makes me laugh each day and gives me the ability to be honest about myself. Also helping clear my mind were Dani and Roda, my Spin instructors, who provided freakishly hard (and fun) workouts, and my triathlete friends in the International Tri-Blogger Alliance.

A special thanks to my one and only journalism teacher, Joseph N. Bell, the first person to tell that I could be a professional journalist. And to college classmates W. Tom Davey and Greg Hardesty, who showed me how thrilling reporting can be—even at a school newspaper.

Finally, I am most thankful to those people who have appeared in my stories over the years, giving me their time and sharing their heart, especially the survivors of clergy sexual abuse. You are always in my thoughts. I thank you for telling your stories, and I admire how you strive each day to reclaim your life.

"If you would be a real seeker after truth, it is necessary that at least once in your life you doubt, as far as possible, all things."

RENÉ DESCARTES

CONTENTS

ONE

"You Need God"

> "For I know the plans I have for you," declares the Lord,
> "plans to prosper you and not to harm you, plans to give
> you hope and a future."
>
> — JEREMIAH 29:11

BY AGE 27, I had screwed up my life. I had married my volatile high school sweetheart five years earlier, mostly because it seemed easier than breaking up. When I left her, I didn't follow through with the divorce. Dealing with her in court would be messy, so I just bailed. In the meantime, I happily jumped into an adolescence delayed by my fidelity to the first girl I'd ever loved. Before long, I managed to get a girlfriend pregnant. I loved my newfound bachelorhood, and I was petrified by the prospect of another marriage and my first child (leaving aside the fact that my divorce to my first wife couldn't be finalized for at least six months).

I ran away as fast as I could, concluding that I had only a few months left in the wild before the baby arrived and a lifetime of responsibility would kick in. I needed to pack in as much living as I could. I drank away many nights. I caroused with friends. And I'm forever shamed to admit that I cheated on my pregnant girlfriend.

Other parts of my life weren't much better. My journalism career had stalled at a local minor-league magazine, where I worked long hours for low pay covering "business lifestyles" about which I couldn't have cared less. My digestive system waged daily war on me. I developed acne that I had been spared as a teenager. When I combed my hair each morning at the bathroom mirror, I couldn't look myself in the eye. When I turned 28, I could barely admit it was my birthday. I couldn't stand the person I had become. I found no reason to celebrate my life.

But then our son, Taylor, was born. I found myself staying up deep into most nights, holding my child tightly, staring at his innocent face, letting his chubby fingers wrap around mine and knowing it was time for me to grow up if this kid was going to have a fair chance at life.

A month after Taylor arrived, I married Greer in a Las Vegas wedding at a small chapel on the Strip presided over by a drunken pastor and his dutiful wife. They were our only witnesses. We spent the first part of our wedding night watching a comeback concert by Tony Orlando and Dawn. I gave our marriage about as much chance as the over-the-hill singing trio performing in that half-empty casino concert hall. Though she would not say it, I knew Greer had grave doubts about me, too, but she wanted her son to have an in-the-home father—something missing from her childhood—and was generous or desperate enough to give me a chance.

Soon after the wedding, on an especially low day, I had lunch with a good friend named Will Swaim. A fellow journalist of my vintage, Will is rail-thin, with a handsome face whose broad features seem to be made from stone. He has a kinetic energy that brings to mind someone who drinks way too much coffee. He is also one of the smartest and most searching people I know. Not yet 30, his career ambitions had swung wildly from Roman Catholic priest (he decided not to go into the seminary) to punk rock star (he was the lead singer for a group named the Barking Spiders) to aspiring guerrilla fighter (an unexpectedly pregnant wife caused him to give up his one-way plane ticket to Mexico City, the first leg of a journey that would have taken him to Nicaragua to fight with the Sandinistas) to peace activist (he worked for three years to ban nuclear weapons). He finally settled into journalism, where he's made a national reputation for himself as an alternative weekly editor and publisher.

Seated at a booth in an upscale coffee shop under the flight path of the John Wayne Airport in Orange County, California, he started a conversation in the usual way.

"How's it going, Billy?"

I hadn't told anyone the extent of my troubles. From the outside, my life didn't look *that* bad. I was married to an intelligent and gorgeous woman, had a healthy baby boy and was president of a local media company. But I was dying inside. And Will was too good of a friend. I couldn't lie to him by saying I was fine. Taking a deep breath, I decided, for once, to tell the truth. I described, with deep shame, every last humiliating detail of my life. It wasn't cathartic for me—it just filled me with more self-loathing.

Will's reaction was unexpected. He didn't seem fazed by any of it. I couldn't detect any judgment or disapproval. His response was matter-of-fact. He first asked if I was suicidal. I wasn't, though I conceded that I did believe everyone in my life would be better off if I were dead. Then, with the certainty of someone describing the law of gravity, he concluded, "You need God. That's what's missing in your life."

God? I hadn't given Him much thought since I stopped going to church the first chance I could, at age 17.

"Everyone has a God-shaped hole in their soul," he continued. "We all try to fill it with something—drugs, alcohol, work, sex—until we stumble upon God. He's the only thing that fills that hole. I was a lot like you until I surrendered my life to God. Why not try it? It can't hurt. Look at where you are with you in control. Get yourself to church, Billy."

It sounded right. More importantly, it felt like a way out. If Will had said in the same confident tone, "You need crack cocaine. That's what missing in your life," it probably would have sounded good, too. I was desperate enough to try anything that would get rid of the pain that had enveloped me like quicksand.

"I'll go to church this Sunday," I said numbly. "Just tell me where."

TWO

Born Again

... [I]f you confess with your mouth, "Jesus is Lord," and
believe in your heart that God raised him from the dead,
you will be saved. For it is with your heart that you believe
and are justified, and it is with your mouth that you confess
and are saved.

— ROMANS 10:9–10

AS A KID, our family—my mom, dad, sister, two brothers
and myself—piled in the station wagon and drove to downtown
Long Beach, California, to attend services at St. Luke's Episcopal
Church. For my parents, going to church was like brushing their
teeth. It was something they just did. For me, it felt more like
pulling teeth. The service—which could stretch to nearly an hour-
and-a-half—seemed more like a test of patience and endurance
than anything else. It certainly wasn't a sacred moment of contact
with the creator of the universe. We sat through ancient hymns
with stilted lyrics ("Lamp of our feet, whereby we trace our path"),
a long list of prayers and readings and a liturgy that changed only

slightly throughout the year. The rector, Roy Young, was a sensitive soul with a gift for storytelling, so I often enjoyed his sermons. But that was it.

My younger brother Jim and I had a routine at the end of each service. When Father Young turned to the congregation and said, "Go in peace to love and serve the Lord," we'd respond with the people, "Thanks be to God." But then we'd turn to each other and whisper, " . . . that church is over!"

I watched with envy as my big sister and then older brother stopped going to church about the time they graduated from high school. I impatiently waited my turn, which never seemed to come. I often passed my time inside the cold church, trapped between the vaulted ceiling and stone floor, trying to quiet some nagging doubts about Christianity. As a kid, I didn't believe faith could be questioned, so I kept these heretical thoughts to myself. But my young mind remained busy working to solve my faith's seeming contradictions.

For instance, I wondered how the Holy Trinity was even possible—how could the Father, Son and Holy Spirit be just one God? I also second-guessed God's sacrifice of His son as the best way to square things with His perpetually sinful children. As a boy, I was fascinated with the Aztecs, and when it was mentioned in church that the Lord sent Jesus to die on a cross for our sins, I often thought of an Aztec chief pulling out the still-beating heart of a young beauty to please the gods. If the Lord was the Lord, there had to be a less primitive way to get us back on the path to salvation.

Some Sundays, I'd look over the congregation and find it odd that the parishioners were mostly white and middle to upper class, when the church was in one of Southern California's toughest neighborhoods. They didn't match who Jesus's followers were in the Gospels. Where were the poor, the sick and the hungry? To find them, all parishioners had to do was step off church property. But they were nowhere to be seen inside the church. I found it curious that the local bishop received a grand reception fit for a king whenever he visited our church. Jesus washed the feet of his disciples and told his followers that the first shall be the last, but the bishop was treated literally like royalty. It seemed backward.

My doubts about faith were often amplified after church by the sounds of my father yelling at us, sometimes before we even pulled out of the parking lot. We had just spent more than an hour trying to get closer to God, praying for help and guidance, singing His praises, listening to His words in Scripture and being told to humble ourselves and love our neighbors—and even our enemies—as ourselves. Though church bored me, I couldn't help but absorb some sense of holiness during the services and often felt spiritually uplifted by the time I walked out those huge wooden doors. This same feeling apparently escaped my father. My dad's tirades after church struck me as a blow against Christianity. How could we so easily discard His teachings even before we made it home?

Like my sister and brother before, I stopped going to church at age 17. My last church service felt like the final day of school. To have Sunday mornings free—to sleep in, to watch NFL games, to go surfing—was a wonderful luxury that I had been denied. Now I was free. I never thought of going back—or rather I considered the possibility with a deep sense of dread. Because by this time, I had fused together the image of God and my father. To me, the Lord acted like my dad: quick to anger, capricious in his wrath, willing to withdraw His love and never satisfied. In other words, like the God I knew from the Hebrew Scriptures, someone who wiped out entire populations, including children, in angry fits. I was scared to be around that God, just as I was sometimes scared to be around my father.

My dad grew up desperately poor during the Depression. His family survived on the bag of groceries a generous grandmother would drop off each weekend. He was a tough man who set high standards for his children. My grandfather, whom I never met, was the town drunk and rarely at home. Through relentless hard work and sacrifice, like many children of alcoholics, my dad became a self-made millionaire. His job as a father, as he saw it, was to churn out high-achieving children. He vowed to raise no quitters or failures. So for us kids, nothing was ever good enough. If we did something well, he warned us not to "rest on our laurels," because we needed to do even better next time. Love was conditional, doled out in proportion to our performances. In some respects, he did a great job (and, to his credit, evolved into a mellow old man). Two of my siblings received undergraduate and graduate degrees from Stanford University, with my sister finishing near the top of her law school class. My older brother and I claimed more modest academic achievements but did well in school and played college water polo. All of us became achieving machines who would climb to great heights in our professions. But the price has been a high one. Among the four of us, you'll find alcoholism, depression, stress-induced physical ailments and crippling anxiety.

I decided in my late teens that I didn't want to worship a God who was that demanding, vengeful, difficult to predict and hard to please. So I didn't. At least not for another dozen years, when Will Swaim suggested I go back to church. He pointed me to Mariners Church, a nondenominational congregation based in Newport Beach. The next Sunday I decided to scout it out alone.

When I stepped onto the well-manicured Mariners campus, I immediately saw that I wasn't at my father's church anymore. As thousands of congregants streamed into the mega-church's sanctuary for one of four weekend services, volunteers served coffee drinks on the patio from cappuccino machines, not silver drums. Classy kiosks—not card tables—ringed the patio, marketing all kinds of church activities and clubs designed to appeal to young singles, older singles, elderly singles, young married couples, married couples with children, older married couples, stay-at-home moms, junior high school students, high school students and college students.

As I entered the church itself, a friendly usher handed me a program—not a copied sheet of paper put together by a church secretary, but a multi-page brochure with a hip, professional design. I took a seat near the back of the large auditorium, which had no church trappings except for a plain wooden cross at the rear of the stage. The building had the feel of a tony playhouse with its padded rows of seats, top-drawer lighting and sound system and wide stage. The church was packed with good-looking people who wore stylish but casual clothes. They greeted their church friends with hearty handshakes and hugs before the chatting and laughter began. Even before the service started, I started to yearn to be part of this appealing club, to get some of what they appeared to have—simple happiness.

When the church band began to play, the crowd rose and sang along with lyrics projected on a big screen. The energy spiked instantly. Instead of hymns, the band—an electric guitarist, bassist, pianist, drummer and several singers—played what's known as worship music, modern songs with simple lyrics repeated again and again. St. Augustine wrote that "to sing is to pray twice," and he was right. Singing words repeatedly, propelled by a catchy melody, allows you to enter a meditative state where you can find God. It would take me more than a year to understand this and fall in love with the musical form.

At first, I just didn't want to sing. I didn't have a good voice, and I felt self-conscious—it all seemed so touchy-feely. As they sang, some parishioners held up their arms to the heavens; others closed their eyes and swayed to the beat. For my first year as a churchgoer, I arrived 20 minutes late in order to avoid all this. But the music slowly worked on me, and I began to understand what they were feeling. When you enter that zone, it feels like you are having an intimate conversation with God and that He is bathing you with love.

The main draw at Mariners is the sermon by Kenton Beshore, the church's senior pastor and its primary draw. The son of a preacher, Kenton had taken over, at age 30, the remnants of an aging, split church. In one of his first moves, he threw out the organ along with other traditional trappings. His ministry focused primarily on people who had been turned off from church for one reason or another. The congregation rapidly grew, drawn to this good-looking pastor with the boyish face, a shock of brown hair that he often pushed off his forehead, a sharp intellect and quick wit. But most important, he delivered stirring sermons—called "messages"—that weaved together humor, his own vulnerability, biblical history and Scripture, making Christianity come alive, giving it relevance in the modern world.

Kenton's talks reminded me of the only time in my youth when I found the church compelling. In confirmation class, Father Young read to us 12-year-olds from Dick Gregory's *Bible Tales*, a collection of biblical stories that the African-American social activist put into the street language of the day. In one chapter, Gregory recounted the story Jesus told his disciples about how they will be judged in heaven, citing a parable in Matthew 25. Here's how Gregory told the ending of the story:

And the bad folks will say, "Lord, you're wrong! We never did that to you. We may have done it to those bothersome poor folks, or those useless old folks, or those dirty hippies, or those niggers, kikes, commies, faggots, and spics, or those muggers, winos, junkies, and rapists. But never to you, Lord!"

And the Judge will say, "You've just condemned yourselves. Every time you did it to one of those—even the very least of those—you did it to me. So sweat it out in hell, while I takes these other folks to heaven with me."

I had forgotten about *Bible Tales* until hearing Kenton on my first Sunday at Mariners. A natural entertainer, Kenton got the congregation to laugh with him at the start of the sermon and cry with him at the end. In my first months at Mariners, I sat spellbound as he delivered his message series on topics such as "Top Ten Surprises of Jesus's Life," "God's 9-1-1: A Series from Hebrews," "Hope in the Storms of Life" and "Life at Its Best: Fruits of the Spirit."

Here's a typical way Kenton kicks off a message series:

The world is fast changing, it's moving quick, and there's a lot going on. Where's the market going? Where are your investments going? Where's business going? Where's politics going? How about relationships in your life? Changing fast. Where do you go to find the truth that you need in a fast-changing world?

We go to God's Word because the Bible isn't just another book. The Bible is a book God has put together for you. To give you principles, truth, that will guide your life in an ever-changing world.

. . . Our challenge when we read the Bible, if we want to understand it better, is to understand the person who wrote any individual book [of the Bible] and the time and the culture in which they wrote it and the people to whom it was written. And when we understand that, then what we can do is understand the Bible as it was written in [that] context and then we can take those truths, those timeless principles, and transport them to the 21st century, to our lives today, and then begin to apply them.

For someone who was basically illiterate when it came to the Bible, these messages fed a hunger in my soul. It was like discovering a great new author, only the writer of this book—or at least the one who inspired it—was the creator of the universe. I thought, finally, I had found the answers to living a quality life. The secrets had been there all along—in "Life's Instruction Manual," as some Christians call the Bible.

Most of the lessons in the Scriptures were just common sense, but they carried the weight of God. Among them: Love the Lord with all your heart and love your neighbor as yourself. Forgive and even love your enemies. Honor your wife. Be open and honest. Take care of the poor. Don't gossip. Don't run up financial debt. It all sounded good. And the Bible's promise—God's promise—was that it would lead to a fulfilled life.

From that first day at Mariners, I began to fall in love with a God different from the one I had grown up with. This God loved me perfectly. He didn't love me any more or any less, no matter what I did. I eagerly lapped up the unconditional love. He was a rock upon which I could build my life. He laid out exactly what kind of life to live in His Holy Book. It was a relief to have someone else in charge of my life.

I began making baby steps as a Christian. I not only went to church each weekend, I looked forward to it. I prayed in the morning and at night. I told Him my dreams, including the desire to get out of my dead-end job, to have my wife forgive me for the mess I made before our marriage and to find a cure for my intestinal problems. Despite my enthusiasm, I was reluctant to dive into Christianity headfirst. I wasn't comfortable calling myself a Christian because of all the baggage that went along with it. Outside of church, I couldn't even say the J-word. The word "Jesus"—or "JEEZ-us," as I heard it in my mind, complete with a Southern accent—had been so thoroughly corrupted by televangelists and other Bible thumpers, so mocked in television and movies and so trivialized by professional athletes claiming that "I want to thank Jesus my Lord and Savior for giving me this win," that it was embarrassing for me to say aloud. I kept my budding faith very private and didn't mention it to most co-workers, friends or even family.

I worried that if I came out of the evangelical closet, I'd be labeled a religious kook, or worse. I knew I didn't have the ability, as a young Christian, to defend my faith in an argument. So like the skinny kid who worried about having sand kicked in his face, I strengthened myself as a Christian in secret. I started by devouring books about Christianity. First, I bought a study Bible with maps and detailed notes, and proceeded to read the New Testament nearly all the way through, stopping short of Revelation—I was too intimidated to tackle the Apostle John's vision of the end of days and its monstrous beasts, plagues, earthquakes and floods, and bloody wars. I also read books written by Christian apologists, intellectuals who defended the faith using science and other academic means. C. S. Lewis was no longer just a children's author to me, but one of the great Christian minds of the 20th century—

I especially loved *Mere Christianity, The Great Divorce* and *The Screwtape Letters*. G. K. Chesterton's brilliant writings moved me (including *Saint Francis of Assisi* and *Saint Thomas Aquinas: The Dumb Ox*), as did the story of Charles Colson, President Nixon's hatchet man who found Christ just before he went to jail for Watergate-related crimes. Since his release, Colson has selflessly served prisoners and their families around the world through his Prison Ministries. His memoir, *Born Again,* is a classic of evangelical literature. And I eagerly read *The Case for Christ* by Lee Strobel, a former business reporter with the *Chicago Tribune* who set out to find the truth about Christianity and concluded that Christ was both a historical figure and the Son of God who died on the cross for our sins and was resurrected.

As I slowly gained confidence in my faith, I managed to talk my reluctant wife into coming to Mariners. Because of her Catholic upbringing, Greer found my mega-church too foreign and casual, but she attended for me. She liked the changes she was starting to see in her husband. I had devoted myself to our young family and was fulfilling my responsibilities as a spouse and father. We usually went to Saturday-night services, which allowed us—young parents on a tight budget—to have a night out. Mariners had excellent child care, so we'd drop off Taylor and attend services. Afterward, we'd grab a cheap dinner out.

After a year back at church, the whole God thing seemed to be working for me. I found a new circle of friends who were committed Christian men, and we met once a week for Bible study and to talk about the challenges of marriage, family and life. My once-shaky marriage improved enough that Greer started to talk about having a second child. Though we didn't have much money, we started giving to the church and other Christian charities.

I prayed for a new job, and soon found something beyond my

imagination: the editorship of the local newspaper. At age 29, I was the youngest editor in the *Newport Beach–Costa Mesa Daily Pilot's* 83-year history. My publisher gave me a nice salary (about double what I was making before), a mandate to save the dying newspaper and all the freedom I needed to do it. I couldn't imagine a better professional challenge.

My health started to improve, too. My acne disappeared, and I found a cutting-edge doctor to treat my intestinal problems. I believed God had done all these things because I had started to listen to Him and follow His Word. Scripture says you'll be made new through Christ, and I was slowly transforming myself into a different, better person.

I gained a spiritual mentor, Hugh Hewitt, who would soon become my best friend. Our relationship started in the late 1980s, when I was looking for a conservative voice for the business lifestyles magazine I was editing. Hugh, an attorney and talk radio host who worked for Presidents Nixon and Reagan, was perfect. Articulate, intelligent, funny, insightful and never in doubt (even when he was wrong), he made the perfect columnist.

When I told Hugh, an evangelical Christian, that I had found God, he was ecstatic. He introduced me to his Christian friends, patiently answered my seemingly endless series of questions and continually urged me to go deeper in my faith. Our relationship quickly went from professional to personal. On the surface, we were an unlikely pair. Though he once ran a three-hour, 12-minute marathon, Hugh looks like a policy wonk. Prematurely gray, he wears wire-rimmed glasses and fights to control his weight. He is a staunch conservative with a passionate dislike for the mainstream media. By contrast, no one would mistake me for an intellectual. Politically, I'm in the middle of the road. And I am a card-carrying member of the mainstream media—or MSM, as Hugh ominously abbreviates it. People who know us independently are surprised to find out that we are friends.

By 1992, two years into my spiritual walk, I still felt nowhere near to being a fully developed Christian. My faith continued to feel a little foreign and uncomfortable, like wearing a new pair of shoes out of the store. I had all kinds of deficiencies as a Christian. In my Bible study, I felt hopelessly over my head when it came my time to pray. I couldn't do some of the simplest things demanded of me by Scripture, such as stop gossiping. And I couldn't imagine embarking on any kind of mission, even to Tijuana two hours to the south. Hugh kept telling me that the Christian life wasn't meant to be easy. He continually pushed me outside my comfort zone.

Classic evangelical testimony stories always reach a climax with "The Moment," the experience of being born-again, of falling on your knees and accepting Jesus Christ as your Lord and Savior—and feeling Him come into your heart. I had not had such a moment, and I didn't think it would ever happen. My faith was more in my head than in my heart. One day, Hugh insisted that I attend a men's weekend retreat at the Thousand Pines Christian Camp & Conference Center in the San Bernardino Mountains, about a two-hour drive from Los Angeles. I didn't want to go. I told Hugh I'd take a pass. I was just a Christian toddler. I needed time to grow.

"Listen, you're going to the retreat," said Hugh, never one for subtleties. "I've already paid for you. It's a done deal. You need this, Billy. You need to get closer to God. You're going to have to trust me. I'll pick you up Friday afternoon."

An introvert by nature, I was horrified by the idea of getting together with nearly 100 strangers from a Presbyterian church I had never attended.

"Hugh, no thanks," I said. "I'll go next year. I promise."

"I'll be at your house at three," he said. "There's no getting out of it."

In effect, he kidnapped me. After a crawl of a drive through Southern California's Friday-night rush-hour traffic, we turned off Interstate 215 and began the 20-mile drive into the mountains, following a long line of cars snaking its way uphill on the narrow two-lane road. My anxiety grew as the brown scrub and chaparral gave way to towering pines. Truth was, I had heard that the weekend would involve singing about God, praising Him, talking about Jesus and doing a lot of sharing. It all reminded me too much of the Christianity I had the most exposure to and hated: the Reverend Jerry Falwell, Pat Robertson and televangelists who talked about "JEEZ-us!" I liked my faith private—and without outward signs of emotion.

Walking into the retreat center's conference room, I noticed how ordinary the members of my retreat looked. They could have been mistaken for a bunch of guys gathered in Las Vegas to watch the Final Four basketball tournament. They ranged in age from late teens to more than 70. The group included students, doctors, attorneys, contractors, repairmen, engineers and retirees. Besides a love for the Lord, their common trait seemed to be an insatiable hunger for junk food. Our meeting room was filled with tables holding buckets of Red Vine licorice, boxes of Hershey chocolate bars, huge bags of M&Ms, bowls of pretzels and cases of Coke and root beer.

The weekend's schedule was simple. The group met in a rustic conference room, with chairs lined up in rows to mimic church pews. A makeshift band—which was surprisingly good—played a series of worship songs, whose lyrics were projected on a screen. A few songs into each session, many of the men, carried away by emotion, began to sing at the top of their lungs, their voices cracking; a few started to cry.

Next came the personal testimonies. The first guy who stood up was Bud, a tall and burly contractor with an oversized personality. He was the retreat's natural leader. Normally the court jester, he got serious quickly as he quietly told the group that his wife of 20 years no longer loved him, that his business was failing and that at age 50, all his life's dreams had been shattered.

"I wasn't the man she needed me to be so she checked out," Bud said, wiping tears from his eyes. "She told me, 'I don't respect you, I don't love you and I don't see how this marriage can possibly work out.' "

Besides a few sniffles, the room was dead quiet. This kind of honesty among men was rare and breathtaking. Bud went on to say that his wife had given him plenty of warning signs that he needed to change, but, thinking divorce wasn't an option for a Christian marriage, he didn't feel the urgency to heed her words. Few people in the room knew of Bud's marriage problems. His confession came as a shock. Bud, knowing this, said men shouldn't keep their pain bottled up inside. He had waited until it was too late. They needed to confess their problems to others and reach out for help when they needed it. It's the way God wants it.

As Bud finished, someone said quietly, "Let's pray for him." Several of his friends got up and placed their hands on his wide shoulders as everyone prayed for him, his wife, their marriage and their three boys.

Hearing Bud's story was both shocking and oddly encouraging. He had made a mess of his life, just as I had. And he believed following God was the way out. But looking at Bud and his gregarious personality, no one would ever have guessed the pain he was experiencing. I felt an instant kinship to him and we remain friends to this day.

The weekend's guest speaker, a retired pastor, then gave a

themed talk about how to live the Christian life. The structure of the weekend, I was beginning to discover, was carefully designed to break down our defense mechanisms. It was exhausting, emotional and active (a lot of singing and talking, not just listening). After more worship songs, we were placed in six-person groups for more intimate talks about our lives. I absolutely loathed this part of the weekend. I didn't know my fellow group members, and people were sharing the most intimate parts of their lives, sometimes for the first time. I said as little as possible. Finally, another round of prayers concluded the session.

This cycle of singing, testimony, preaching, sharing and praying repeated itself Saturday morning, Saturday evening and Sunday morning. Saturday evening, another man—this time a former business executive in his 60s—said he was inspired by Bud to tell his story and ask us to pray for him. He said he had been laid off the year before from his high-paying engineering job and couldn't find any other work at his age. He had gone through his savings and was close to broke when he humbled himself enough to take the only job that would have him—selling cars. There were more tears and more prayers for this stoic guy.

During free time, the guys prayed, hiked, napped or went to town to watch college football on a wide-screen TV at a local restaurant. On Saturday afternoon, many of the weekend warriors played basketball on the outdoor courts, a game that resulted in several pulled muscles, tweaked knees and turned ankles. In between, we ate our meals communally at a dining hall that reminded me of my freshman dorm, but not in a good way. There were other things, besides good food, that you couldn't get at the retreat: television, radios and sleep. The lack of shut-eye came from sharing a Spartan cabin with a half-dozen grown men, whose bodily functions and impressive snoring provided the night's soundtrack.

By design, the weekend left us emotionally raw. Cut off from our regular lives, our facades broke down under the assault of song, prayers, worship, honest sharing and sleep deprivation. With real emotions exposed, I could see the other guys were as screwed up as I was. Some had even more troubles. There was nothing these guys wouldn't share: addiction to pornography, affairs, mistreatment of children, failed business ventures, and alcohol and drug abuse. And they all found comfort and direction in Jesus. They weren't like Falwell or Robertson. They were like me.

It took until Sunday morning, in the retreat's chapel, for my fortified walls to crumble. It wasn't the modern worship songs that got to me, but the centuries-old "Amazing Grace." I felt myself surrendering to God in a way I never had before. I felt those words deep in my soul, especially the third verse:

> *Through many dangers, toils and snares*
> *I have already come;*
> *'Tis Grace that brought me safe thus far*
> *and Grace will lead me home.*

After the music, Mike Barris, a pastor-to-be who conducted the climactic Sunday-morning service, asked the men gathered in the chapel a simple question that I should have anticipated, but hadn't: Have you publicly pronounced Jesus Christ as your personal Lord and Savior? I hadn't. I wasn't ready to. Panicked, my pulse quickened. My eyes darted. I suddenly felt trapped. I didn't want to be a born-again Christian—I knew what I thought of them, and I knew what people less tolerant than I thought of them. I couldn't even say "Jesus" in public, for gosh sakes! The weekend had been such a great spiritual experience, why did Barris have to wreck it by forcing this born-again question on me? My walls quickly came back up. I needed more time to warm up to the idea of being called born-again.

Barris, an athletically built man in his late 20s who looked more like a frat boy than a pastor, went on to say that a public confession of faith was an important part of the Christian journey. He asked us to bow our heads, close our eyes and pray. In a gentle voice, he told those who felt moved to accept Christ into their heart today to raise their hand. My heart beat even faster, but no longer in self-defense. I couldn't believe it, but I felt an urge to lift my hand. But I sure as heck didn't want to be the only one. I took a peek around the room and saw several hands shoot up. What was I going to do? My eternal fate might rest on this decision. Ah, maybe not, said another voice inside my head—this whole born-again thing could be just a bunch of crap. I shut my eyes and prayed. That seemed safe and noncommittal. But there was the urge again to raise my hand—was it from God?

My heart threatened to beat out of my chest. I was at the edge of a cliff, weighing whether to jump. I wanted to take the plunge, but I didn't want to be looked at as a freak. I didn't know how I'd explain my conversion to my atheist friends. I didn't want to imagine how I would change once Jesus truly became the center-piece of my life. Would I be wearing a rainbow wig and handlebar mustache inside a football stadium, waving a "John 3:16" sign at the television camera? Would I be compelled to walk away from material pleasures and devote my life to helping the poor? I didn't want to find out.

Barris was very good at his job. Not in any rush, he said he still felt there were others in the chapel who wanted to become Christians today. He'd wait a few more minutes, in case anyone else wanted to raise his hand. Was he talking to me, I wondered? Or was it God who was speaking? My pulse actually slowed as, at last, I obeyed. My arm seemed to float up on its own until it was over my head.

Barris asked those of us who raised our hands to repeat the sinner's prayer. I don't remember the exact words, but it went something like this:

> *Father, I'm a sinner, and I want to repent. I believe that your son, Jesus Christ, died for my sins, was resurrected from the dead, is alive, and hears my prayer. I invite Jesus into my heart to become my personal Lord and Savior, to rule and reign in my heart from this day forward. Please send your Holy Spirit to help me obey You, and to do Your will for the rest of my life. In Jesus's name I pray, Amen.*

When I repeated the line "I invite Jesus into my heart," I experienced what I can only call a vision. Time slowed. In my mind's eye, my heart opened into halves, and a warm, glowing light flowed right in. As my heart melted back together, it remained illuminated with a soft light from the inside. I felt instantly the light was Jesus, who now lived inside me. A tingling warmth spread across my chest. This, I thought—no, I *knew*—was what it meant to be born-again.

I opened my tear-filled eyes and was quickly surrounded by my new brothers in Christ, men who had been strangers less than 48 hours before. They slapped me on the back, hugged me and shook my hand. They congratulated me on making the best decision of my life, one that would have eternal consequences. As happy as they were for me, I was even happier for myself—I now had Jesus in my heart.

An hour later, Hugh and I were driving down the mountain. I was still trying to sort out what had happened.

"What made you publicly decide to accept Jesus today?" Hugh asked.

"It was the weirdest thing, Hugh," I said, as I steered the car along the road carved into the mountain wall. "I think I had a mystical experience up there."

I told him about my vision. Hugh, born and raised in Ohio, is a guy with Midwestern sensibilities who became a Presbyterian because it was the church in which he was least likely to be hugged. He's an analytical thinker who keeps his emotions tightly under wraps. Yet in a voyeuristic way, Hugh was fascinated by what had happened to me, and he didn't doubt for a minute that it was true.

"Did you see Jesus?"

I explained about the vision and warm light.

"Did you feel His presence?"

I told him about the tingling.

"How do you feel now?" he asked.

"I don't know," I said, still trying to figure it out. "I'm a little stunned, I guess. Excited. Anxious. I don't know how this all will play out."

"You don't have to worry about that," he said. "God will show you the way."

THREE

A God Thing

Now faith is being sure of what we hope for and certain of
what we do not see.

— HEBREWS 11:1

DRIVING DOWN THE mountain, Hugh and I made a pact
to meet each Monday at dawn to run along Newport Beach's Back
Bay, a 752-acre saltwater estuary in the heart of Orange County.
The oasis of open space serves as the community's Central Park,
a haven for cyclists, runners, kayakers and birders, who track the
200 species—from blue herons to brown pelicans to light-footed
clapper rails—that make the estuary their home.

We quickly developed a pattern on our runs. We would spend
the first 30 minutes talking about our week at work, our families,
sports, politics and anything else that weighed on our mind. At
the turnaround point, we stopped chatting and started praying.
Right there on the road, we would talk to God for a half hour,
asking Him for His help and guidance. We weren't bold enough
to pray within earshot of others, so our prayers oftentimes were

interrupted if anyone passed by. Many of our petitions changed from week to week, but several stayed the same: Good health for our families and friends. Peace around the world. Career success. Comfort to those in need. The ritual seemed a little strange at first, but soon it became one of the highlights of my week. The prayers put me into a one-on-one relationship with God. They also made me focus more on others. And it felt like I was actually *doing* something about the problems and injustices in the world.

As the months passed, I also made sure that God knew how thankful I was for all that He had done for me. My marriage had moved to solid ground. Greer had given birth to our second healthy son, Tristan. And my career was taking off as the brass at the *Los Angeles Times*—which owned the *Daily Pilot*—put me in charge of a rapidly expanding chain of local dailies and weeklies, which were winning statewide awards. Wanting to make sure the blessings continued to flow, I went to church each week with my wife and children. I attended a weekly Bible study. I volunteered my journalism skills to edit a book for my pastor, Kenton Beshore. I volunteered to deliver Christmas presents to an orphanage in Tijuana. And I continued to read everything I could to deepen my faith. On my bookshelves, Christian books now crowded out my previous staples of mysteries, biographies and adventure books.

My relationship with God was going well, but it didn't keep me from selfish thoughts. I began to pray for money for my family. In one of his sermons, Kenton advised us to be specific about what we pray for, so I decided to ask for $50,000. I wasn't sure where I got the 50K figure, other than that it seemed like a big round number.

After a few months of praying along these lines, I drove home from work one evening and spotted my old boss in front of my house. Why in the world was he here? The last time I had seen him, I told him that I felt cheated—in an ethical, not legal, sense—when he sold his business lifestyles magazine just after I had left the company for the *Daily Pilot*. I had helped build it. I had owned a 5 percent share in the magazine, which I forfeited when I left. I told him it didn't seem right that he received all the benefit of my seven years of work but because of a very short gap of time—a matter of a few months—my ownership was void. He said he didn't see it that way, but did write me a $5,000 check that he believed was generous considering he didn't legally owe me anything. I thought it was about $45,000 short of what was fair.

Now, months later, he greeted me warmly on the darkened street in a quiet Costa Mesa neighborhood and explained that he and his wife had become Christians, and this rift with me had been bothering them. So they had prayed about it and decided to make things right. He handed me an envelope and told me to open it up with Greer once I got inside my house.

Walking back into my home, I tried to imagine what was inside the envelope. I quickly ruled out the possibility that it held $45,000. My former boss had many good traits, but generosity wasn't one of them. Maybe it was an apology letter. Or an explanation. Or, best-case scenario, another $5,000. I called Greer to the front room and told her about my encounter and held up the envelope.

"Well," my wife said, not wanting to get her hopes up, "let's see what's inside."

I tore it open, pulled out a letter and unfolded it. Tucked inside was a check. My hands started to shake as I read the amount: $45,000. Without a word, I handed it to Greer. She kept looking at the check and then at me. "He just gave you this?" she asked in disbelief.

"Yeah, he said he's become a Christian and this has weighed

on him," I said. "Can you believe this? If you add the $5,000 he had already given me, this is exactly the $50,000 I have been praying for."

"He's a Christian now?" Greer asked, still trying to wrap her mind around the difference between my ex-boss's former and new selves. Together we read the heartfelt note that accompanied the check. He said, in brief, the Lord had told him to give the money to me. I had goose bumps. I hardly needed more evidence of God's existence, but I thought He had just delivered 50,000 more reasons to cement my faith—and He had transformed my former boss.

Since entering the Christian world, I'd frequently heard stories like this—miraculous coincidences and life turnarounds credited to Providence. In evangelical circles, the unofficial term for what happened to me was called "a God thing"—something wonderful and unexplainable that pops up in a believer's life and can only be the work of the Lord. Evangelicals don't think much of coincidence. Wonderful events are God's work. Bad events are attributed to human sinfulness, the devil's work or, when those two are ruled out, a mystery only God can solve.

Believers see God's work everywhere, and the God things I saw all around me cried out to be covered by a journalist. The more I heard about, witnessed and experienced these moments of grace, the greater disconnect I saw between what was happening in the faith community and the coverage of religion in the mainstream media. Why were so many of my journalistic colleagues around the nation missing the real stories on the faith beat? Why were most stories about Christians negative or dismissive? This quickly became a major topic of conversation during my runs with Hugh. We ticked off the outrages in media coverage of religion each week. Too much of the journalism was either repetitive (concentrating on a few issues such as abortion and homosexuality), boring (detailing the latest internal denominational squabbles, usually about homosexuality), lacking in nuance or simply not an accurate reflection of what was going on in the nation's churches, mosques, synagogues and temples.

One example—which became infamous among Christians and is still cited as the nadir of sloppy religion coverage—happened in 1994 when the *Washington Post* casually described conservative evangelical Christians as "largely poor, uneducated and easy to command" in a news story. The characterization provoked a slew of protests and forced the *Post* into running an unintentionally funny correction: "An article yesterday characterized followers of television evangelists Jerry Falwell and Pat Robertson as 'largely poor, uneducated and easy to command.' There is no factual basis for that statement." Can you imagine a journalist writing off any other large group in the United States that way? It's not just that a reporter wrote it; that description sailed past a gauntlet of editors whose job is to scrub away bias. The story struck a chord with Christians because it was hard evidence of how some journalists really thought of evangelicals. Most of the time, the bias was more subtle and harder to put a finger on.

The poor quality of religion coverage in the 1990s (it has improved greatly in recent years) wasn't surprising to anyone who worked in a newsroom during that time. Few journalists volunteered for the religion beat, which was seen as a place to warehouse burned-out or incompetent reporters. It was one step lower than writing obits, traditionally the last rung of the ladder before a reporter was drummed out of journalism (that has changed in recent years, too). Many editors—most of whom didn't regularly attend worship services, according to several studies—saw the religion beat as an antiquated part of newspaper tradition, surviving only because the "Faith" section on Saturdays made money and needed some filler to surround the listings of houses of worship and church advertisements.

I came to view the religion beat as an untapped vein of gold. It offered complex stories of great human interest that could be unearthed with minimal effort. I'd seen lives, including my own, dramatically changed by faith, but most of the stories seemed to be located away from where mainstream journalists liked to dig for their articles.

After months of complaining about media coverage of religion, I had an epiphany that felt as if it came straight from God. "Why don't you become a religion writer?" asked the inaudible voice. "This is a way for you to use your gifts for the Kingdom of God."

The idea excited me. I could be both a mainstream journalist and a devout Christian, simply by writing about the impact religion had on the lives of everyday people. I thought God's plan for me (for such it had to be, I was sure) was ingenious. It played to my strengths—my "gifts," in Christian parlance. I needed only to produce solid journalism about faith in America, and I would be fulfilling God's call *and* my career ambitions.

I told Hugh about my idea—God's idea—but I warned him there were too many barriers for it ever to work. As the editor in charge of the *Los Angeles Times*'s local news division, I was making good money. Taking a pay cut to write for a smaller paper wasn't an option for the sole breadwinner of an expanding household, and I didn't want to uproot my family to work for another big-city paper. Besides, I hadn't been a reporter in more than a decade. Who would hire me at even a low salary to write about religion? My choices narrowed to one paper: the *Los Angeles Times*.

Even there, my ambition seemed impossible to fulfill. I worked for its local news division, and there was a Grand Canyon–sized gap between the local division, where we concentrated on covering suburban city councils, school boards and prep sports teams, and the newsroom of one of the world's largest papers. Bridging the gap would be like having a young minor-league manager in the New York Yankee farm system called up to play center field for the big club. It just didn't happen.

"You're putting limitations on God," Hugh said when I finished explaining why this would never work. "Just pray for the job. He'll find a way to get you it if that's what He wants."

So I began to pray. I asked God for a religion-writing job at the *Los Angeles Times*. I prayed for it in the morning, at night and in between. On my weekly runs, I asked again. So did Hugh. We prayed and prayed and ran and ran—and nothing happened. The prayers continued for four years. But my faith remained strong, and I didn't think about giving up. Sometimes, being a believer means being stubbornly persistent. Moses waited patiently for 40 years in the desert, and he didn't even get to enter the Promised Land. I was certain that getting the job depended on God's timing, not mine.

In the meantime, word began to leak out about my conversion, and I became sought after in some circles because of the shortage of evangelical Christians who were also mainstream journalists in Southern California. When my church organized a 24-hour prayer vigil, I was asked to lead an hour-long prayer session for the media. I was self-conscious and barely managed to stumble through it. Sixty minutes had never gone by more slowly. It was like standing up and giving an impromptu speech in junior high, only this time I had my eyes closed and my audience consisted of not just devout Christians (many of whom had a gift for prayer) but also God

Himself. My voice quaked, and my mind went blank several times as I tried to figure out what the media needed from God. I had to be the worst prayer ever.

I declined an invitation to join an international group of evangelical Christians who worked in secular newsrooms and banded together for support. I didn't see the need. People of faith weren't especially embraced in newsrooms, but they also weren't rejected. When it came to evangelicals, the newsroom had an informal but polite "don't ask, don't tell" policy. Conversations at the water cooler rarely strayed into personal matters of faith.

I was asked to teach a journalism class at a Christian college to show how evangelicals can survive in a secular newspaper. I declined that offer, too. It felt like the educators really wanted me to show how Christians could infiltrate—not "survive"—the newsroom. The covert approach turned my stomach.

I came to believe that if people were going to be drawn to Christianity, it would be because of quiet examples set by Christians. I had adopted the faith because people whom I admired were living more satisfying lives than I was, and a belief in Jesus seemed to be at the center of their contentment. They proselytized simply by living authentic Christian lives, not by preaching, badgering or threatening hellfire. St. Francis of Assisi put it best: "Preach the Gospel at all times, if necessary use words." My faith and experience told me that the lives of nonbelievers would change radically for the better—here and for eternity—if they accepted Jesus, just as I had. I wanted people to see me as an attractive example of the Christian life. It was a goal of which I repeatedly fell short, but toward which I still kept striving.

I started to find excuses for why God hadn't given me the job at *The Times* yet. Maybe I wasn't ready for it. I'd be on a national stage if I got the position, and perhaps this was my time in the desert to pray and fast and prepare. Yet four years into praying, I saw no progress. Finally, I decided to find another way to get my foot in the door. God helps those who help themselves, right? Maybe, I thought, my mistake was trying to find a way to get a *full-time* writing job, and I was praying for the wrong thing. What about starting with something part-time? I could propose writing a regular religion column for the paper's Orange County edition. That way I could still keep my day job and the edition, with more than 200,000 subscribers, would be able to connect more deeply with a remarkably religious community that flourished among Orange County's 3 million residents.

In the fall of 1997, I landed a meeting with the editor and the president of the Orange County edition, both of whom I knew well because of my work at Times Community News. We sat around a small conference table in the president's office. I took a deep breath, said a quick silent prayer and made my pitch.

"What if I told you that you have an institution in Orange County that draws more than 15,000 people a weekend and that you haven't written about it in years despite your army of 200 journalists in the county?"

They shook their heads and said they couldn't imagine such a thing.

"It's called Saddleback Church in Lake Forest. You guys are not covering Saddleback, and it's like not reporting on the Anaheim Ducks or Angels." I looked down at my other talking points and continued. "Orange County also has the second-largest Catholic diocese west of the Mississippi, the largest mosque in North America and one of the wealthiest Jewish communities in the nation. People give more money, by far, to their church, synagogue and mosque than to any other charitable organization in the county. Objectively, this is a huge story that you're just not covering well.

Faith matters to people. It's at the center of their lives. But the Orange County edition tends to treat it as some sort of a novelty act. Not all the time, but too much of the time. Do you know, for example, that thousands of high school and college students from Orange County will spend their spring break this year building houses for families in Tijuana instead of drinking heavily in Palm Springs? That story would be a great read.

"I want to write a religion column that reads like a sports column. Something that's written by someone who actually likes religion and knows it matters in people's lives. This can be a really popular addition to *The Times*'s Orange County coverage."

I slid across the table a list of 30 column ideas. The editor and president looked them over and nodded. They said the idea intrigued them, and they wanted to start something like this as soon as possible. They'd get back to me with the details. I felt like doing a little dance. I shook their hands and thanked them for their time. This was going to work! I had nailed the interview, and once more, God had delivered.

But three weeks went by without a word. And then I opened *The Times* one day and saw an announcement about a new religion column. At first, I thought it was strange to announce my new column without calling me first. But as I read the copy, I discovered that the columnist wasn't me. He was a local college professor who studied religions. My heart sank. They had taken my idea and assigned it to someone else—without even an explanation. How could this have happened? Didn't they think I could pull it off? Was it possible that two people came up with the same idea at the same time, and they decided to go with the academic? I wondered whether I had spent four years praying for nothing. Did I even have God's desire for me right? Had I misunderstood His will? I was experiencing self-doubt, filtered through the conviction that there was a divine plan for each of us. As I fretted, I couldn't bring myself simply to call *The Times* executives to find out the real reason—it was just too crushing.

After days of prayer and depression, I concluded that I didn't have God's will wrong at all. There was no mistaking the strong sense of direction I was receiving from above. I knew God wanted me to be a religion writer. I felt it. *The Times* blew its first opportunity at getting a great religion columnist. There had to be another chance coming, and I would be ready.

This time, it took less than half a year. A new editor took over the Orange County edition, and I quickly made friends with her. Before too long, I made the same pitch for a column and handed her my list of 30 ideas, noting the difference between what I proposed and the more scholarly column written by the professor. She studied my list. Finally she looked up and said the miraculous words: "Let's do it. We can run it every other week. When can you get me the first one?"

I felt like one of the last tumblers in my Christian life had clicked into place. I was certain that God had made it happen; I was just His vessel. A sense of deep satisfaction engulfed me, along with a sense of awe about God's power. I wasn't going to waste this chance. That afternoon, I started to write. I wanted to show that some of the best stories in the paper could be found on the religion beat—dramatic tales that were so good they couldn't be confined to the religion-page ghetto on Saturday, but would be sprinkled throughout the paper, including the front page.

A few weeks later, on December 19, 1998, I awoke to the sound of the newspaper hitting my walkway with a thud, and I jumped out of bed and walked outside to get my hands on it. I opened the paper in the pre-dawn gray, lifted out the Metro section, and turned to B4. There it was, my column profiling John Moorlach, the county's treasurer–tax collector who a few years earlier had been the only person to predict the $1.5 billion Orange County bankruptcy. Though it was never reported at the time, Moorlach says he gained his financial wizardry from the Bible:

> It's not something John M.W. Moorlach shouts from the county Hall of Administration rooftop, but he'll tell you if you ask. The Bible is the first book the Orange County treasurer–tax collector turns to for financial advice.
>
> "The Bible is the greatest self-help financial book ever written," says Moorlach, the Costa Mesa accountant who predicted the Orange County bankruptcy six months before it happened. "I added it up once, and I found more than 2,000 pieces of financial advice in the Bible."
>
> . . . Moorlach knows some of his constituents will blanch at the thought of a devout Christian in control of public finances. But Moorlach points out that Scriptural directives have formed the basis for sound financial planning for thousands of years—and their secular cousins are easily recognized.
>
> "The Bible tells us to be content, to save, to avoid get-rich schemes, to diversify, to be honest, to be consistent, to exercise fidelity and stewardship," says Moorlach, a 43-year-old married father of three who attends church at Costa Mesa's Newport-Mesa Christian Center. "The Scriptural principles work, even if you're not a Christian."

As a believer, I loved the idea that Moorlach's reliance on the Bible might have helped him, somehow, to predict the county's shocking meltdown. Yet as a journalist, I also was drawn to the debate it would generate. I knew Moorlach's admission would drive nonbelievers crazy—for them, it was like having a government employee consult an astrologer to determine where to invest tax dollars. I took a middle ground, believing that Moorlach's basic financial principles were likely gleaned from the Bible but his ability to spot the impending bankruptcy was due more to his knowledge of Wall Street investing principles than to anything he found in Proverbs. Moorlach's success was clear, yet believers and skeptics had no trouble explaining it from entirely different points of view. I knew in my gut that this type of controversy was deeply engaging—and that there were many more stories like this out there. I had struck a rich, largely untapped vein of journalism for which I had been searching.

· F O U R ·

Answered Prayers

This is the assurance we have in approaching God: that
if we ask anything according to his will, he hears us. And
if we know that he hears us—whatever we ask—we know
that we have what we asked of him.

— JOHN 5:14–15

AS I SUSPECTED, I didn't have much trouble gathering material for my "Getting Religion" column. I kept stumbling across
one interesting religion story after another that illustrated how
faith shaped people's lives. I met extraordinary people everywhere
I turned.

One was Madge Rodda, an elderly church organist, who woke up
at three each Sunday morning and headed to a nearby Denny's for
some "spiritual Wheaties"—Bible study, quiet time and breakfast.
It was the 70-year-old's way of getting ready for 7:30 a.m. church
services at Calvary Chapel of Costa Mesa.

One Sunday at the restaurant, Madge went to the restroom.

Hiding in the stall next to hers was a transient carnival worker named James Bridle. High on cocaine, he had been reading a pornographic magazine. With a knife in one hand, he was ready to attack. Madge said that when she emerged from the stall, there he was. The attack was vicious and long—maybe 15 minutes. After wedging the door shut with the porno magazine, Bridle choked her, bashed her head repeatedly on the tile floor, cut her throat and tried to sexually assault her.

Madge put up an amazing fight against the strapping 23-year-old attacker. She stands all of 4 feet, 11 inches and weighs 100 pounds. She said she hit and kicked and screamed out prayers ("Lord, help me! Lord, save me! Dear Jesus, only you can save me!"), though no one in the restaurant could hear her through the bathroom's double doors. When the attack was over, she said Bridle turned to her—Madge's white blouse was soaked in blood, her face swollen and bruised—and said, "I believe in God, too. But Satan is poisoning my mind. I need help. I know I need help." And then he fled, but he didn't get far. A Denny's manager chased him down, then tackled and pinned him until police arrived.

This was where the story would usually end. "Elderly church organist attacked by carnival worker" might have rated a couple of paragraphs in the local paper. But in her bed at Hoag Memorial Hospital Presbyterian in Newport Beach, Madge changed all that with the first words she whispered to her daughter after the attack: "That poor man. That poor man. We must find a way of getting him a Bible."

Not a lot of people understood what she was doing. The rape counselors insisted she was in denial and pleaded with her to "get [her] anger out." Others thought she was a saint, a theory Madge laughed at. "It's my nature to hold a grudge," Madge said. "I can remember things from years and years ago that everyone else has probably forgotten." Madge's explanation is simply that the spirit of God moved her. "This wasn't natural, it was supernatural."

Madge and her attacker met again, this time in court. After a judge sentenced Bridle to 17 years in prison—which Madge thought was fair—she gave her assailant a Bible with verses she had highlighted to help him on his spiritual journey. And she began to set up a support network of Christian men to counsel Bridle when he is released from jail—most likely long after Madge has passed away.

"God knew this attack was going to happen," she told me. "So he sent a little old lady organist who'd have no better sense than to stand up in court with a Bible and say to her attacker, 'The word of God is all you need.' "

Another one of my stories profiled Donna Boggess. The natural impulse is to feel sorry for her. The relentless 30-year march of multiple sclerosis through her central nervous system has caused her body to mutiny. Her legs abandoned her long ago; her arms recently stopped working. She now relies on others to get her out of bed, help her to the bathroom, bathe her, comb her hair, put on her makeup and help her eat. And that's before 9 a.m.

Yet if you meet Boggess, pity is the last thing you'll feel. Try inspiration, awe and humility, for starters.

Sitting in a wheelchair, her arms frozen in the ever-tightening vise of multiple sclerosis, she tells you that because of God, her life is great. And the weird thing is, right off the bat, you believe her. You can see the evidence all around her.

First, there are her friends. She has lots of them. The phone rings constantly in her Mission Viejo apartment, and her home is filled with guests and laughter. On some days, a friend will come over, put Boggess in her red Miata convertible and drive, top down, all over the county, logging up to 150 miles in a day.

"The world gravitates toward Mom," said daughter Keri, 26, who lives with her. "She touches everyone she talks to."

Second, she has a budding career developing her own ministry. She gives Christ-centered inspirational talks, has produced a motivational tape ("A Walk to Joy") and is writing—with the help of a voice-activated computer—a book.

This is in addition to her part-time work for Saddleback Church, where she makes phone calls each evening to remind parishioners of meetings and offer encouragement. She also runs a support group out of her apartment for chronic illness sufferers. And she's most proud of the work she's done raising two beautiful daughters.

And third, she's just plain happy.

"I'm humbled because she has so many obstacles, and she handles them all with such grace," said Jan Muncaster, Saddleback's administrator. "She helps people with perspective. She literally never complains about her situation."

The obvious question: How can a wheelchair-bound woman who needs help even to brush her teeth think life is so wonderful?

"God's given her this happiness," Keri said. "Maybe that's God's gift to her. People are drawn to that contrast—tragedy and happiness at the same time."

Boggess has a different thought. "My problems aren't any bigger than anyone else's," she said. "It's just that mine are right out there for everyone to see. Some people struggle with bigger problems that they hold inside."

When talking with Boggess, it's not hard to imagine that 31 years ago she was a song leader at Tustin High School. At 49, she's still cheerleader cute (and her daughter wants any eligible "godly men" out there to know that Mom's single) and an extrovert who's half Rosie O'Donnell, half Mother Teresa.

Since being diagnosed with multiple sclerosis at 19, Boggess has spent the past three decades battling the progressive disease and shaping her attitude toward it. She's gone from cane to walker to wheelchair to electric wheelchair. Each year, the illness has chipped away at her freedom and made her increasingly dependent on God.

"I never know what my body's not going to do today that it did yesterday," Boggess said. "God's with me every minute of the day, and I don't know how I could do it by myself . . . I've learned to put all my worries at his feet. And when I do, the heavens open up and the blessings come down."

Even after meeting Boggess, I still had to ask: "With everything that's happened to you, do you ever wonder if there's really a God?"

"How could there not be a God?" Boggess responded. "How could I do all this without God? God is my hope, my joy, my strength. He's the love of my life."

Just one more example: Sister Mary Norbert. She's young, bright and attractive, razor sharp, once a promising litigator and partner in a Minnesota law firm. Now she lives a cloistered life in the Tehachapi mountains. She shares the modest convent with five other women from Orange County's St. Michael's Abbey, which recently launched the only house of Norbertine nuns in the United States.

St. Norbert, a German, lived in the early 12th century and gave up his wealth for life as a poor priest who followed a strict regimen of prayer and penance.

"There comes a point when you have a conversion, and everything changes," said Sister Mary Norbert, who joined the order a year ago after feeling disenchanted with her career. "Part of the change in my life was my work. I was pushed out of the legal system, but there was also a pull from God."

It has to be a strong pull. For the rest of their lives, the sisters will follow the same daily routine. They will rise at 4 a.m., go to sleep at 10 p.m. and get up again for midnight prayers. Prayer will take up most of their time, but they will also sing, study and develop a cottage industry (maybe data entry for companies on the Internet) that will make them self-sufficient. They will get one hour of free time each day.

It's a lifestyle stripped down to essentials. There is no television, radio or newspapers, and there are few visitors and no trips off the 475-acre grounds except for doctor's appointments and family emergencies.

The pioneering sisters volunteered for this austere life because they believe prayer matters. Intercessory prayer—prayer that asks God to help someone—works, they insist. And the best way to pray is to reduce life to its basics, allowing no worldly diversions to come between those praying and God.

A contemplative life is something not many people can understand, including some of the nuns' family members and friends.

"When you live a life in the world and live that lifestyle, everything is normal," Sister Mary Norbert said. "When you start to make changes, oftentimes those changes become frightening, and people are challenged by it because it makes them look at their own life.

"This was a conscious choice to give my life to God. It's pretty radical, but Christ's gospel is demanding. We're here to save souls."

Sister Mary Norbert, her eyes wide and alive, said of the day she became a nun, "I had a lot of peace, a lot of joy. I was ready for this. There is nothing else. God is everything. There is no other choice."

. . .

I quickly found the religion beat to be different from others at
the paper. One of my first interviews was with a pastor who had
walked away from a six-figure job as a commercial real-estate bro-
ker to follow God's call. He once had ordered custom dress shirts
but was now shopping at the Goodwill so he could start a new
career ministering to God's people.

After escorting me into his tiny office, he said, "Do you mind
if we first pray about your job and your responsibility?"

Praying with a source wasn't the type of thing that was covered
in the *Los Angeles Times's* code of ethics, but it didn't seem right.
Was it a conflict of interest? Should I just pretend to pray so as not
to offend him? The pastor kept looking quizzically at me, wondering why I was taking so long to respond.

"Sure," I finally said, not wanting to make a big deal out of
it. He bowed his head and started to pray. I lowered my head but
kept my eyes open—that was the best compromise I could come
up with at the moment. This would happen often on the faith
beat, no matter the religion I was writing about.

More often than not, people I interviewed asked me first about
my own faith. In covering other stories over the years, people rarely
asked me personal questions, at least not right off the bat, and never
about religion. Now I was treated either as suspect or possibly as a
target for proselytizing. It wasn't just paranoia among the faithful.
Often, when it comes to stories about believers or religious questions, there is an unbridgeable gap in perception between believers
and others. It is an extreme example of the proposition that what
we bring to life determines what we take away from it.

My first reaction was to keep my faith private, because an answer
might imply that my religious views would color my reporting.
But since I wanted the interviewees to open up to me, I decided

the least I could do was to give them a direct answer to their simple question.

"I'm a Christian," I would say, and provide more details only if they asked. They often asked.

People of faith—it didn't matter whether they were Christian, Jewish or Muslim—almost universally expressed relief that a journalist who was religious was assigned to write their story. This reaction was the mirror opposite of some newsroom talk that, in its most polite form, went like this: "Can an evangelical Christian cover faith objectively?" My feeling was that you could cover faith well whether you were an atheist or devoutly religious. What mattered was a desire to write about religion accurately, with context and nuance.

The same kind of question was rarely asked, especially in the newsroom, about other beat reporters. Could a reporter who's a Democrat cover a Republican presidential primary fairly? (Indeed, the overwhelming majority of national political reporters are Democrats. Republican candidates are suspicious of them, and though I believe a liberal slant slips into media coverage, most of the bias reflects the laws of the marketplace. Bad news is easier to report, and it sells. Scandals and controversy get a lot of attention, regardless of party identification. Deep analysis of health care plans or Social Security reforms holds little popular appeal.) And what about sports writers who report on their favorite team? Or committed environmentalists whose beat is development? Every journalist is biased. What matters is the accuracy of the story. The readers and editors know soon enough if a reporter has an agenda, especially in the age of the Internet watchdog.

My only agenda was to make religion as fascinating to others as it was to me. Though I considered myself an evangelical Christian, I didn't think my role was to promote the faith. First, the rules of journalism prohibit it. Second, it wasn't my style. And third, a ham-fisted approach like that wouldn't have worked with readers and would have led to the quick demise of my column.

Writing "Getting Religion" was a part-time job. I worked on it weekends and at night and then e-mailed the column to my editors. Yet I thought about it night and day. I felt as if I had been handed the key to an utterly fascinating world, and I was determined to explore every inch.

In retrospect, I can now see there were patterns in my columns. Whenever I had a question of faith, the answer found its way into my writing. For example, I doubted the wisdom of giving 10 percent of my income to the church. It felt like a bit of a gimmick by religious leaders to make sure their organizations were well funded. Plus, did God really expect someone on a journalist's salary, living in Orange County with a growing family, to hand over 10 percent of his income (pre-tax, pastors always pointed out) to Him? I wasn't sure I could afford it. But then I wrote about a multimillionaire named John Crean who gave half his income (50 percent of $176.8 million the year that I interviewed him) to charity. A half century before that, he had begun to tithe on the advice of his pastor. At the time, Crean was a struggling businessman whose company was $250,000 in debt.

"The preacher said if you were to give—and not expect anything in return—you'll get your investment back tenfold in blessings," said Crean, a recreational-vehicle tycoon who has since died. "That sounded like a pretty good deal. It was worth giving it a shot, anyway."

As soon as he started giving, his fortunes turned around, and he told me he couldn't give away his money fast enough. It just kept coming in. So I started to tithe, too, and I found that I really didn't miss the 10 percent I gave away.

I frequently worried that my faith would end up costing me a lot more than a portion of my salary. So I wrote often about people who had made much greater sacrifices because of their belief in God. None regretted what they had done. In fact, they always said their lives had never been fuller. In one column, I explored the price of faith by interviewing a former Muslim and Orange County resident who was leaving the United States to go undercover as an evangelist in the West Bank, a calling that put his life at risk. (In fact, it would lead to a series of threats by the terrorist group Hamas.)

"I've always felt a call to be a missionary to Muslims," said Steve, who didn't want his real name used because, if caught, he faced death under Islamic law. "Muslims are great, wonderful people—more pure than a lot of Christians. Muslims are willing to die for their religion, but Christians won't sacrifice a TV show to go to church."

Steve sold all his possessions except for some clothes, a few books and a guitar to finance his new life.

"I'm not going to be afraid," he said. "I believe that God wants me to do this and He will protect me."

I also wrote about people who had been beaten down by life but still didn't blame God. These people were better Christians than I. I reported on the funeral of Ethan Shigeru Sechrest, a premature baby who had once made the evening news when he came home after spending his first three months at the hospital. Ethan weighed 14 ounces at birth.

After his birth, the Sechrests, devout Christians, and their friends rallied people around the world to pray for the infant. One of his doctors, trying to explain Ethan's miraculous survival, said he had been "prayed into life."

But then, at eight months old, Ethan caught a respiratory virus. His body hadn't developed a robust immune system, allowing a series of illnesses to overwhelm him. With Ethan's death, the Sechrests, their pastors, doctors and friends—everyone the baby touched—had to struggle with a question: Why didn't God step in to save him again? I went to the funeral because Ethan's tragic story was gripping. But I also attended because I wanted to hear the answer to that question.

Pastor J. P. Jones told mourners that Ethan's death "reveals our deepest fears" about God. And the honest answer, he said, is that we don't know why God allowed Ethan to die. And we won't fully know until "we pass from this life into heaven when we see things as God sees them."

It was one thing for the pastor to say that, but what would the parents say? If it were my child, I would rage at God for what He allowed to happen—especially after answering so many prayers for Ethan. It seemed cruel.

The Sechrests, who lost their first child to a stillborn birth, were confident they'd see glimpses of God's plan in the years to come.

"After the death of our first son, I couldn't see any blessings in that," Alan Sechrest said. "But over time, I could. Our marriage got stronger. We became better parents. But we just couldn't see it right away.

"We're going to be okay. Not today, not next week. But we're going to be okay because we trust in God."

Using the Sechrests as a yardstick, I had a long way to go in my faith. They provided inspiration and a model for me.

I still felt like I was a relatively new believer, and I had lots of questions about my faith. Scripture—the Bible—was a major source of them because, at least to a close reader, the Word of God contains contradictions, bizarre laws and hard-to-believe anecdotes. For me, the Bible was a puzzle I hadn't figured out yet. I found great wisdom in Scripture when I cherry-picked the passages. Among my favorites: "Have I not commanded you? Be strong and courageous. Do not be terrified; do not be discouraged, for the Lord your God will be with you wherever you go." (Joshua 1:9) "Do not be anxious about anything, but in everything, by prayer and petition, with thanksgiving, present your requests to God. And the peace of God, which transcends all understanding, will guard your hearts and your minds in Christ Jesus." (Philippians 4:6–7) And, "But the fruit of the Spirit is love, joy, peace, patience, kindness, goodness, faithfulness, gentleness and self-control. Against such things there is no law." (Galatians 5:22–23)

But trying to read the whole book through—which I attempted unsuccessfully several times—I bumped up against long recitations of boring genealogies (the opening chapters of First Chronicles), several of God's laws where the punishment didn't quite fit the crime (the Book of Leviticus recommends the death penalty for cursing your mother or father, for being a medium or "spiritist," for committing adultery, incest, bestiality or acts of homosexuality and for blaspheming the name of the Lord) and a wilder and more angry Jesus than I had known (the Gospel of Mark). I certainly didn't take everything in the Bible literally, but even viewing some passages figuratively didn't help—what was I to understand, metaphorically, about God and His plan for me when he kills "every firstborn in Egypt, both man and animal" because Pharaoh won't free the Hebrews? That God was a son of a bitch when messed with? Still, I didn't doubt the Bible was inspired by God; the trouble, I believed, was my ability to interpret it.

Several of my columns dealt with Christian apologetics—the study of the historical accuracy of the faith. I needed to hear Christians more intelligent than I who had the utmost confidence—and evidence to back it up—in what the Bible said, even those uncomfortable passages that most believers skip or ignore. That was why I loved interviewing people like Bill Creasy.

When he started working on his doctorate in medieval literature, a friend warned Creasy, "Don't waste your career being the world's leading expert on a third-rate Victorian poet. Choose a major author or a major work."

"So I chose God and the Bible," Creasy told me. "God's a world-class poet."

By day, Creasy, then 52, was a popular English professor at UCLA. By night—and on early mornings and weekends—he was a tireless Bible instructor. He strove to teach the Good Book cover to cover, verse by verse, to as many people as possible.

"The curtain goes up in Genesis and goes down in Revelation. It's a very linear story," Creasy said. "You can't possibly understand Revelation without reading the 65 books before it."

I attended several of Creasy's classes. He was a rich storyteller who combined encyclopedic knowledge with a sense of humor. His approach, a popular one in the modern era, was to teach the Bible as literature. His goal was to get his students "inside the narrative," just as they would with any book, instead of "standing outside the text."

"The people in the Bible are as real to me as you are," Creasy said. "And I think I make them come alive in class."

The problem that most people have studying the Bible, he added, was that they read it in bits and pieces. His students read the Bible straight through in two years.

"It's like listening to a Beethoven symphony a few bars at a time in random order," Creasy said. "Many people always wanted to read the Bible all the way through, but they bog down around Leviticus. I'm a scout. I've been down the trail before."

Though it has at least 44 authors and was written over 1,500 years, Creasy sees the Bible as a unified literary work that is the Word of God. "The main character is God, the conflict is sin and the theme is redemption," he says. "His face is on every page of Scripture; His voice is in every word . . . [The Bible] brings us ever closer, moment by moment, to the living Lord."

Yet most college professors who teach the Bible as literature aren't doing so as, or for, believers. Usually, this approach is merely an introduction for students who are biblically illiterate and feel obliged to learn something about what is called history's most influential book without wanting to commit themselves on the big questions. Indeed, reading the entire Bible means facing *all* the potential contradictions. The Apostle Paul wrote, "God is not the author of confusion," yet the Bible is perplexing enough to spawn thousands of different interpretations and Christian denominations. Even theologians arrive at different answers to questions large (can we be saved through works or by grace alone?)—and small (did Jesus have brothers?). What is a believer to make of all this? By incorporating historical context and scholarship, Creasy provides nuanced answers for each troublesome verse of the Bible.

For example, to a casual reader, the Book of Genesis turns into a horror story when God tests the faithfulness of Abraham. The Lord tells him to take "your only son, Isaac, whom you love [and is an adult], and go to the region of Moriah. Sacrifice him there as a burnt offering on one of the mountains I will tell you about." (Genesis 22:2)

It seems like a sadistic request, especially when God abruptly stops Abraham just as he's about to plunge a knife into his son. But Creasy, in a 95-minute lecture which he pulls from geography, history and other parts of the Scriptures, explains that Abraham knew Isaac would either be saved or resurrected by God because the Lord had promised Abraham earlier that Isaac would have many descendants. God always keeps His promises, and how could Abraham's son have children if he were dead?

Others may disagree with Creasy's analysis, but I found it comforting that someone of his intellect didn't flinch as he made his way through the Bible.

It didn't escape me that I had the best part-time job in the world. Whatever interested me, whatever I wanted to know about religion, I could pick up the phone and call some of the country's greatest experts, and they would talk with me. Or I could visit someone who would testify about God's miracles. I got up each morning excited about the prospect of reporting and writing another column. I didn't mind, for instance, spending a Friday night at the hottest high school dance in Orange County, which happened to be put on by the Mormon Church. Or driving to Tijuana on a weekend to watch orphans open Christmas presents sent by churches in the United States. Or taking a Saturday morning to watch a teacher at a synagogue make the story of Noah's Ark come alive by having her children make a ship out of pita bread and, with a layer of frosting in the hull, place Animal Crackers inside.

The work gave me goose bumps. I framed my first column and hung it in my office at Times Community News. I had found my calling and tried to figure out a plan to move over to *The Times* full-time. My hopes rose when my editors started to wonder how I found much more interesting stories in a few hours a week than their Orange County religion writer did full-time. As the column developed, I'd occasionally get two equally good and timely column ideas and the editors would give me the green light to write one of them as a regular story. This allowed my work to start appearing on the front of the Metro section and get more attention.

Best of all, covering religion was deepening my faith. By 1999, it had been seven years since my mountaintop conversion. I felt a growing muscularity to my Christianity. I was learning more and more about the Bible. I wanted to plunge deeper into belief, history and custom. I didn't need as much self-help as I had earlier; my life had long ago gotten out of intensive care and had stabilized. I started to feel claustrophobic at Mariners Church. Its seeker-friendly services—which had drawn me so effortlessly back to Christianity—now seemed simplistic. I wanted to strip away the happy songs, the upbeat, black-and-white messages and the cappuccino machine. I wanted something more authentic, more raw, even. I was grateful for my time at Mariners, but I felt I had graduated. We stopped going as a family one day and slipped away. Nobody noticed. That was the blessing and curse of belonging to a mega-church. No one knows you've arrived and no one realizes when you've gone.

Greer still dreamed about attending the Catholic Church of her youth. Like a lot of cradle Catholics, she never felt entirely comfortable in other denominations. She liked the ritual, the formality and the familiarity. We made a test run at our local parish, but it ended badly when Father Jerome Karcher (son of Carl's Jr. founder Carl Karcher), with a kind smile on his face, explained to Greer that she was an adulterer because she hadn't gotten married in the church.

"You don't really believe that," Greer said, laughing.

"Oh, absolutely," Father Jerome assured her. "Jesus said it."

We didn't go back.

Yet I felt a growing attraction to the Catholic Church, its complex 2,000-year-old history, its stories of the saints, the breadth and depth of its theology, its beautiful liturgy and its big-tent tradition that allowed for ultra-liberals and ultra-conservatives, the rich and poor, majorities and minorities to worship in the same parish. Not too long ago—within living memory of some—the centuries-long conflict between Protestants and Catholics still had sharp edges in the United States. When Al Smith was the Democratic nominee for president in 1928, vitriolic anti-Catholic literature and speakers flourished. (One perennial bestseller claimed to report on baby burnings from inside a convent.) Republican operatives spread the rumor that Smith was secretly extending the Holland Tunnel 3,500 miles to the Vatican. Today, evangelicals and Catholics still have an uneasy relationship, with many evangelicals viewing Catholics' devotion to the papacy and their praying to the saints as unbiblical, at best. For their part, many Catholics simply ignore evangelicals because they aren't part of the One True Church.

Greer and I compromised for the moment, agreeing to attend St. Andrew's Presbyterian Church in Newport Beach. Pastor John Huffman, a longtime friend, had run the church for decades. At six-foot-four and 220 pounds, John was a teddy bear partial to sweater vests and neatly pressed slacks. An intellectual with a fondness for politics and golf, John was mentored by Norman Vincent Peale. He had been one of President Richard Nixon's spiritual advisors when John was pastor of a Presbyterian church in Key Biscayne, Florida, where the president often vacationed. With his booming baritone voice and sharp mind, John gave thought-provoking sermons with academic overtones for churchgoers who wanted to believe with both heart and mind.

We started attending services in 1999 and put our three (soon to be four) boys in their youth programs, which they loved. We kept our tradition of attending church on Saturday evenings and stayed afterward for pizza and salad with friends. St. Andrew's also had a great Bible study on Wednesday evenings, along with a parallel children's program. Saturday and Wednesday evenings served as the tent poles of our family life.

. . .

I knew I was maturing in my faith because I had become less worried. It didn't kill me to know that my full-time job at Times Community News was on the chopping block—actually, my whole division was on the chopping block. We had new owner-ship and changing strategies, and our unit had staggering annual losses than ran into the millions. Over the past three years, *Times* executives had made a push for local news by starting nearly two dozen community dailies and weeklies. We had hired close to 200 young journalists and opened ten offices. Yet the expansion had not translated into new advertising revenue.

In 2000, when the Tribune Company bought the *Los Ange-les Times* and a new management team arrived, the community news concept was ripe for reexamination. Though no one told us directly, we knew our days were numbered. We stopped hiring. We tried to slip our most talented people into positions at *The Times*. We advised our reporters, photographers and editors that it might be a good time to get their résumés together. We were dead journalists walking; we just didn't know our execution date.

I had always been an anxious person and still am one. I bite my fingernails until they bleed. My stomach can churn up at a moment's notice. I have anxiety nightmares more nights than not. But in 2000, I didn't have the usual crippling apprehension. My situation was nerve-racking and filled with anxious moments, but I wasn't overwhelmed by it. This feeling—of well-being? I wasn't even sure what to call it—was odd. I hadn't felt it in my first four decades of life. The stakes were high. I had hired most of the people who were about to be laid off, and I felt responsible for them. And I didn't have a pile of money or any job prospects to fall back on for myself. My family—now complete with four boys—lived pretty much paycheck to paycheck. I was a 40-year-old journalist who specialized in low-paying community news at a time when the industry was quickly downsizing.

Yet I sensed, deep in my soul, none of it mattered. God loved me perfectly. He would take care of my family and me, whatever happened. Perhaps subconsciously preparing for the end, I had written several columns about people who had lost everything yet came back ever stronger because of their belief in God. I was on vacation in Kauai when I got the call.

"Bill, sorry to wreck your vacation, but I thought you'd want to know," said an executive with *The Times*. "We're closing down most of Times Community News. We're going to make an announcement next week. I don't want you to worry personally. Everyone loves your work, and you'll have a job with *The Times*. We'll have to work out the specifics later."

Within a week, I stood at the front of a large meeting hall packed with worried young journalists. Someone within *The Times* had leaked the news of the layoffs to other media organizations. Many of my people found out they didn't have a job by listening to the radio on the drive to work.

I confirmed for them the bad news. I told them how proud I was of our effort. We had done great work against long odds, and that's something no one could take away from us. I also said that as shocking as this day was, I was confident that all of us would go on to much greater things, and this was just a speed bump in our careers. I said this with conviction because I believed that God would take care of them, too. I don't think many of them believed me.

I still didn't know my own future, despite what I had been told. I desperately wanted to be a full-time religion writer, and I didn't see how that could happen. *The Times* already had a full complement of religion reporters, including one in Orange County. Yet instead of worrying about it, I tried to look at this turn of events as the start of another adventure with God. Where would He put me next?

The answer came almost instantly. The editor of the Orange County edition called me soon after the meeting and asked if I could come to her office. There she said she wanted to know if I was interested in a crazy idea she had.

"What if I told you I was interested in having you write about religion full-time?"

My heart pounded in my chest. Was she kidding? We had never talked about the possibility before.

"I'd love the job," I replied. "But what about the current reporter?"

"We'd move her to another beat," she said.

I hated to bring it up, but I told her it would be difficult for my family if I had to take a pay cut to become a reporter.

"Don't worry, I'll take care of that," she said. "So, do you want to do this or what?" She smiled broadly. She was excited to have me. She had no idea that I was even more thrilled.

"I'd be honored."

Two weeks later, I walked into *The Times* as a full-time religion reporter.

As a college student, aside from sports (and sex and beer), I had a passion for news. I considered myself a news junkie. I adored reading newspapers and magazines. In the pre-Internet days, I often went to the library at the University of California, Irvine, and spent hours just looking through newspapers from around the country and reading magazines. The stories—whether they were breaking news, funny little features or complex narratives—intoxicated me. My favorite novel, by far, was Hunter Thompson's *Fear and Loathing in Las Vegas: A Savage Journey to the Heart of*

the American Dream, a story about a journalist's drug-filled weekend during which he was supposed to cover a motorcycle race. I
still have the novel's first line memorized: "We were somewhere
around Barstow on the edge of the desert when the drugs began to
take hold."

At the end of my junior year, I didn't have any career plans. I
was a political science major, and, unlike most of my classmates, I
didn't want to go to law school. I hadn't met too many happy attorneys. Panicked at my looming graduation, I sought the counsel of
a wise family friend. He told me to find something I loved to do
and do it for a living. That way, it really wouldn't be like working
and my passion would ensure career success. Maybe, I thought,
I could be a journalist like Hunter Thompson or his mainstream
counterparts, Woodward and Bernstein.

I said to the family friend: "Well, I love journalism. Maybe I
could be a reporter."

"Then get your butt down to the college paper and give it a try."

I sat in the courtyard outside the offices of the *New University* (the
name of UC Irvine's weekly student newspaper) for an hour, trying
to get up the courage to go inside. With my heart in my throat, I
walked up the stairs to the paper's second-floor offices and stepped
through the open door. It was love at first sight—the relentless ringing of the phones, the clacking of the keyboards, the smell of scraps
of old pizza in oily boxes on the floor, the mess of old papers and
documents stacked everywhere. This was heaven. I felt at home.

"Excuse me," I stammered lamely to the first person I saw
behind a desk. "I'd like to be a reporter, maybe covering sports."

"Well, I'm the sports editor," he said. "What are you doing this
afternoon?"

I shrugged my shoulders. He reached inside his desk, pulled
out a skinny reporter's notebook and shoved it in my hand.

"There's a men's tennis match starting in ten minutes. Go cover it and have the story in by tonight."

I hustled out the door, stoked at landing my first assignment. A few days later, I opened up the *New U* and saw *my* byline over *my* sports story. My name, my words in print. I was a writer. I was a journalist. Eighteen years later, I walked into *The Times*'s Orange County newsroom for the first time as a reporter—and as a full-time religion writer, to boot. It lacked some of the characteristic shabbiness of my previous newsrooms. This was, after all, The Show, the major leagues of American newspapers. Expensive signage pointed visitors to the Metro, Calendar and Sports departments. A news rack outside the editor's office held neatly placed copies of the *New York Times, Wall Street Journal, USA Today* and *Orange County Register*. Off in the corner was a library, equipped with computers linked to special databases, bookshelves full of reference materials, a morgue of newspaper clips going back decades and a counter full of current magazines. Still, at heart, my new newsroom wasn't that much different from those at smaller papers. The phones rang, the keyboards clacked and the desks were covered with stacks of reports and newspapers. The most important difference was *The Times*'s newsroom was home to some of the world's best journalists.

I had made it. I credited my faith and constant prayers. God had answered my prayers more completely than I could have ever imagined. Now I would be paid to learn everything I could about religion, and I would be able to help shape religion coverage at one of the nation's largest media outlets.

It seemed too good to be true.

Shot Out of a Cannon

Delight yourself in the Lord and he will give you the desires
of your heart.

— PSALMS 37:4

A FEW WEEKS into the job at *The Times*, in November 2000,
a colleague stopped by my cubicle with a story tip.

"Hey, Bill," said Jean Pasco, one of the most respected reporters
in the newsroom. "You ever hear of Father Michael Harris?"

I shook my head. Jean, a top political reporter in her 40s who
spent her free time running sub-four-hour marathons, was the
dean of Orange County journalists. Her list of sources was roughly
the thickness of a small city phone book.

"He was principal at Mater Dei and Santa Margarita high
schools," she said in a voice that was famous for booming
throughout the newsroom. "Raised something like $26 million
to build Santa Margarita. Anyway, he's named in a clergy sexual
abuse lawsuit, and someone leaked me these documents." She

dropped a stack of legal papers on my desk. "They look interesting. Maybe we can team up for a story when the case goes to trial or gets settled."

I thumbed through a few of them—depositions, reports and motions. They formed a big pile. I promised myself I'd look at them by end of the week at the latest. But I never got around to it. At the time, it was an isolated, sordid story that didn't set off any journalism alarms in me. I didn't see that right in front of me was a tale that would cause upheaval and historic reforms within the Roman Catholic dioceses of Orange and Los Angeles, generate the first of more than $1 billion in payouts to hundreds of victims of sexual abuse by priests and foreshadow by almost two years the church's national sex scandal. Fourteen months later, when the Catholic sex scandal broke from Boston to Hawaii, it would be searingly clear that Father Harris's case was a bellwether of news to come.

I was distracted by some much more inspiring stories I was attending to. In my first year of full-time religion, I felt like I had been shot out of a cannon. I wrote 145 stories for the paper. Each article led to something better, more inspiring, more engaging. I saw it as the subtle hand of the Lord at work. Another God thing.

I was fascinated by people who seemed holy—the Madge Roddas of the world who instantly forgave their rapists and would-be murderers. There were many of them, living on the edges of each major faith. This was nothing new. The roster of saints in Catholic history is filled with people who were thought to be lunatics at the time, and I met a lot of modern equivalents.

One of the most beloved saints, Francis of Assisi, was initially mocked and scorned by his wealthy family and friends when he

changed his life. A hard-drinking son of a prosperous businessman, he was inspired, in part, by a sermon based on this passage
in the Gospel of Matthew:

> *As you go, preach this message: "The kingdom of heaven is*
> *near." Heal the sick, raise the dead, cleanse those who have*
> *leprosy, drive out demons. Freely you have received, freely*
> *give. Do not take along any gold or silver or copper in your*
> *belts; take no bag for the journey, or extra tunic, or sandals*
> *or a staff; for the worker is worth his keep.*
>
> — MATTHEW 10:7–20

Francis stripped away his possessions, right down to his shoes.
He put on a rough tunic and belted it with a rope. He went bare-
foot. He began to treat lepers in that simple outfit that would
become standard dress for the Franciscans, the order founded on
Francis's principles.

When I found Christians on the religion beat who radiated
holiness, they intrigued and frightened me in equal measure. They
were true believers who simply couldn't live out their faith in a
moderate fashion. God required more from them. They had been
radicalized by Scripture to follow the words of Jesus. That often
meant living among the poor and serving food and providing various services to them. It also could translate into politics, in battles
to stop abortion, to allow Christianity in the public square or to
save the environment—God's creation.

It wasn't until after that first year, when the ether of unbounded optimism wore off, that I began to see in many of my stories a wide chasm between the lives of the average believer (this group included myself and most pastors I encountered) and those of true believers—people who lived their lives as if the Scriptures were true.

This gap first struck me during an interview with one of the richest couples in the world, Susan and Henry Samueli. A former UCLA engineering professor, Henry Samueli co-founded Broadcom Corporation in 1991, which went public seven years later. When I talked with the Samuelis in July 2000, their wealth was estimated at $5.1 billion and they had spent the past year giving away $27 million to the University of California, Irvine, $25 million to UCLA, $5 million to Opera Pacific and lesser sums to a variety of nonprofits. I wanted to talk to them about their latest donation, $3 million to help build a permanent home for a Reform synagogue in South Orange County that had operated for years in a series of trailers.

I arrived at the Samuelis' oceanfront home perched on a cliff in Corona del Mar with *Times* photographer Mark Boster. After being questioned by one of the compound's bodyguards, we were escorted inside the house. I was nervous—it wasn't every day I interacted with billionaires—but the Samuelis, especially Susan, made us feel at home in the multimillion-dollar mansion with sweeping views of the Pacific Ocean and California coast. Henry, a trim man with a dark mustache and full head of short-cropped brown hair, had the demeanor of the engineer that he was: quiet, reflective, intelligent and precise. He carried himself ramrod straight. Susan, a stylish woman, was the extrovert of the pair, with an easy laugh and an enthusiasm that was quickly fired up. She grew up in a Jewish neighborhood in Los Angeles and said her strong faith, a constant since childhood, had made instant wealth easier to handle.

The Samuelis said they were brought up in the Jewish tradition, which teaches *tzedakah*, the Hebrew word for justice. It can also be translated to mean charity. Henry, whose parents were Holocaust survivors, said he had been troubled that his synagogue, Temple Beth El in Aliso Viejo, existed in a series of trailers that "had the implication of nonpermanent."

The couple also disclosed for the first time that they were trying to give permanence to the emerging liberal Reform movement in Israel, a country dominated by Orthodox synagogues. At the time, of the estimated 20 Reform temples in Israel, only four had their own buildings. The Samuelis had already given $2.5 million to a Reform temple near Tel Aviv.

Henry Samueli, then 45, described himself as "very much a moderate in all aspects of my life." When he spoke of his religion, his voice rose in passion only on the subject of fundamentalism.

"Broadcom is probably the most multicultural company on the planet Earth," he told me. "We have every race, creed, color, religion, which is great. I love that.

"One of the things I like most about Reform Judaism is that it promotes tolerance of various religions and cultures. I'm very much against orthodox religions of all kinds, including Judaism. They don't have their heads on straight."

Henry Samueli's only harsh words of the morning stayed with me. He inadvertently had hit on a religious paradox that would become one of my preoccupations. Are true believers crazy and misguided or do they just take their religion more seriously than others? Evangelicals ask each other an interesting question: If you were arrested for being a Christian, would there be enough evidence to convict you? For many people, the answer would be no. I loved to write about people who put their faith above all else—not in words, but in deeds. They were just so *different*. Down the road, when my faith faltered, I held onto these stories of pure belief like a life preserver. They reminded me that holiness could be achieved.

For instance, there was Pastor Ed Salas. If you want to see whether your pastor's faith is real, watch how he reacts after a tumor is found inside the brain of his ten-year-old son. Study whether his faith wavers after the doctors remove a quarter-sized mass from his child, after a biopsy reveals an aggressive cancer, and after his son is left dizzy and so nauseated that he drops from 84 pounds to 67.

On a Sunday service that was supposed to celebrate his church's move into a larger facility, Salas told the congregation about his son Timothy's cancer. He delivered a sermon about how to stand firm in faith. He chose Daniel 3:17–18:

> If we are thrown into the blazing furnace, the God we serve
> is able to save us from it, and he will rescue us. . . . But even
> if he does not, we want you to know, O king, that we will
> not serve your gods. . . .

"Faith doesn't depend on circumstances," he told his congregation. "It depends on who God is."

Then there were Leia and Dwight Smith. The couple had carved out successful careers in sales. She sold textbooks; he worked for 3M. But as middle age approached, they determined that they weren't following Christ's admonitions to live a selfless life and help the poor.

"You just can't say Jesus is your Savior," Dwight says, "you have to act like it."

They quit their jobs for a life in the Catholic Worker, an independent poverty-relief group with a branch in Santa Ana, California. Living in a donated two-story Craftsman home in a hardscrabble section of the city, the couple began to take in homeless people, especially women and children. Soon, bodies of every shape and size filled their house and then their backyard each evening. At the end of each month—long after the government checks had run out—the crowds swelled to almost 200 people. The lines for the three bathrooms were constant. Feeding the visitors each night out of one kitchen turned into a Herculean task. Still, the Smiths didn't turn anyone away.

"It got to the point where I couldn't decide which middle-aged woman with health problems to throw back on the street so they could be robbed or raped," Dwight told me. "These people are so disenfranchised, the only person who will stick up for them is Jesus Christ."

Dwight is a large, balding man with a loud voice, keen intellect and a quirkiness that fits in well with his homeless guests. Leia is a quiet force who mixes the stubbornness of a pit bull with the kindness of a saint to somehow make the chaos swirling around Catholic Worker work. The Smiths live on the second floor with a handful of other Catholic Workers. No one receives a salary—just room and board and a few dollars a week for spending money.

Social activist Dorothy Day started the Catholic Worker movement in 1933, during the Depression. One of its founding principles was to provide the poor with dignity, along with food and shelter. I've spent many hours at the Santa Ana Catholic Worker, surrounded by the sick, the mentally ill, the downtrodden, the addicted and the flat-out unlucky. These troubled souls share a very small space and have no privacy. Arguments are frequent; problems and demands arise quickly among these high-maintenance guests. Dwight and Leia set about their work like emergency room doctors, working on the critical cases first, but in the end, ministering to all.

It is a frenzied, heartbreaking but occasionally uplifting

scene, as when some of the homeless children received free music lessons, practiced their instruments (mostly violins) regularly amid the bedlam that engulfed them and ended up playing in an all-star middle-school orchestra at Carnegie Hall in New York City. Most other miracles at the Catholic Worker are more modest: a father stops taking drugs for a night; a transient mother enrolls her children in school; a family sleeps with a roof over its head.

During the Thanksgiving and Christmas holidays, the single phone line at the Catholic Worker rings endlessly with people who feel the urge to volunteer. Though the Smiths don't need the large influx of help, they accept each volunteer with a warm embrace. They understand that at this moment the volunteers need the experience of helping others, even if the homeless shelter is overflowing with helpers. With any luck, the volunteers will return during the year, when the help is really needed.

I've sometimes thought that Dwight and Leila are hopelessly idealistic, downright masochistic or just plain nuts. I've come to realize that they simply believe in Christianity as much as they believe in breathing. They can behave in no other way.

Mega-church pastor and best-selling author Rick Warren is a Christian about whom I was quite skeptical at first. He had built Saddleback Church in Lake Forest, California, from scratch into one of the largest congregations in the world. More than 20,000 people attended weekend services. The ten-acre campus has the feel of Disneyland (no coincidence, since Disney engineers helped with the design), with modern, cheerful buildings and gorgeous landscaped grounds that include a stream that parts like the Red Sea and a boulder that rolls back to reveal a model of Jesus's tomb. My distant impression of

Warren was that his ministry was driven more by slick marketing than by God's word.

But then I spent some time with Warren, his staff and other pastors he had mentored shortly after his *Purpose Driven Life* book hit the stores, and I realized I was wrong about the mega-church pastor. First, there's nothing slick about him. His language is simple and straightforward. He wears khaki pants and untucked Hawaiian shirts, even for Sunday services. He prefers bear hugs to handshakes. He reflects the laid-back nature of his rural upbringing in Northern California, seemingly having time to chat with anyone who crosses his path. He comes across more like a guy on your bowling team than a superstar pastor.

"Rick is just a normal guy," a pastor of a small church told me. "There's a feeling that if he can do it, so can we."

Thousands of pastors around the world credit Warren's purpose-driven formula for creating thriving churches. The plan focuses on attracting seekers to church and then getting them, step by step, involved in ministry. I talked with scores of purpose-driven pastors, and many talked about a second Reformation that Warren was leading within Christianity. Warren, despite a self-deprecating style, speaks in similar terms of his movement: "The first Reformation clarified what the church believes—our message and doctrine. The current Reformation will clarify what the church does—our purpose and activities on Earth."

At the same time, Warren seems genuinely bewildered by his success. He frequently mentions how many millions of books he's sold as if he still can't believe it. He talks the same way about getting a fan letter from President George W. Bush or how NASCAR drivers are using the *Purpose Driven Life* for Bible study.

With so much at stake, and with a profile so high, Warren

is careful to keep clear of controversy. He has declined numerous opportunities to have a regular television program—not wanting to be associated with televangelists—and has been generally media-shy, preferring to work through pastors and churches. He drives a three-year-old Ford truck and announced to his congregation that he had paid back 23 years of salary to Saddleback Church with the royalties from his book. He now "reverse tithes," giving away 90 percent of his book's royalties to ministry.

"Now that our church knows I've done this, I'm eager for the nonbelieving public to know it too, because it counteracts the popular perception by skeptics that all ministers are all in it just for the money, especially large-church pastors," Warren told me.

To eliminate gossip and temptation, Warren has vowed never to be in a room alone with a woman except his wife, Kay. Even if an elevator door opens and there's only one woman inside, Warren said that he lets that one go and waits for another—or takes the stairs.

Following Warren around for a few days is exhausting. Part of his genius is that he has attention deficit syndrome, which allows him to generate idea after idea (though he not surprisingly has disdain for meetings). It's not hard to imagine him back in his high school days, when as a skinny, long-haired guitar player with John Lennon glasses he started a Christian club on campus, sponsored rock concerts after school, gave out New Testaments, produced a Christian musical and published an underground Christian newspaper. Today, Warren is in an even bigger rush to win converts.

"[God] wants His lost children found," Warren told me. "I decided a long time ago I'm not going to waste my life. Life is too short and eternity is too long."

After my story ran, Warren gave me his private e-mail and cell phone number in case I ever needed someone to talk to. It was a gesture I suspect he made to almost everyone he came in contact with for more than a few minutes.

It is refreshing to see a man of God, at the height of his powers, remain grounded. Later on the religion beat, I would watch a Catholic cardinal step out of a limousine and extend his hand to a parishioner who asked "His Eminence" if she could kiss his bishop's ring. I would investigate high-profile pastors and find they owned several mansions, late-model luxury cars, custom-made suits, jets and yachts. And I've watched as Christian leaders, from congregations large and small, tumbled into sexual affairs because they didn't see the danger in being alone in a room with a woman. Rick Warren was different from most.

You didn't have to have a powerful position to be holy. Jen Hubbard believed in her faith enough to risk her job and take on one of the best-known names in the evangelical community. At the time I met her, Jen was a gung-ho 27-year-old evangelical fresh out of college. She landed what she thought was a dream job, working for Hank Hanegraaff, the best-selling Christian author and theological watchdog known for his syndicated radio show, *The Bible Answer Man.* Jen worked for Hanegraaff's umbrella non-profit organization, the Christian Research Institute, then based in Orange County, California.

Jen oversaw communications to and from potential donors, working to get people to give money to the ministry and feel like their money was making a difference. In the office, she sat near the women who paid the ministry's bills and processed donations. Jen soon grew alarmed that donor money seemed to be paying for the personal expenses of Hanegraaff and his family. His ministry paid for, among other things, a luxury sports car, a large salary for his wife who rarely worked in the office, and country club dues. Jen and other employees took their concerns to their managers, who told them to keep quiet because "dealing with the issue was not within our sphere of influence. . . ."

After her co-workers went home, Jen started to copy any questionable invoice that she saw, including ones for a board-approved 2003 Lexus sports car and smaller items, such as repairs to Hanegraaff's children's computers, meals at the country club and birthday flowers for his mother.

"Donor money shouldn't have been used for these things," Jen told me. "I worked with donors, and they expect their money to be handled wisely, not spent lavishly."

When management learned she had been making copies of the invoices, she was fired. Her actions, though, spurred an audit by the Evangelical Council for Financial Accountability that resulted in what it called a "significant reimbursement" to the ministry.

"I felt angry and broken that the Christian community did not apologize to me," Jen told me. "I felt like I did this thing that felt in line with my faith, and here I was shunned by the most 'powerful' people within that faith group."

She acted on her responsibility to God to safeguard the donors' money, and her actions left her unemployed and her boss still in ministry. How could that be? I often thought of Jen when I saw Christians lacking the courage needed to make a sacrifice required by their faith (a category in which I often found myself). If this young woman could take on a national evangelical leader, what was stopping the rest of us from practicing a more radical form of Christianity?

True believers were by no means limited to Christianity. On the religion beat, I had gotten to know a rabbi named David

Eliezrie, who founded a Chabad-Lubavitch synagogue in Yorba Linda, California. The Chabad-Lubavitch movement is known for its rabbis who wear long beards, black suits and fedoras. The Lubavitchers, a small but rapidly growing part of Judaism, interested me because they are so different from other Jews. Their passion in their beliefs and quest for innovation allow them to break many of the cultural traditions surrounding their faith and reach out to disenfranchised Jews. The Lubavitchers don't isolate themselves from the world as do other Orthodox Jews, but embrace it. For example, they were one of the first religious groups to harness the power of the Internet to connect their members around the world, to attract new recruits and to serve as a research tool for any Jew.

The Lubavitchers have become an island of growth, innovation and success at a time of aging synagogue memberships and stagnant population elsewhere among American Jews. The beliefs of the Lubavitchers seemed far-fetched to me—for instance, that God wants men and women segregated inside the synagogue, or that menstruating women cannot have sexual relations with their husbands and must take a purifying bath after their period before resuming sex. But I was intrigued by the confidence they have in carrying out their faith, especially in bringing nonreligious Jews back to the fold.

"When a Jew alienates himself from his people, God forbid, it is only because he is thirsty," said their late leader, Rabbi Menachem M. Schneerson. "His soul thirsts for meaning in life, but the waters of Torah have eluded him. So he wanders about in foreign domains, seeking to quench his thirst.

"Only a shepherd who hastens not to judge the runaway kid, who is sensitive to the causes of its desertion, can mercifully lift it into his arms and bring it back home."

I wrote two lengthy features about the Lubavitchers, describing how the followers, inspired largely by the teachings of Schneerson—who died in 1994 and wasn't replaced—have taken the Jewish world by storm (and generated plenty of controversy by doing so). In keeping with Schneerson's ideas, Jews exploring their faith in Chabad centers don't have to accept all—or even any—of the group's Orthodox practices. They need not join a synagogue or pay dues. The idea is to patiently lead Jews back to Orthodoxy one small step at a time—by getting them to attend a Sabbath service, light candles Friday night, listen to a lecture from a Jewish scholar.

The success of the Lubavitchers can be measured two ways. First, there are the hard numbers. The number of Chabad rabbis and their families who now serve lifetime assignments has doubled in the past decade to more than 4,000 in 61 countries, according to Chabad statistics. In an era where some denominations, including Roman Catholicism, have left pulpits empty because of clergy shortages, the offspring of Chabad rabbis are following in their parents' footsteps in such numbers that a surplus of about 200 new rabbis and their wives is now staged in Brooklyn, awaiting assignments around the world. Schneerson said there was no higher calling.

"A Jew may say to you, 'Why can't you leave me alone?' " Schneerson told his followers. " 'Why can't you just go and do your thing and let me do mine? What does it bother you if I drill this little hole in my little boat?'

"You must answer him, 'There is only one boat, and we are all in it together.' "

Lubavitch officials say a new Chabad center opens every ten days somewhere in the world. Chabad's fundraisers, including its widely publicized West Coast telethons, bring in more than

$800 million annually. The movement's outreach is so good that it attracts money from other Jews who see it as simply a good investment for Judaism. A New York investment manager has given millions of dollars to support newly ordained Chabad rabbis and their wives each year. Among other things, he has sponsored 35 couples to open Chabad Houses at colleges across the country and 33 others to expand adult Jewish learning in the United States. The banker, who attends a Modern Orthodox synagogue, said Chabad's emissaries provide the most cost-effective way of strengthening the Jewish community, whether it's at an American college or in Africa.

The second measure of Chabad's growing influence is the controversy it generates, much of it from Jews frustrated at the movement's success and worried that the Lubavitchers' brand of Judaism will become too influential.

Schneerson's charisma was such that in the final years of his four decades of leadership, increasing numbers of Lubavitchers believed the rebbe was the *moshiach*, the Messiah. A dozen years after his death, the belief that Schneerson is the Messiah has waned dramatically, at least in public.

"The Jewish community is becoming deeply dependent on them for religious services and ceremonies, education and social services," said David Berger, an Orthodox rabbi and a history professor at Brooklyn College who has written a book on Chabad. "It's a clear and present danger to Judaism."

Danger? Here's what I saw: a group of people who, on the whole, lived out their Jewish faith in a way that outshined most of Judaism. Their leaders, rabbi-and-wife emissary teams called *schluchim*, didn't mind doing the dirty work—living in remote outposts in lifetime assignments, earning modest salaries and ministering to nonreligious Jews. From my reporting and talking to others who had covered the movement, I found most Lubavitchers to be happy and content with their lives. The evidence for that is in their children; the majority of them—more than 70 percent in California, where the best statistics are kept—also become *schluchim*. Imagine what would happen to any faith group if 70 percent of its pastors' offspring became pastors themselves. It always struck me as ironic that one of the best evangelical denominations was found in Judaism among the Lubavitchers. For me, their actions produced an attractive portrait of faith in action.

I found radical believers easy to spot, because they shined so brightly among the gray of the spiritual pack. I didn't even know if *I* wanted to be holy. I feared where God would take me. I liked my life. It was comfortable. I had money and a nice home. I didn't live among the poor and sick; visiting once in a while was enough. When these thoughts crept into my mind, the words of C. S. Lewis from *The Weight of Glory* haunted me:

> *Indeed, if we consider the unblushing promises of reward and the staggering nature of the rewards promised in the Gospels, it would seem that Our Lord finds our desires, not too strong, but too weak. We are half-hearted creatures, fooling about with drink and sex and ambition when infinite joy is offered us, like an ignorant child who wants to go on making mud pies in a slum because he cannot imagine what is meant by the offer of a holiday at the sea. We are far too easily pleased.*

I thought Lewis might be right, but I lacked the courage to test the premise. I'd stick to making mud pies in a slum. He was writing about nonbelievers, but the words applied to Christians, too. Was I doing enough? Was I truly dedicated to God? Or was I making convenient compromises? It seemed to me that all Christians had to come to grips with another challenge from Lewis, who wrote in *God in the Dock*: "Christianity, if false, is of no importance, and if true, of infinite importance. The only thing it cannot be is moderately important."

I started to view the moderates of my faith (myself included) as people who didn't fully believe the radical, uncompromising message of the Gospels. We didn't turn our lives entirely over to Christ. We stored up treasures on Earth and not in heaven. We didn't go too far out of our way to help the poor or make real sacrifices in the name of Jesus. We lived a version of Christianity Lite, a feel-good brand of faith that didn't extend much past Sunday morning.

My Ten Commandments

Do your best to present yourself to God as one approved, a
workman who does not need to be ashamed and who cor-
rectly handles the word of truth.

— 2 TIMOTHY 2:15

IT WASN'T EASY writing about the faith of a true believer.
Journalists like to trade in facts. In many ways, sports teams and
courthouses are among the easiest beats for reporters because the
action happens in real time, right in front of them. There is a clear
winner and loser, and statistics to detail what happened. At the
game, you can even watch instant replay in case you missed the
action the first time. In a courtroom, you can get a transcript and
other legal documents to refer back to if you're hazy on a point.
On the religion beat, you're dealing in facts mixed liberally with
matters of faith. It's drilled into journalists that "if your mother
tells you she loves you, better check it out." But such journalistic
standards can't be applied to much of faith reporting. It's impossible to check whether God is real, or whether someone's conver-

sion is authentic. Large portions of religion stories are ultimately unknowable.

It wasn't my job to prove the Lord's existence or the worth of someone's faith—unless its worth could actually be proven. I operated on the premise that God and their faith were real to the people I interviewed. This allowed me to slip into their skin and feel what they felt. David Waters, a *Washington Post* editor and one of the country's best religion writers, developed a list of Ten Commandments for reporters on the faith beat, which I followed probably better than the Bible's Ten Commandments.

First Commandment: "God is real. For billions of people on this planet, God is more than a fact. God is a central factor in their lives, their values, decisions, actions and reactions." This was easy for me. It was the reason I got on the religion beat.

Second Commandment: "God is everywhere. Don't think of it as the religion beat. The world is our beat. Worship attendance is 24 to 40 percent [of the American population]. But belief in God is more than 90 percent." I tried to find stories in places other than church, as they made for richer tales: the struggle of a Jewish father to get his son's prep football game moved from Friday night because it fell on Yom Kippur; the controversy over a Muslim football league whose team names included the "Infitada," "Mujahideen" and "Soldiers of Allah"; and the success of UCLA scholars in building a virtual-reality theater that acts as a time machine, dropping visitors off onto the dusty streets of Santiago de Compostela in northwestern Spain in 1211 to tour the cathedral there.

Third Commandment: "God really is in the details. John Ashcroft's father, a Pentecostal preacher, died the day after his son was sworn into the U.S. Senate. 'John,' his father said to him the night before, 'I want you to know that even Washington can be holy ground.' " David's point is that stories about God can be found everywhere, even in throw-away lines in articles or interviews. Also, he advises us to dig deep in our interviews. I almost always uncovered the most revealing insights at the end of my interviews, when everyone was relaxed and less guarded.

Fourth Commandment: "God is the object, not the subject. You don't have to write about God (or religion) to write about the difference God makes in the way we live." This is great news for religion writers, because it means that almost any piece of news can be turned into a religion story. In July 2001, I wrote a front-page story about how church leaders were taking advantage of the $600 tax rebate Americans were getting from the federal government by asking their congregations to simply sign over their checks.

Fifth Commandment: "God is good. Behind many if not most stories of hope, struggle, sacrifice, survival, forgiveness, redemption and triumph is someone's faith." I found if I probe deep enough into any dramatic story, I find religion near its roots. I did a story about a guy who ran across the country at the pace of a marathon a day (26.2 miles). The reason? He had prayed for a way to raise money for needy children—and he heard God tell him to run an extreme distance.

Sixth Commandment: "Don't just write for the Church Page. God created the world in seven days, not one. No need to cram all the God-related copy in one weekly 'Faith & Values' section or page. Write for every section. Write for every day of the week." I had a running competition with a colleague whose beat included Disneyland over who could get their stories in the most sections of the paper. In one year, I was able to get onto the front page and in the Metro section, the Sunday magazine, the Calendar section and the business section. (She still beat me.)

Seventh Commandment: "Don't take weekends off. Friday night through Sunday night is Game Day for most religious folk.

You can't understand someone's faith unless you experience the public expression of it." I found this to be invaluable in learning about different faiths, though I tended to find my actual stories outside of the religious services.

Eighth Commandment: "Don't spend too much time in your head. Faith isn't just expressed. It's experienced. It's belief and behavior. It's intellectual, emotional, and, above all, spiritual." I tried to report on mystical experiences with the same level of objectivity as a denominational squabble. When the marathon runner said he was ordered by God to run across America, I wrote it in a straightforward manner, without a snicker. For context, I did contact those around him to see if his behavior had changed since becoming a Christian, and checked criminal and civil court records to see if anything interesting turned up. But as for people's alleged interactions with the Lord, I simply reported what their experiences had been. I tried to follow the example set by Supreme Court Chief Justice William O. Douglas, who in 1944 wrote the majority opinion in the *United States v. Ballard* case. Guy Ballard claimed, through mass mailings, to be a healer and prophet of God (he also claimed to be Jesus, St. Germain and George Washington). The government convicted him of fraud, which he had undoubtedly committed. But the Supreme Court overturned the conviction, with Douglas stating:

> *Heresy trials are foreign to our Constitution. Men may believe what they cannot prove. They may not be put to the proof of their religious doctrines or beliefs. Religious experiences which are as real as life to some may be incomprehensible to others.*
>
> *. . . The miracles of the New Testament, the Divinity of Christ, life after death, the power of prayer are deep in the*

religious convictions of many. If one could be sent to jail because a jury in a hostile environment found those teachings false, little indeed would be left of religious freedom.

Ninth Commandment: "Fear not. Even God had editors. They might not always get what you're trying to do or say, but keep at it." Religion frightens a lot of editors, many of whom aren't used to the subject and are uncomfortable with expressly religious terms. For one of my early stories, I covered the Harvest Crusade in Anaheim, California. The three-day event is designed to convert nonbelievers to Christianity. I wrote a line in the story that went something like this: "About 20 percent of the crowd came out of the stands and onto the outfield to accept Jesus Christ as their personal savior." The editors on the copy desk flipped over that line. They said it implied that Jesus Christ was everyone's savior. No, I replied, it said that these people accepted Jesus Christ as *their* savior. It was just a fact. That's what happened. That was the whole point of the Harvest Crusade. They thought the line was still offensive and wanted to change it to something like "About 20 percent of the crowd came out of the stands and onto the outfield to *express their new belief in God.*" I actually had to appeal to some supervising editors to keep the reference to Jesus Christ in the story.

Tenth Commandment: "Forget the flood. Interview God. No matter the story, ask people about their faith and how their faith guides their thoughts and actions." For me, this is derivative of Waters's Fourth and Fifth Commandments. I suspect that my friend had a hard time coming up with a fresh Tenth Commandment, and David Waters's *Nine* Commandments didn't have the proper ring.

. . .

Waters's Ten Commandments served me well on the religion beat, and the Seventh Commandment—thou shall not take weekends off— allowed me on a personal level to sample a wide variety of Christian denominations and churches and find where I wanted to make my spiritual home. We had left the feel-good theology of my mega-church for a Presbyterian setting with more rituals, traditions and probing sermons. Yet mainline Protestantism felt to me one step short of my final destination, the Catholic Church. In my decade as an evangelical Christian, I had studied the Bible, especially the New Testament, extensively—something most Catholics don't. Yet that knowledge gave the rituals of the Catholic Church deep meaning and beauty. Attending a Mass, I felt like I was standing on the shoulders of 2,000 years of Catholics who went before me, an unbroken line that could be traced directly back to Christ and His apostles. This filled me with a sense of awe and humility—and a little pride.

I did have problems with parts of the Catholic theology, including its sexual teachings (for example, a ban on condoms, even if it meant millions dying in AIDS-plagued Africa). More fundamentally, I couldn't accept transubstantiation, the climax of the Mass when, according to the church, bread and wine are literally turned into the body and blood of Christ. Of course, I wasn't alone. Millions of Americans—whom some orthodox Catholics derisively call "Cafeteria Catholics"—don't agree with many of these teachings (40 percent don't even go to confession, a basic requirement of the church). If Catholics truly believed they were in the real presence of Jesus during the Eucharist, they would fawn over and worship the Blessed Sacrament, the unused but consecrated bread and wine that is placed, in most churches, in a golden tabernacle; the Blessed Sacrament usually sits off to the side of the altar, ignored by the faithful, except for a few true believers who can occasionally be found before it in prayer and adulation.

I didn't only rely on the comfort of the crowd. Written into the Catechism of the Catholic Church—a reference book that outlines church teachings—is a wonderful loophole called "personal conscience." If something, even church doctrine, goes against your conscience, you're allowed to follow the moral voice inside your head. As the Catechism says, "A human being must always obey the certain judgment of his conscience. If he were deliberately to act against it, he would condemn himself."

My conscience allowed me to practice birth control without guilt or fear of eternal damnation. It allowed me to view the Eucharist as only a symbolic representation of the Last Supper. I planned on being a Cafeteria Catholic, picking which parts of church doctrine I would keep and which I would ignore. But my selection was based on conscience, not convenience.

To become a Catholic officially, I needed to go through a year-long process that consisted of some introductory courses and then months of classes. I signed up in the summer of 2001. Greer wanted a refresher course in her childhood faith, so she came along. We had a vague idea that after I was received into the church, we would have a proper church wedding and get rid of the Catholic stigma that we were adulterers not worthy to receive Communion.

On Tuesday evenings and Sunday mornings we arrived at Our Lady Queen of Angels in Newport Beach to learn about the church, its history and its doctrine. Father Vincent Gilmore led the program, which was called the Rite of Christian Initiation of Adults (RCIA). Father Vincent was part of the conservative Norbertine order, on loan to the Queen of Angels parish because of a priest shortage within the Diocese of Orange. In his late 30s, he rode mountain bikes and was a gifted teacher who believed squarely in the church's teachings. He explained them passionately, simply and thoroughly. I was also assigned a sponsor. I was fortunate to get Bob Gannon, a lanky gentleman with salt-and-pepper hair whose decency and kindness knew no bounds. Though soft-spoken, he was a prosecutor in the Orange County District Attorney's Office, so I knew he could be tough. To me, he was a loving soul who patiently answered every question I threw at him.

As the people in the class began to get friendlier, some discovered that I was a religion writer with *The Times*. The recognition wasn't unpleasant. Some remembered stories I had written before the class started. A few talked about a story I had written just before Easter, some months before. It focused on retired Bishop Norman McFarland, a giant of a man at least six-foot-four with a wide girth and booming voice. He was known for his gruffness. When his successor, Bishop Tod D. Brown, publicly released the diocese's finances for the first time, many priests within the diocese heralded the move as the start of a new era of openness. They implied that Bishop McFarland had run the diocesan finances with an iron fist and in secret.

I had called him on a Sunday afternoon to get a response. Knowing his reputation, I dialed his number with trepidation. The bishop's phone rang several times before he picked it up and growled an irritated, "Hello!"

"Hi, Bishop, this is Bill Lobdell with the *Los Angeles Times*," I started, trying to keep the quiver out of my voice. "I'm working on a story and would like to get a comment from you." I paused, trying to think of something to break the ice. "How are you doing today?"

"Pretty good until you called and interrupted my goddamn football game," he barked. "What do you want?"

The conversation didn't get any better.

My Easter story, written much later, put Bishop McFarland in a far different light. I watched him and Father John McAndrew minister to inmates inside the Theo Lacy Branch Jail in Orange, California, on the eve of Good Friday. There I met inmate Anthony Ybarra, who claimed he was experiencing the best day of his life. He had been upset because he didn't know when he would see his two-week-old son, and was crying hard. But a priest was washing his feet, just as Jesus did for his 12 surprised disciples at the Last Supper. Father John McAndrew cleaned and kissed Ybarra's feet, along with those of 11 other prisoners. Bishop McFarland then heard Ybarra's confession.

"My heart is still pounding," Ybarra told me afterward. "Things just flowed out. He told me God loves me no matter what I've done. Something just came over me—a peace.

"The feeling is a better high than any drugs I've had. It was quite a surprise. This service is the best thing that's happened to my life so far."

The services took place in a stark chapel. White plastic chairs served as pews. Four sheriff's deputies took the place of ushers. In between squawks on the deputies' radios, the prisoners sang, took Communion, joined hands and got down on their knees on the polished cement floors to pray. And they cried—often.

"This is a wonderful moment," McFarland had told the 28 inmates in orange jumpsuits gathered for one of two afternoon Masses. "There are very few times in our lives where we can say we're doing exactly what God wants us to do."

McFarland's interest in the inmates at Theo Lacy began three years earlier, when the bishop faced a life-threatening aneurysm. At the time, a jail chaplain had the prisoners write get-well letters to McFarland. The bishop could still recite by heart one of those 40 letters, which read in part:

Dear Bishop McFarland,

Hi there, Norman. I'm a prisoner here in Theo Lacy because of something I've done. You're a prisoner because of your health.

The writer of the letter went on to tell the bishop that he was praying for him because he could identify with being helpless. The letters touched the bishop. He received hundreds of get-well cards, but saved only those from prisoners.

Soon after that, Bishop McFarland accepted an invitation to visit the inmates for the first time. Indeed, it was his first jail visit during his 11-year tenure as bishop of Orange. He gave a homily on Christ's conversation with the two criminals who were crucified alongside him. The inmates gave the bishop a standing ovation.

Father McAndrew told me the story: "It was hard to tell at that moment who was more moved. Beginning with that experience, there was some sort of connection that spoke to some place inside of him that no one ever got access to."

My story on the softer side of the bishop surprised many Catholics, creating a nice buzz. I'm sure it didn't exactly hurt my standing with Father Vincent at Our Lady Queen of Angels, either. Shortly after that, I stumbled upon another Catholic-based story that became much talked about. In the lead of the story, I called it "Eight Weddings and a Fiesta," the real-life drama of a pastor of an impoverished Latino parish eager to see his congregation's couples married in the church.

For the eight brides and eight grooms who said "*Si, te acepto*" on a Saturday night when I visited Our Lady of Lourdes Church in Santa Ana, Father Bill Barman offered the deal of a lifetime: a wedding they otherwise couldn't afford, along with a chance to get back in harmony with the Catholic Church. Unable to shoulder the financial burden of an expensive church wedding, many of the working-class couples already had tied the knot in civil ceremonies. But those weddings aren't recognized as valid church unions. Father Bill's weddings offered them an easy way back. He gave a Mass wedding, picking up the bill for the photographer, decorations, three-tiered cake, deejay and flowers. The brides and grooms needed to do only three things in return: attend a 12-week marriage class, find something to wear on the big day and have their families bring their favorite Mexican dishes to the reception.

Father Bill's idea was so clever and the night so joyous that I didn't think about the absurdity that underlined the story: that his parish's married couples—devout Catholics—had been barred from the Lord's table during Communion because they could afford only a civil marriage. As a journalist, it pains me to say that the thought never crossed my mind. It wouldn't have changed what I had written, but I should have thought about it.

The absurdity didn't bother most people. The story was picked up by *The Times*'s wire service and ran nationally. After reading about it, priests in other poor parishes in America started the multiple wedding concept. And the article raised my profile a little higher in my conversion class. I didn't mind the minor celebrity status—at least not then, when my stories on the Catholic Church had a feel-good quality to them.

In August of 2001, Jean Pasco again stopped by my desk.

"Hey, you remember those legal documents I dropped off some months back about the Father Harris case?"

Crap. I had forgotten all about them. As Jean stood before me, I guiltily unearthed the papers from a pile on my desk.

"These?" I said. "I'm so sorry, Jean, but I haven't looked at them yet."

"Well, you better now. There's a big press conference later today at the courthouse. They are going to announce a settlement in the case. We are the only ones who have all the documents, so we'll have the best story."

I immediately fished a yellow highlighter from my drawer and began to read.

SEVEN

Father Hollywood

> Dear friends, do not be surprised at the painful trial you
> are suffering, as though something strange were happening
> to you. But rejoice that you participate in the sufferings
> of Christ, so that you may be overjoyed when his glory is
> revealed.
>
> — 1 PETER 4:12–13

WITH THE NEWS conference starting in a few hours, I had
The Times librarians pull all newspaper clips about Michael "Father
Hollywood" Harris. Within minutes, a virtual stack of stories
landed in my e-mail inbox. I printed the articles and started to
read them in chronological order. They were mostly fawning. I
learned about the Michael Harris most people knew, loved and
even idolized.

"Father Hollywood" received his nickname from students
because of his movie star–like presence. He was athletic and tall,
with a mop of untamed brown hair, piercing blue eyes, a chiseled

chin and a warm smile. His charisma, it was often noted, enabled him to dominate every room he entered.

In 1978, Harris was named principal of Mater Dei High School, advertised as the largest parochial school west of the Mississippi. He was all of 29. Under his guidance, Mater Dei reached national prominence in academics, athletics and the arts. He was ubiquitous on campus, attending nearly all extracurricular events and hugging students as they passed by.

Harris's popularity with the students didn't end at school. He outfitted his home with a state-of-the-art movie system and filled his bookcases with hundreds of films. The priest frequently invited students—a mix of athletes, drama club members and kids in the band—over for pizza, sodas and popcorn, where they watched movies or TV or played games. Oftentimes, Harris encouraged male students, especially those who were having trouble at home with their parents, to spend the night. His students devoted multiple pages in their yearbooks to photos of "Father Mike," venerating him like a saint. Families of his students invited him on luxury vacations, thankful for the guidance he had shown their teenagers.

"To a man or woman, we all thought Mike Harris was as great as you're going to get," one parent told me later. "He was a Godlike presence on campus."

For a time, Father Mike drove a white Corvette to school provided to him by a grateful Catholic—until his superiors told him it was too flashy. He became a sought-after guest on the Orange County social scene, even modeling in charity fashion shows. One year, he wore motorcycle leathers as one of "Heaven's Angels."

In the mid-1980s, the Diocese of Orange decided it needed to build a state-of-the-art high school in fast-growing South Orange County. But the church hierarchy was filled with mostly introverts and bureaucrats who had limited ability to raise the needed $26 million for the school. So Harris, quite content at his Mater Dei post, was drafted—and basically sent out on his own to find the money. Trained in obedience, Harris followed orders and tapped into his strong friendships with local entrepreneurs and millionaires to raise the funds.

At the 1987 opening of Santa Margarita High School, Harris dramatically ripped open his black clerical shirt and revealed a T-shirt with the Superman logo on it. The crowd roared its approval. The "S" stood for Santa Margarita High School, but it sent another message: Father Harris was Superman. Three years after the school's opening, Pope John Paul II made Harris a monsignor, an honorary title that translates to "My Lord."

In 1991, Father Harris penned a commentary—in hindsight, one filled with Freudian projection—for *The Times*, urging parents to teach their children to abstain from sex.

"As an educator faced with the challenging task of helping teenagers develop values, it is time to confront the compulsive hedonism that plagues adolescents," he wrote. "In order to accomplish anything of value, we need to learn to delay gratification."

In January 1994, Superman unexpectedly hung up his cape. Harris shocked the community by announcing he was taking a leave of absence as principal of Santa Margarita because of "stress."

"Although very difficult for me personally, there is a need to take some time for prayer, rest, retreat and restoration," Harris, then 47, wrote to parents and students. "The impact of accumulated stress over the years has taken its toll."

He resigned a month later.

In September 1995, a former student filed a lawsuit, accusing Harris of molesting him. Two other accusers stepped forward, but the diocese and community backed Harris. The lawsuit was thrown out because the statute of limitations had passed, and Harris—his reputation largely untarnished—faded from public view and reinvented himself as a developer specializing in low-income housing, a venture backed by his wealthy Catholic friends, among them a prominent retired judge, a land baron and a national homebuilder.

Nothing in the clips mentioned the lawsuit filed in 1996 by a young man named Ryan DiMaria against Harris and the dioceses of Los Angeles and Orange. The epic legal battle that would be the harbinger to the national Catholic sex scandal had taken place entirely under the media's radar. I grabbed my coat and headed to the Orange County Courthouse for the press conference, wondering what else I would find out about Harris.

Attorney Katherine K. Freberg, a former Texas Tech basketball player who stood six-foot-one—and this Monday afternoon was even taller in two-inch heels—strode to the bouquet of microphones on the second floor of the Orange County Courthouse in Santa Ana. In a large half-circle around her, about two dozen journalists stopped their casual talk and whipped out their notebooks, turned on their tape recorders and rolled their cameras. The word had leaked out that a historic settlement had been reached in the sexual abuse case against Harris.

I hated press conferences. They made me feel part of a wolf pack, waiting for someone to throw out scraps we would fight over. It was more satisfying to hunt for a story by myself. I kicked myself again for not looking into the Harris legal documents sooner. Not everything was lost, though. We had the papers, and no other journalist did. This would keep us ahead of the competition for months to come.

Unused to standing before the media, Freberg's shaky voice

was amplified by the microphones. Reading from a prepared statement, she told the journalists that the Roman Catholic dioceses of Los Angeles and Orange had agreed to pay her client, Ryan DiMaria, a record $5.2 million to settle the case he brought against the dioceses and Harris five years earlier. Harris continued to deny he had molested Ryan, but agreed to leave the priesthood as part of the settlement. The news produced a buzz among the reporters—a record settlement and Harris's high profile meant a big story and good play for their reports.

In addition to the money, Freberg continued, the Diocese of Orange had agreed to apologize to four other alleged victims of Harris. But most importantly, the dioceses of Los Angeles and Orange—formed from the southern section of the Archdiocese of Los Angeles in 1975—agreed to institute 11 changes in the way they handled clergy sexual abuse claims. In hindsight, these reforms appear to be commonsensical, but the settlement was reached five months before the Catholic sex scandal would erupt in Boston and then spread across the nation. In August 2001, DiMaria's settlement was unprecedented within the Catholic Church.

Among the new procedures: Any priest with a credible allegation of molestation in his past would be removed from ministry. (Amazingly, even in 2001, this wasn't the case. Orange and Los Angeles dioceses had many prominent priests working in parishes who had admitted to molesting a minor—in Los Angeles, two clerics remained on the job despite being *convicted* child sex offenders.) The church also promised to assign alleged victims of clergy sexual abuse an independent advocate who would help with their claims. (In the Diocese of Orange, the bishop initially assigned a church attorney to be the "independent" advocate.) The dioceses agreed to set up a toll-free hotline and website for victims to use, anonymously if they preferred. Priests were barred from being alone in social settings with minors. Bad behavior by a priest could no longer be hidden in secret files that prosecutors and plaintiff attorneys didn't know existed. And the dioceses pledged to enact an educational program on sexual molestation prevention.

The Catholic Church didn't start out to create an institution that protected pedophiles. The clergy had been trained in a hierarchical culture that valued obedience and loyalty and disdained scandal and secular interference. The priests also had been taught about the power of redemption. So when faced with a priest who had raped a boy, anyone with knowledge of the incident knew to keep quiet. The victim and his family were dealt with in a manner that would avoid scandal—sometimes they were lied to, and other times shamed or threatened into silence. If those tactics didn't work, a secret financial settlement was offered. Never did the church officials voluntarily report the crime to civil authorities. Sometimes, they transferred the offending priest to an unsuspecting parish, relying on his word that he had repented and wouldn't sin again. Other times, the priest was sent secretly to a Catholic treatment center, where psychiatrists and psychologists would eventually assure the priest's bishop that the pedophile was no longer a danger to children. Then the cleric would be quietly put back in ministry. From the bishops' worldview, they were taking care of a delicate problem by providing a cure for the priest—through the power of God, psychiatry or psychology—and avoiding tarnishing the church. Justice or help for the child who had been raped or sodomized didn't figure into the equation, because it wasn't part of the culture of the Catholic clergy when faced with a scandal. This didn't happen in just a few dioceses across the country; it was standard procedure in nearly all of them.

Ryan DiMaria said that's why he pushed for reform. He told me, "The lawsuit was always about making a change and slowing [clergy sexual abuse] down or stopping it."

I wanted to believe Ryan, who was then 28 and fresh out of law school. A slight man with some leftover adolescent acne, he seemed sincere, and everyone I talked with said he pushed hard for the 11 changes in the church's policy despite stubborn opposition from the dioceses. The judge confirmed that Ryan took less money in exchange for those reforms. But the size of the $5.2 million pay-out bothered me. I knew from the lawsuit that Ryan claimed to have been sexually abused twice by Harris, about a decade earlier. I didn't see how that, as bad as it was, equated to $5.2 million. Why spend so much energy going after the church and its money for a ten-year-old incident? Wouldn't it have been healthier for Ryan to focus on getting over it and then moving on with his life?

Back in the newsroom, I called Mary Grant, who founded the Southern California chapter of the Survivors Networks for those Abused by Priests (SNAP), for a little perspective. In 1991, she received a $25,000 settlement from the Diocese of Orange after Father John Lenihan, a dynamic Irish-born priest, admitted to having sex with Mary, then a teenager, for four years. Mary had been one of the few tireless voices for reform of clergy sexual abuse policies within the Catholic Church. One of her goals was to get her abuser removed from ministry, but church officials refused. Lenihan's career continued to thrive despite his confession, and in the fall of 2001, he was the beloved pastor at an affluent parish in Dana Point overlooking the Pacific Ocean. Mary and other advo-cates like her couldn't get any traction. Civil authorities, perhaps reluctant to take on the church, had let the statute of limitations pass in Mary's case. The media locally and nationally were gener-ally unresponsive as well, with a few notable exceptions. But now, she told me, Ryan had finally found a way to force change on the church. Finally, a victory.

I wrote down her quotes and then asked, "But Mary, what

about the money? Does $5.2 million seem like the right amount for what happened to Ryan?"

She immediately knew what I was getting at. She asked gently, "Have you ever been to a survivors' meeting?"

I said I hadn't.

"There's one this week in Long Beach. Why don't you come and sit in? I think you'll better understand this whole story if you do."

I agreed to meet her there later that week.

The news of the settlement—my story ran on the front page of *The Times*—rocked the Catholic community. Among the clergy, the new reforms were a bombshell. Catholic leaders soon would be combing their files to find credible allegations of sexual abuse. What constituted "credible"? What if a crackpot had falsely accused them of molestation years ago? Who would make the decision? Who would be kicked out of ministry? Where were the protections for the good priests when an anonymous caller could phone in a complaint on the victims' hotline?

I received many angry calls from readers who yelled at me for ruining the reputation of Father Mike. They couldn't believe the allegations, despite the record payout, apologies, reforms and Bishop of Orange Tod D. Brown's statement that he had "grave doubts about [Harris's] innocence in these matters, taking into consideration the number of complaints made against him, the similarity of those complaints and the apparent sincerity of the persons making these statements."

Harris's supporters clung to a statement issued by his attorney that said he had done nothing wrong and that the diocese settled for "business reasons."

"Monsignor Harris is extremely proud of his work with high school students and counts hundreds of them close friends and supporters," the statement read.

The Harris fans were the Catholic version of the O. J. Simpson jury; they refused to acknowledge the mountain of evidence against their priest. At first, I tried to argue with the callers. Nothing I said would change their mind. Eventually, I stopped arguing and just listened to them vent. There was desperateness to their outrage. It was as if their carefully constructed world of faith would come tumbling down if Harris had molested boys. As a Catholic in training, the truth about Harris didn't threaten my faith. I knew about the sinfulness of man. It was the whole reason Christianity was necessary—to bridge the yawning gap between God and his perpetually misbehaving children. Every faith has its Monsignor Harrises, but that doesn't disprove God, nor even necessarily taint organized religion. I saw exposing what Harris did as cleaning up, not hurting, Catholicism.

Blind loyalty to a member of the clergy would be a recurring theme during my next five years as a religion writer. For Catholics, the bond between parishioners and their priests was particularly strong. Unquestioning loyalty was one of the most cherished values in the Catholic hierarchical pyramid—from pope to cardinals, cardinals to archbishops, archbishops to bishops, bishops to priests and priests to the people in the pews. In my Catholic conversion classes, I was taught that priests were people set aside by God and endowed with special powers that allowed them alone to dispense the sacraments of the church. A layperson could recite the liturgy of the Eucharist perfectly, but, according to the church, he or she could not turn the bread and wine into the literal body and blood of Christ. The laity couldn't grant someone absolution after hearing a confession, or give Last Rites to expedite passage into heaven. Only a priest had those powers. This separation between the clergy and laity served to emphasize the dependence, deference and loyalty expected of the parishioners to their "Fathers." In that light, it was easier to account for the defensive reaction Catholics had to the Harris news.

Jean Pasco and I told our disbelieving editors about the groundswell of support in the community for Harris, and we agreed we should produce a detailed profile that would explain how such a beloved priest, who did so much good, could hide such a dark secret for so long.

A few days later, I found myself in Long Beach, walking into a nondescript therapist's office on Atlantic Avenue with Mary Grant, the survivor of clergy sexual abuse who had invited me to witness her support group. The seven survivors gathered there had been told I would be joining them.

Entering the room, I awkwardly said hello to everyone, and they introduced themselves. I was struck by the range of ages in the room: from 30-something to more than 70. The first person to speak was the mother of Rita Milla. Her neck was being gently rubbed by her daughter, who sat next to her. From earlier news accounts, I could only vaguely recall the bare outline of their story, and I had to look up the details the next day at the office. As an awkward, overweight young teenager, Rita Milla had caught the eye of a parish priest named Santiago "Henry" Tamayo at St. Philomena Church in Carson, California. In 1978, after grooming her with special attention and visits to her home, the priest first molested Rita, then 16, through a broken screen in the confessional. He later introduced her to six other priests, who took turns having sex with her—once allegedly at a hotel room that was rented by the hour and then in the parish's rectory. When Rita became pregnant in 1982, Tamayo wanted her to get an abortion, but she refused. So instead, he shipped Rita off with $450 to the Philippines, where she and her baby almost died in childbirth.

When the scandal came to light two years later, Bishop Juan A. Arzube of Los Angeles—who later would be accused of molesting an 11-year-old boy—blamed Rita for luring the priests into bed.

"This girl has had very bad actions even with altar boys," the bishop told a Spanish-language television station in 1984, responding to a $15 million lawsuit she filed against the priests and Archdiocese of Los Angeles. "She is a person of bad reputation."

Not that it mattered, but Rita said she was a virgin until the priests got a hold of her. On the day her civil suit was filed, all seven priests disappeared from their posts. Later, church officials encouraged Tamayo to stay in the Philippines to avoid the authorities and to keep quiet about the archdiocese's continued payments to him. Rita's initial case was thrown out because of the statute of limitations. None of her alleged rapists was arrested.

In 1991, Tamayo returned to the United States against the wishes of the archdiocese and publicly apologized to Rita. He died in 1996.

That was Rita's story, but that night in the Long Beach therapist's office, her mother's anguish dominated the room. Through sobs and tears, Rita's mother talked, in a heavy Spanish accent, about how honored she had been that Father Henry had taken an interest in her daughter. Father Henry, she had believed, was a godsend. With bitterness dripping from her voice, Rita's mother recalled how she would send her daughter off with Father Henry into the night, even when Rita begged to stay home. She believed that her daughter was being mentored by a man of God.

"Why didn't I see what was going on?" she said between heartbreaking sobs. "Why did I keep making her go with him?" Her face contorted in agony. "Why did they do this to us?"

I'd never seen such raw pain. It had been nearly 20 years since the last of the rapes, but the mother's guilt and sense of betrayal were still fresh. My heart pounded, and tears welled in my eyes. I felt ashamed just to be there. I was a voyeur, peeking into another world. I hadn't earned this kind of intimacy. I just stared at the floor as she talked. Rita kept rubbing her mother's back and telling her it was okay.

I learned several facts that night about survivors of clergy sexual abuse that would inform my reporting in the months ahead when the Catholic sex scandal burst open. These insights haunt me to this day.

I discovered that as horrific as the abuse was, most survivors experienced the most lasting damage from church leaders whom they approached for help. Instead of receiving protection and justice, these children and their parents were vilified for coming forward, called liars or accused of being bad Catholics for trying to bring scandal upon the church. The victims and their families were routinely told that they were the first to complain about a priest's behavior, though it often wasn't true. Church leaders acted as though "they had no fear of God," as Rita Milla put it. Sitting there, listening to the victims, I couldn't imagine why any bishop, upon hearing about an abuse claim, would not immediately pick up the phone, call the police and bar the cleric from ministry pending the outcome of a criminal and church investigation. It rarely, if ever, happened.

I also learned that the media's terms "sexual abuse" and "molestation" were far too neutral to describe what happened to most of these people. (The church even shied away from those terms, preferring instead such Orwellian language as "boundary violations" and "inappropriate conduct.") During my time covering the Catholic sex scandal, I tried in vain to get my editors to use more accurate and graphic descriptions: "child rape" and "sodomy," to begin with. The more descriptive words in my copy were always changed. They were considered too graphic for a family newspaper. I thought our readers were grown-up enough to handle the more precise description. Molestation or sexual abuse could refer to a child being fondled through layers of clothing. That was bad, but it didn't compare to violent sex acts performed on children. I always thought there would be less loyalty and more outrage if the laity knew exactly what their molesting priests had done.

By contrast, *The Times*'s editors saw the wisdom of using graphic descriptions when the paper published a story in 2003 about women who claimed Arnold Schwarzenegger, then a candidate for governor of California, made unwanted sexual advances and behaved cruelly in front of them. *The Times* wrote that one woman said Schwarzenegger "whispered in her ear: 'Have you ever had a man slide his tongue in your [anus]?' "

In another section of the story, we ran a quote from a waitress who said Schwarzenegger beckoned her to his side. "I bent down to listen to him," she recalled. "He said, a little louder than a whisper, 'I want you to do a favor for me.' I thought, OK, maybe he wanted more bread. And he said, 'I want you to go in the bathroom, stick your finger in your [vagina], and bring it out to me.' "

I admired the editors for not patronizing their readers with vague paraphrases of Schwarzenegger's alleged quotes. They put them right out there with only the thinnest of filters (e.g., the word was not "vagina"). But how can the accuracy of a salacious quote be more important than the accuracy of actual behavior? I never got a satisfying answer. I don't think there's any conspiracy here; I just think that the very idea of priests sodomizing a boy on an altar until he defecates, or plunging an aspersorium, used to sprinkle holy water, into a girl's vagina, or a little boy hiding his bloody underwear from his mother was too much for even jaded journalists to consider.

The last thing I learned that night from the survivors concerned the deep wounds and permanent damage inflicted on children who were sexually abused by priests. The acts badly twist and retard a child's spiritual and sexual development. Children simply have no way to process what's happening to them when a religious icon performs sex acts on them. When the Catholic faithful say victims filed suits primarily for the money, I learned quickly not to argue with them. They wouldn't understand until they attended a therapy session of survivors of clergy sexual abuse.

On the road to Damascus, a light from heaven blinded Saul of Tarsus, who had been attacking Jews who believed Jesus Christ was the Messiah. He fell to the ground and heard God's voice ask, "Saul, Saul, why do you persecute me?" Three days later, a disciple named Ananias restored Saul's sight and baptized him. From that moment, Saul—with the new name Paul—dedicated his life to spreading the Gospel of Jesus Christ, becoming one of history's most influential figures. I didn't have a sudden conversion—or rather, de-conversion—after meeting with the sexual abuse survivors, on the 30-minute trip from Long Beach to my home in Costa Mesa. But looking back, it now appears to me as a Road to Damascus moment that I kept safely locked away in my subconscious. I drove in almost a trance. I had written so much about the redemptive power of faith, but I had never seen, in a real and personal way, the opposite: the damage religion could do in the hands of bad people. I looked back on what I had seen on the faith beat and started to wonder, for the first time, about the low level of holiness I was seeing. It was the reason why stories were so easy to spot—the people with deep faith, real faith, shined brightly against the dullness of the spiritual pack. This short supply of holiness was something that began to stick in my throat, a disconcerting fact that I washed down with prayer and Christian aphorisms such as "Don't mix up man's shortcomings with God." It would take a lot of processing and several years for my conscious thinking to catch up to my gut.

When I got home, I tried to tell my wife what I had seen at the survivors' meeting, but it was impossible to properly put into words. The closest I could come was to say these people had had their souls shattered, and they would never be whole again. I would later run across a better description given by Father Thomas Doyle, whose career was stunted by church leaders after he became, in 1985, a leading advocate for victims of clergy sexual abuse. Molesting priests and their superiors, he said, were committing "soul murder."

A Spiritual Body Blow

Then we will no longer be infants, tossed back and forth
by the waves, and blown here and there by every wind of
teaching and by the cunning and craftiness of men in their
deceitful scheming. Instead, speaking the truth in love, we
will in all things grow up into him who is the Head, that
is, Christ.

—EPHESIANS 4:14–15

BACK IN THE newsroom, I started to do what I should have
done nine months earlier when Jean Pasco dropped the stack of
legal documents on my desk: put together the story on Michael
Harris. Thanks to the DiMaria lawsuit, which caused the church
to disgorge documents from their secret files and forced church
leaders to testify under oath in depositions, Jean and I were able to
piece together an in-depth story of Father Harris and his fall from
grace. I had glanced through the documents on the day of the
settlement press conference, gleaning a few highlights for the next
day's story. But now, I had the time to put together all the pieces

of the puzzle. This was one of the best positions for a journalist to be in—to be able to draft a story from hundreds of pages of highly revealing, exclusive documents. For most articles, you had to fight for scraps of information, file public records requests to pry information from the government and beg sources for copies of key documents. But DiMaria's attorneys—Freberg and her partner, John Manly—had already spent five years wielding the court-backed power of discovery, as it is aptly named. And their work was in front of me now. The story could be something special, and I attacked it as a journalist, leaving behind any questions of faith it raised. For now, it was all about the story.

The documents showed—with remarkable clarity—the gaping difference between how an ancient structure and modern society dealt with sexual abuse. The real shock wasn't what Michael Harris allegedly had done. The story turned out to be the behavior of his superiors and colleagues, who lied to and misled the victims, their families and the public to avoid a scandal and protect their brother priest. Going through the pile, I found the story of Vincent Colice, a student at Mater Dei High School when Harris was principal from 1977 to 1979. After being diagnosed with AIDS in 1992, Vincent confessed to his mother that during his junior and senior years, Harris had molested him. He asked her not to tell anyone. The secret weighed greatly on her. Two weeks before his death, in the fall of 1993, Vincent released his mother from her vow of secrecy. After her son died, Lenora Colice sat down and wrote Harris. It was Thanksgiving Day. A copy of the neatly written note was included among the documents.

"Today of all days I have to write, to finalize my thoughts and put them to rest," Lenora Colice began. "Over the years I thanked God many times for the support and love you showed to my family through times of adversity and sorrow." She went on to state that Vince had told her that he had been molested by Harris after going to him for counseling.

"I will never ever forget or forgive what you did to my son. Only God in his merciful way knows how you feel for what you have done and continue to do to others. My prayer for you is that you seek help and you never ever again do to any young boy what you did to Vince. [No one should] have to live with the torment that Vince did.

"The anguish he lived with can never be taken back. I only hope that his life and death were not in vain. He is at peace now."

Next was a copy of a handwritten card Harris sent to Lenora Colice a week later: "Through counseling and other resources I have endeavored to work through many things. Hard work and prayer have helped. It may not be any consolation, but I am very sorry."

Was it a tacit confession? Colice thought so, and she took it to church officials in December. She wanted Harris removed as principal of Santa Margarita. Around the same time, the diocese had been contacted by an attorney who claimed she had two clients who also were sexually abused by Harris. She wouldn't reveal their identities, perhaps fearing the power and retribution of the church.

Worried about Harris's note and the anonymous allegations, diocesan officials shipped Harris off to the St. Luke Institute in Maryland for an in-patient evaluation. St. Luke was the preeminent Catholic psychiatric facility, specializing in treating priests with sexual problems. It was standard practice in those days, when faced with a credible allegation of sexual abuse, for the church to send a priest for counseling. Though the acts in question were felonies, civil authorities were kept out of the matter. Usually, after treatment, the priest received a clean bill of health. His bishop would then place him in a new, unsuspecting parish. All too often, he would molest again.

Before the Diocese of Orange sent Harris away, Harris and church officials concocted a cover story about his "stress" and need for time away from his job to recuperate. They didn't explain that they had sent him across the country to psychiatrists to determine whether he was a child molester. They certainly didn't ask whether anyone had information about Harris that would be useful to the church's investigation.

I turned to the deposition of Monsignor John Urell, the church's chief investigator into the Harris accusations. A rising star in the diocese, Urell was rumored to be in line for appointment as a bishop. With sandy brown hair, a round, boyish face and an easy manner, Urell looked as though he would fit in on a country-club golf course or in the halls of Congress. He was also a good friend of Harris.

John Manly, one of DiMaria's attorneys, took the deposition in July 2001. Manly was an aggressive lawyer whose temper and wild streak scared church leaders. He was also a cradle Catholic and the product of a Catholic education. His principal at Mater Dei had been Michael Harris. Manly felt that church leaders had forsaken the Catholic principles of morality and justice that were drilled into him during his schooling. In the deposition, he didn't hide his disgust.

I skimmed down to the section where he asked Urell about the apparent letter of confession. Manly asked whether he considered the note an admission of guilt. Urell gave several conflicting and evasive responses, including "I did not consider it an admission because it doesn't say it was an admission of it. So I did not consider it an admission. I considered it very troubling and concerning to me."

Later, Manly asked Urell whether he thought the diocese's cover story blaming "stress" for Harris's abrupt departure from Santa Margarita High School was misleading.

URELL: *No, I did not . . . . I believe he was under tre-mendous stress at that time.*

MANLY: *That's not the reason he took a leave. He took a leave because you made him take a leave because he had been accused of child molestation.*

URELL: *He was on administrative leave.*

MANLY: *Because he had been accused of child molesta-tion.*

URELL: *Because there had been an accusation made by the parent of someone who was not alive to talk about it, yes.*

MANLY: *You think this statement and article is consistent with the bishop's motto of "walk in truth"?*

URELL: *Yes, I do.*

In the stack of documents, I next turned to the key piece of evidence generated in the DiMaria case: a psychological report written by Harris's doctors during his five-day stay at the St. Luke Institute. Their findings were so damaging to the church's case that its attorneys appealed to the California Supreme Court to prevent its release. They lost. The 12-page report—first delivered to the diocese in March 1994—would become a part of the public record.

Doctors at the Catholic facility diagnosed Harris with same-sex paraphilia (deviant sexual behavior) and ephebophilia (a sexual attraction to adolescent boys). Harris would not confirm or deny the alleged molestations because he knew his superiors would be receiving the report, but the institute's doctors were unequivocal: "Our clinical team believes that there is substance to the allegations. It has been our experience that in many cases like these, the allegations that have surfaced are only a few of the actual incidents of abuse that have occurred." Indeed, Harris was eventually accused of molesting a dozen children, and the church has paid out more than $15 million to settle claims against him. He has always maintained his innocence.

At St. Luke, doctors noted that Harris was depressed and anxious as he revealed disturbing childhood secrets, but still impressed them with an external demeanor "striking for its calmness." Harris's appearance was so polished that other patients started to confide in him "as if he were a therapist," according to the report.

"Michael has always been most concerned about appearances and his reputation at the expense of his own healing and inner health," wrote Dr. Stephen J. Rossetti. "As a result, he has been applauded by the community, but he has become isolated, confused, anxious and depressed."

Harris told doctors he had suffered from sexual conflicts for years and suggested that his affection for students could have been misinterpreted. He admitted his sexual development appeared to be arrested in adolescence, when he went into the minor seminary. He also said he sometimes was sexually aroused by hugging high school boys.

For devout Catholics, one of the priest's most striking confessions was that he was engaged in virtually no prayer life "except for a few minutes of the Rosary before he falls asleep. He used the Rosary not only as a prayer but as a repetitious act to help him fall asleep.

"Upon inquiry, Michael said that he is afraid to spend time alone praying. He is afraid of what will surface."

By March 1994, top officials in the Diocese of Orange knew from the St. Luke report that Harris was sexually attracted to boys and that he was likely a serial molester. But they kept the information a secret, even to another Harris accuser who had come forward.

Larry Rehab claimed that Harris had sexually assaulted him in counseling. Rehab, who was 20 at the time, had been struggling with his sexuality when he turned to Harris. Rehab claimed that after one counseling session at Harris's home, his car wouldn't start and Harris offered to let him spend the night. During that evening, Rehab claimed that Harris sexually attacked him by ramming his penis forcefully into his mouth.

Rehab detailed the sexual encounter to Urell, who confronted his friend about the allegations. Urell testified that Harris—a priest who had taken a vow of celibacy—admitted to having sex with Rehab, claiming it was by mutual consent. After hearing Rehab's story, Urell attended an intimate farewell dinner for Harris that very night given by his close friends in the diocese.

An incredulous Manly asked Urell in his deposition if "it was appropriate to go to dinner with somebody who admittedly sexually assaulted somebody and was accused at this point by a whole bunch of people of molesting children . . . ?"

"I can say now I believe it was inappropriate to go, yes," Urell replied. "We were all—we had been all friends and co-workers for many years, so yes."

"Monsignor, can you see how this looks very, very bad?" Manly asked. "Can you see where someone would look at this and say, 'You have . . . the person who is investigating the matter going to a dinner with him, who is an accused child molester?' Can you see how people would perceive this as—I mean no disrespect—but duplicitous?"

"Yes, I can," Urell admitted.

As each duplicitous move by the diocese was revealed, I cheered a little. It meant the story was getting even better. For the moment, the case of Michael Harris had nothing to do with my faith. What I was experiencing was just a pure, journalistic adrenaline rush. Each time I thought there was no way church officials could act any worse, they did. I greedily gathered the information that this rare peek inside the Catholic hierarchy provided. I felt that the gods of journalism were looking after me. I did have some sense of bewilderment that an entire diocesan team could act so contrary to the Gospel, but those feelings were simply overwhelmed by the thrill of the hunt.

In September 1994, David Price became the first person to publicly accuse Harris of molestation, filing suit against the priest and the diocese. The former Mater Dei student had first met privately with church officials and told them that Harris molested him repeatedly when he sought counseling after his father's death in 1979. Price said he had remembered the episodes during a series of therapy sessions years later. Church officials did nothing. "Instead of apologizing that day, Monsignor Urell lied to me," wrote Price in his self-published memoir, *Altar Boy, Altered Life*.

"The truth was that he and the church knew at this time exactly who Monsignor Harris was and what they were dealing with . . . But nobody at the diocese offered to help me, or offered any hint of an apology.

"I was told by Monsignor Urell that, 'First and foremost, the Catholic Church is a business, and secondly it's a religion . . . The religion part is church on Sundays, but we're not talking about church right now—we're talking about business.' "

Two months later, after hearing nothing from church officials, Price filed suit. Larry Rehab and another victim also went public to bolster Price's allegations. The documents revealed what kind of treatment the diocese gave Price and Rehab when they spoke out about their alleged abuse. First, an outraged Monsignor Lawrence Baird, the spokesman for the diocese, told an *Orange County Register* reporter that Harris was "an icon of the priesthood."

Next, Harris's top defense attorney, John Barnett, savaged the three accusers in the press. He called the alleged victims "liars" and "sick individuals" who were just after money. Barnett compared the allegations to those at "the Salem witch trials of 1692, in which 29 people were executed in Massachusetts after being falsely accused of being witches." Again, no one within the diocese stepped forward to defend the victims or simply to tell the truth about Harris.

In November 1994, more than 350 Santa Margarita High School students and their parents held a rally for Harris at a park near the school. Among them were the parents of Ryan DiMaria, who, unbeknownst to them, had been molested by Harris. The crowd sang "For He's a Jolly Good Fellow." At one point during the 45-minute gathering, an airplane flew overhead with a banner that read: "We Love Father Harris." Several prominent Orange County leaders spoke in an impassioned defense of Harris's innocence.

"He is a victim," said Sharon Cody, a Mission Viejo councilwoman, at the rally. "I believe in the end we will find he has done nothing wrong. But in the meantime, the real sadness is that his life will forever be changed because of this. This is not deserved."

Church officials again decided to let the lies go unanswered.

Finally, the church's attorneys were let loose on Price in May 1995. By Price's count, they deposed him for 11 days, eight hours a day, despite repeated motions to the trial judge to end the ordeal. In his memoir, Price wrote that he was questioned by about a dozen attorneys who represented the church or Harris. They asked about his sexual history, whether he liked the way Father Harris touched and sucked him, if he fantasized about having sex with his father, if he ever resisted the sex acts, and if he welcomed the sex acts. They also asked, "What do you think God thinks of your lawsuit?"

When his suit was eventually tossed out of court because of the statute of limitations, he said the diocese threatened him with $60,000 in legal bills unless he dropped his appeal. Not wanting to go deeper in debt, Price agreed.

The diocese's strategy of using disinformation and hardball legal tactics worked. Harris's accusers—already emotionally fragile—faced the wrath of the public, a battery of church attorneys and an expensive legal battle. Who would want to take on such formidable opponents?

Ryan DiMaria didn't want to sue the diocese. He only wanted an apology, and some money for counseling for what he claimed Harris had done to him as a high school sophomore. In 1988, when Ryan was despondent over a friend's suicide, his parents had asked Harris to counsel the boy. Ryan said Harris took him out for dinner and a performance of *The Phantom of the Opera* in Los Angeles before returning to the priest's house, where the boy spent the night. Ryan said Harris invited him to share his bed. He refused and slept on a couch in another room. The next morning, Ryan said, Harris repeatedly abused him.

Ryan spent the next six years battling depression and thoughts of his own suicide. He wanted to tell his secret, but to whom? Who would believe his word against Father Hollywood's? His parents had even attended the rally to support Harris. Ryan vowed he would go to his grave with the secret—and he wanted that grave to be an early one. In 1996, after a night of drinking, Ryan called his father and said he was going to kill himself. He started to explain how to access his various bank accounts. Ryan's family rushed to his home in time to stop him. Finally, the secret came out.

Ryan brought his case to the district attorney's office, which declined to press charges in what was then a six-year-old incident despite pleas made by Ryan and his parents the day before the criminal statute of limitations expired. In the fall of 1996, church officials met with the family, but offered no apology.

"We thought we were doing the church a favor," his mother, Diane DiMaria, told me. "What we found out a long time later is that they knew much more [about Harris] and really didn't care. They were trying to keep us quiet about it."

Unhappy with the church's response, DiMaria filed a civil law-suit in 1997.

His attorneys had no experience in clergy sexual abuse cases, and most of their colleagues advised against taking Ryan as a client. They took the case anyway and spent the next four years fighting the dioceses of Orange and Los Angeles. At the time, few people had ever beaten the Catholic Church in a clergy sexual abuse suit. The bishops had superior resources. They also maintained a secret set of files where sensitive documents were stashed, unbeknownst to plaintiff's attorneys. The statue of limitations was often a prob-lem because victims of childhood sexual abuse usually don't come forward until well into adulthood. The victims and their families were frequently told by bishops, parishioners and friends that the church shouldn't have to endure a scandal.

Getting ready for the DiMaria trial, his attorneys spent more than $150,000—a fortune for a small law firm. Along the way,

Ryan's team floated various settlement offers: $100,000, $150,000 and, as the case got closer to trial, $1 million.

"They basically told us to drop dead," Manly recalled. "That's how stupid they were."

As the trial's opening neared in the summer of 2001—and a judge gave the okay for Ryan's attorneys to depose Cardinal Roger M. Mahony, the powerful archbishop of Los Angeles—settlement talks accelerated. Mediated by Judge James Gray in Orange County Superior Court, the two sides agreed to an unprecedented $5.2 million settlement, and at Ryan's and Gray's insistence, to a new set of rules the church would enact when dealing with allegations of clergy sexual abuse.

The negotiations got stuck on two points. First, Ryan's attorneys insisted that Harris be removed from the priesthood. The priest, who continued to deny any wrongdoing, didn't want to leave the clergy. It took hours before church officials and Ryan's attorney could extract that concession. Harris reluctantly agreed to ask Pope John Paul II to release him from his vows.

Second, Judge Gray wanted to get a promise from Ryan. He asked the young man, who often had suicidal thoughts, to vow to him that he would live a long and happy life. It took most of a day, but the judge finally got the promise.

Our lengthy profile, "Sins of the Father," came out in November 2001, two months after the settlement. It portrayed a deeply conflicted man who spent the vast majority of his time in saintly pursuits that positively affected thousands of students and parents, but who harbored untamed demons that turned him into an alleged predator.

Yet there was a bigger, deeper story here that I didn't fully recognize at the time: the response to the victims by the bishop and his lieutenants. They had acted more like Mafia bosses than shepherds. I wrote off their actions as the work of a single, morally corrupt diocese. I filed the story neatly away in a compartment in my mind. And even if all of organized religion were somehow fundamentally corrupt, that didn't mean God isn't real. It seemed a ridiculous thought. Besides, I was still quite sure that organized religion was not inherently bad—only a few individuals were, as is the case in every organization. I had just gotten an unvarnished look into a single diocese that had forgotten what it was about.

I was attending my Catholic conversion classes twice a week and was being fed all the rich teachings of the church. I felt inoculated from an attack on my faith from the likes of Father Harris and the Diocese of Orange.

In a boxing match, a powerful body blow early on might not seem too damaging to the fighter. But it can have a devastating effect. The boxer who is pounded hard in the ribs will instinctively lower his guard to protect against another blow, leaving his chin open to attack. He'll be sapped of strength. And he'll think twice about aggressively punching away, knowing that he'll be exposing his tender midsection.

For me, the Father Hollywood story was a spiritual body blow, but I didn't sense it at the time. Of course, it wasn't an isolated story for the Catholic Church, as we now know. I have also come to realize the widespread church corruption reflected in the sex scandal is not isolated to the Catholic institutions. Much that would trouble me about my faith in the next five years of reporting was neatly contained in the Father Hollywood story. Hypocrisy at all levels of the church, innocent people put in harm's way by the church's "shepherds," self-interest triumphing over Christian values, lies big and small and a general lack of courage among followers of Christ, especially those in power, would be recurrent subjects of my reporting.

My reporting on Michael Harris had one other effect. It made me realize I had a knack for investigative reporting, and that the world of religion offered fertile ground for my use of that God-given gift. I still didn't think it would harm my faith. My beliefs were too strong, too real. Father Vincent had taught me to pray the Rosary. I studied the Bible. I walked the Stations of the Cross inside my parish. I read books about St. Francis of Assisi, St. Augustine of Hippo, St. Theresa of Lisieux, St. Ignatius of Loyola, St. Thomas Aquinas and St. John of the Cross. I prayed that I would experience a sense of holiness that infused the saints, and occasionally—surprisingly—got glimpses of it. I wanted to be like the biblical David, a deeply flawed person who was still described in Scripture as "a man after God's own heart."

My faith was as natural—and essential—to me as breathing. I thought nothing could take it away.

·NINE·

The Golden Rule

. . . If your enemy is hungry, feed him, and
if he is thirsty, give him something to drink . . .

— ROMANS 12:20

MOST PEOPLE OF faith don't spend a lot of time consider-
ing beliefs different from their own. For Christians, for example,
it is comforting to believe that all denominations—Protestant or
Catholic—share the same belief in Jesus as their Savior and the
Bible as Holy Scripture. Most differences between Christians can
be chalked up to hair-splitting. But as a journalist, I was exposed
to a much wider range of religious experience and needed to take
all seriously. I covered many stories about Judaism and Islam, in
addition to having some contact with Buddhists, Unitarians, Hin-
dus, Sikhs, Scientologists, Jains and Baha'is. This can raise questions most of us don't usually confront. What would you do if you
met people you admired greatly, who reminded you of the best
examples of your fellow believers, yet whose faith rested on what

you saw as patent absurdities? In my case, I met such folks when I covered Mormonism.

I found Mormons mesmerizing—especially their generally high moral conduct—even though I didn't believe a word of their doctrine. In a nutshell, the Church of Jesus Christ of Latter-day Saints teaches that an angel named Moroni led Joseph Smith in 1827 to discover a divine set of golden plates buried in a hillside near his New York home. God provided the 22-year-old Smith with a pair of glasses and "seer stones" that allowed him to translate the "Reformed Egyptian" writings inscribed on the plates into an additional revelation from Jesus called the "Book of Mormon." Mormons believe this scripture restored the church to God's original vision, leaving the rest of Christianity in a state of apostasy.

The book's narrative focuses on a tribe of Jews who sailed from Jerusalem to the New World in 600 BC and split into two main warring factions. The God-fearing Nephites were "pure" (the word was officially changed from "white" in 1981) and "delightsome." The idol-worshiping Lamanites received the "curse of blackness," turning their skin dark. The resurrected Jesus appeared in the Americas in about 34 AD and gave instructions on how his followers should conduct themselves. This ushered in 200 years of peace until the Nephites and Lamanites began fighting again. By 385 AD, the dark-skinned Lamanites had wiped out their Hebrew enemies. The Mormon church calls the victors "the principal ancestors of the American Indians."

Independent scholars have dismissed this account as implausible. In 1996, the Smithsonian Institution responded to rumors that it was using the Book of Mormon as an archeology guide. It issued a stinging eight-point statement on why there was "no direct connection between the archeology of the New World and the subject matter of the [Book of Mormon]." Smithsonian officials and others point out that the Book of Mormon contains a long list of anachronisms unknown in ancient America, including such animals as cattle, horses, oxen, domestic sheep, pigs and elephants; such metals as steel; such weapons as swords; and such inventions as the chariot.

"Reports of findings of ancient Egyptian, Hebrew, and other Old World writings in the New World in pre-Columbian contexts have frequently appeared in newspapers, magazines, and sensational books," the Smithsonian wrote. "None of these claims has stood up to examination by reputable scholars."

Of course, absence of evidence is not always evidence of absence, but you won't find many Mormon archeologists digging up the Americas in expectation of unearthing ancient chariots and swords. And the best Mormon apologists can say is that the text is rich, complex and written in a revelatory style that Joseph Smith, a rural man of simple education, wouldn't have been capable of producing.

But those are minor problems compared to recent DNA evidence that shows the descendants of Native Americans came from Asia, not the Middle East. This knocks away the underpinnings of the Mormon scripture, though church officials are hurriedly reinterpreting the Book of Mormon on the fly to account for the absence of Hebrew blood in Native Americans. These hastily constructed explanations, mostly by Brigham Young University scholars, contradict 150 years of teachings by the church and its prophets, but have been mostly unquestioned by the Mormon faithful—if they are bothered by the controversy at all.

Mormons also believe the leader of their church, called their president and prophet, has the ability to receive direct revelations from God. For example, Joseph Smith learned from the Lord that the Garden of Eden had been in Jackson County, Missouri, and it was there that Jesus Christ would return to Earth.

In a revelation that became better known, God instructed Smith in 1831 to begin the practice of polygamy within the church. Smith later explained that he had no choice but to take multiple wives (33 in all, most historians believe, ranging in age from 14 to 58 at the time of the marriage).

"God commanded me to obey it," Smith said. "He said to me that unless I accepted it, and introduced it, and practiced it, I, together with my people, would be damned."

But in 1890, long after Smith's death, the Lord instructed another Mormon prophet to halt the practice. The timing was fortuitous, as federal opposition to Utah's statehood was gaining strength because of the Mormons' polygamous practices. God also sent a message in 1978 to the Mormon prophet that blacks should be treated equally in the church and should no longer be barred from ministry. This particular revelation came 116 years after the Emancipation Proclamation and 13 years after passage of the Civil Rights Act.

Cosmologically, Mormons believe that human souls begin as a pre-human spiritual—but also physical—presence on a crystal orb in outer space. These spiritual children are made by God the Father and His wife procreating and eventually make their way to Earth. After humans die, they have a chance to become gods themselves and live on their own planet. Mormons are also taught that once our planet reaches its "sanctified and immortal state," it too will turn into crystal.

I thought this was all quite nutty, yet from what I could see, Mormons faithfully lived out their beliefs in far greater numbers than other Christians. Most of them tithed, giving 10 percent of their income to the church, as instructed. This provided the church with a large revenue stream for building projects and for charity. The church had developed a private welfare system that would be the envy of any government, creating a large safety net for Mormons down on their luck. Members in good standing neither drink nor smoke. Their clergy comprise a nearly all-volunteer force, with most of the church's paid members headquartered in Salt Lake City. Their members observe Family Home Evening, a weekly at-home event where the television is turned off and the parents and children sit down for spiritual lessons or board games, conversation and special treats. About 40 percent of young Mormon men agree to go on a two-year mission where they spend their days in short-sleeve, white dress shirts, ties and black slacks, knocking on doors and telling people about the Mormon faith. Can you imagine any other Christian denomination where nearly half of the young adult males sacrifice two years of their life to go and make converts?

Jesus said a person's faith could be judged by the fruit it bears:

> *Watch out for false prophets. They come to you in sheep's clothing, but inwardly they are ferocious wolves. By their fruit you will recognize them. Do people pick grapes from thornbushes, or figs from thistles? Likewise every good tree bears good fruit, but a bad tree bears bad fruit. A good tree cannot bear bad fruit, and a bad tree cannot bear good fruit. Every tree that does not bear good fruit is cut down and thrown into the fire. Thus, by their fruit you will recognize them.*

> — MATTHEW 7:15–20

Judged by its fruits, Mormonism compares favorably with other Christian denominations, even as many Protestants dismiss the Latter-day Saints as a non-Christian cult. So why do many Mormons practice so many of Christ's teachings better than "real" Christians? As a mainstream Christian and budding Catholic, I often was amazed at how devoted and unquestioning Mormons could be to a faith that seemed so preposterous—not to mention racist—on its surface. I knew doctors and lawyers and other professionals at the top of their field who were practicing Mormons. How, I wondered, did they suspend their disbelief long enough to get around the many common-sense obstacles put in their path by the Book of Mormon and the life of Joseph Smith? Around the world, the church was (and still is) recruiting new members at an explosive pace, approaching 500,000 per year, according to church figures (numbers that critics say are inflated). Do they all believe the tenets of the faith? Do they look the other way theologically in order to join a lifestyle they admire? No one seemed bothered in the least by the speed bumps I encountered through a simple reading of their holy scriptures and the tiniest bit of research. For them, there was no need to debate their faith, just as there was no reason to bicker about whether the Earth was round.

Many non-Mormon Christians share my reaction to Mormon doctrine. Yet what's so strange about Mormonism compared to traditional Christianity? At the time, I didn't see any parallel between the Mormons' fidelity to the claims in the Book of Mormon and my allegiance to the New Testament, which included stories of a virgin birth, water turning into wine, two people rising from the dead, a coin to pay a temple tax being found in a fish's mouth, Jesus walking on water, five loaves of bread and two fish feeding 5,000 families, and Jesus and his apostles curing people of crippling and fatal illnesses. And that's just the New Testament.

The Hebrew Scriptures talk about a global flood, people living well into their hundreds, a parted sea, a vast exodus not yet found in the archeological record, bread falling from heaven daily for 40 years and a man living three days inside a whale before being spit out. The details of Mormonism are fresher, but not much more strange and mythical. I just happened to have grown up with the stories of the Bible. I was more used to them.

I was drawn to Mormons because they seemed to be in a spot similar to mine: they were people who believed deeply in their faith despite its challenges to rationality. At this point, after a decade of the Christian life, I wasn't worried about specific details of my faith not making sense. I just assumed man's hand in writing the Bible had injected some harmless contradictions into the Holy Book, and many of the wilder stories were simple allegories. But I did ponder deeper theological problems—the why-do-bad-things-happen-to-good-people kind of thoughts. Why are some prayers answered directly while others appear to be ignored? When a little girl gets raped and killed, where is God? Why might a busload of Christian high school athletes crash on the highway? Why does God play a hide-and-seek game with us, making it difficult to figure how He wants us to act?

I often felt silly just having these kinds of doubts because the questions seemed so elementary. By this point, I thought my faith should have been more advanced. I saw it as a defeat, in a way, as if I had lasted long into a marathon and now was forced to go back to the starting line. I fought back with heavy doses of Christian reading, church services, prayer and long talks with my friend Hugh. On our weekly run around the Back Bay, I'd bring up the suffering of innocent children, and Hugh admitted that there wasn't an easy answer to the pain they suffered, and that it broke his heart—and the Lord's—to see it happen. But, he would always tell me, "Compared to eternity, we're on this Earth for less than a blink of an eye. With that perspective, any suffering here is so minimal, and we won't know why we even have that until we see the Lord. It will all be made clear, Billy, in less than a blink of an eye. I can wait. Heaven will be a wonderful place."

In retrospect, the Mormons were also part of my therapy. In them, I could see people living a faithful life while relying on a doctrine that to me seemed wildly flawed. Perhaps what mattered wasn't theology, but the quality of life it created. I admired them because they lived a healthy and holy life. They were more admirable than I was. Yet I also thought my Scriptures, though they contained some contradictions, made far more sense. Was I thinking too much? At some point, didn't I need to take a leap of faith? That's why it's called "faith" and "belief." Science couldn't prove or disprove the existence of God. Perhaps I could learn from the Mormons and conclude that intellectuals far wiser than myself had explored the tenets of Christianity and found them solid. I didn't have to reinvent the wheel. Still, I wondered, Jews, Muslims, Mormons, atheists and others each had their own scholars, who tackled great questions and confidently reached conflicting answers. These arguments would ricochet in my head until I just didn't want to think about them anymore.

I longed to be Mormon-like, accepting my faith and moving on to more productive matters—such as living it. I wrote often about Mormons, covering everything from their paradoxically hip teenage dances, which attracted 700 students from across Southern California, to the success of Mormon temple weddings, which boast a low divorce rate of 6 percent (the born-again Christian divorce rate is about 27 percent). I reported on a trio of moms who talked a Nordstrom department store into holding a fashion show that featured dresses that Mormon (and Orthodox Jewish and Muslim) teenagers could wear at their proms to retain their modesty.

I even spent a day and night as part of a wagon train that journeyed 800 miles across the deserts of the Southwest, from Salt Lake City, Utah, to San Bernardino, California. The trek commemorated the Mormons' first settlement in Southern California in 1851. I marveled at the commitment by the 60 or so Latter-day Saints who volunteered for the 50-day journey. Dressed in pioneer garb, they rode in seven covered wagons, which included a two-seater "potty wagon," over the dirt trails, dried creek beds and some paved roads that roughly paralleled Interstate 15. They braved 100-degree-plus desert heat and fierce sand storms. They washed their clothes in tubs or over rocks. They settled squabbles in group meetings before each day's ride.

During my short time on the trail, I began to appreciate what the Mormon pioneers had gone through. The combination of the wooden-plank seats and rocky trail pounded relentlessly at my kidneys. The novelty wore off quickly, replaced by boredom. The desert landscape passed at less than five miles per hour. I especially felt for the young mothers on the trip. I have enough trouble entertaining my kids on car trips, even with an array of electronic devices at my disposal. These modern mothers had nothing, but somehow kept their young sons and daughters entertained for nearly two months, trapped in a tiny wagon.

I had come to expect this kind of devotion to faith and family from Mormons. I could often spot a Mormon among other strangers in any given setting. They tended to be clean-cut, bright-eyed, conservatively dressed and surrounded by young children. And they just gave off a Mormon vibe, a Boy or Girl Scout goodness that made you feel at ease in their presence. That's how I longed to live my faith—with so much integrity that everyone would instantly recognize me as a religious man.

My story of the Mormon wagon train sparked an e-mail

invitation to the inaugural Ex-Mormon General Conference in Salt Lake City the following month to see a different side of the Latter-day Saints. The conference was designed to run parallel to the Mormon General Conference, a semiannual meeting that draws more than 30,000 Latter-day Saints to Utah from around the world.

Before heading to the hotel headquarters of the ex-Mormons, I walked through historic Temple Square, the Vatican of the Mormon faith. The General Conference attendees swamped the ten-acre parcel that is home to Salt Lake Temple (built under the watch of Brigham Young) and the Tabernacle (home to the Mormon Tabernacle Choir). I also passed by the church's conference center, a granite fortress of a facility with a capacity of 21,000.

A block away, I found about 60 ex-Mormons gathered in a small, dingy meeting room at a second-rate hotel. These people lived mostly in the Mormon "Jell-O belt"—Utah, Idaho and Arizona—so-named because of the plates of Jell-O that inevitably appear at Mormon gatherings. They would spend the next three days trying to answer one question: How can a former Latter-day Saint carve out an acceptable life within the immense shadow of the clannish Mormon church, which claims roughly 70 percent of Utah residents as members?

"In Utah, the church has created an almost impossible box to climb out of," said Sue Emmett, then 60, a great-great-granddaughter of Brigham Young who left the church in 1999.

Over the next few days, I saw something familiar at that hotel room: the tremendous pain that had been inflicted on people's souls by men and women of faith. This time, the victims hadn't been raped by priests and kicked around by church leaders; they had simply admitted that they didn't believe in their faith anymore. Their punishment came from the laypeople: rejection by Mormon spouses, children and relatives; the disappearance of Mormon friends; the end of a social life; and sidetracked careers.

Mormons who openly abandon their faith are relatively few. Most Mormons who fall out of belief don't admit it. Called "Jack Mormons," these people are believed, by some estimates, to represent about 25 percent of Mormon rolls, but they don't dare come out of the closet because of the anticipated backlash. It took 16 months for Suzy Colver—another attendee at the ex-Mormon conference—and her husband to work up the courage to quit the Mormon church officially. They worried about what would befall them once word of their defection spread through their Mormon-dominated town of Ogden, Utah.

They didn't have to wait long. Colver told me that her family instantly became the neighborhood pariahs. She lost every one of her Mormon friends, even though she'd been a leader in the Church of Jesus Christ of Latter-day Saints' local Relief Society. She wasn't asked to volunteer at her kids' elementary school anymore. Her decision was so unspeakable, she said, that when her brother-in-law visited he was afraid to even acknowledge it, despite the visual taboos: the coffeemaker on the counter and the bottle of chardonnay in the refrigerator.

"If Mormons associate with you, they think they will somehow become contaminated and lose their faith too," Colver said. "It's almost as if people who leave the church don't exist."

The people at the ex-Mormon conference were an eclectic bunch: novelists and stay-at-home moms, entrepreneurs and cartoonists, sex addicts and alcoholics. Some were depressed, others angry, and only a few had successfully moved on. But they shared a common thread: They wanted to be honest about their lack of faith and yet continue to be loved by family and friends. In most pockets of Mormon culture, that wasn't going to happen.

The ex-Mormons warmly welcomed me, as had the victims of clergy sexual abuse. They were thankful that someone—even a stranger, even a journalist—would listen to them. They didn't have many friendly ears to bend on most days. Over the three days, we talked. And talked. We had a few drinks and talked some more. They wanted me to know the hardships they had experienced simply because their faith had evaporated.

One expressed relief after moving out of state to a non-Mormon neighborhood: "It was so nice to go to the grocery store and know no one's going to look down on you."

Another told of the pain she felt from the response of her grown children, who believe she's been influenced by the devil: "They see me as an enemy, as a heretic and as a threat to their children."

A third—someone who was having problems in her marriage—told me that she quit going to bed with her husband because he refused to stop wearing his sacred Mormon undergarments, worn day and night by the devout. She wanted a respite from symbolism.

"That church was right there in the bed with us," she complained. Eventually, he quit wearing the underwear to bed, and she stopped wearing her "Have You Hugged an Apostate Today?" T-shirt.

Though it was often covered by laughter and gallows humor, a deep sadness filled the conference. Part of what drew me to Christianity were the radical teachings of Jesus—to love your enemy, to protect the vulnerable and to go to any length to lovingly bring lost sheep back into the fold. As I reported the story from Salt Lake City, I wondered how faithful Mormons could embrace so many of Christ's teachings but miss so badly on one of His primary lessons: to love your neighbor—even an ex-Mormon—as yourself. The lost faces of former Mormons and the callous treatment they suffered stuck with me. Their tormenters were not conspirators; the church did not need to order anyone to freeze them out. Surely the remarkably harsh and widespread reaction against them was a sign of insecurity: declaring Mormon belief a house of cards was a serious threat that evoked defensive hostility.

At the time, I didn't analyze it; I just instinctively felt for the victims. I did the only thing I thought I could do at the time: I prayed for the former Mormons and I prayed for Mormons who caused them such pain. I prayed for understanding and reconciliation. I asked for God's intervention to bring love, understanding and healing to the people involved.

When translated into English, the shortest sentence in the Bible is "Jesus wept" (John 11:35). He cried in front of the tomb of his friend Lazarus, whom he would soon raise from the dead. Evangelicals love the brevity of the sentence because it underscores the tenderness and human empathy of Jesus. After my trip to Utah, I imagined Jesus weeping over the treatment of the former Mormons I had met. And I was right there crying with Him.

· T E N ·

Millstones Around Their Necks

"But if anyone causes one of these little ones who believe
in me to sin, it would be better for him to have a large
millstone hung around his neck and to be drowned in the
depths of the sea."

— MATTHEW 18:6

FORMER MORMONS LET down by their church, family and
peers was one thing. Catholics let down by a church that covered
up sexual abuse was much worse, and it involved criminal acts on
a national scale. Little more than a month after my ex-Mormon
story, on January 6, 2002, the *Boston Globe* published the first of
a two-part series that described in devastating detail the extent of
the clergy sexual abuse scandal in the Archdiocese of Boston. This
would permanently change the arc of my religion-writing career—
and my spiritual journey. I was just a few months away from converting to Catholicism. Those weeks would raise a deep question:
If an institution is corrupt, does that have any bearing on God? At

the time, I thought the answer was obviously negative. But now I think I was wrong.

Globe reporters, who would win a Pulitzer for their body of work, highlighted the case of Father John Geoghan, a priest who had been accused of molesting at least 130 boys, most of them in grammar school. The youngest was four years old. What made the story even more appalling was that Cardinal Bernard Law had known that Geoghan was a sexual predator in 1984, his first year as archbishop of Boston, but did nothing to stop him. (Geoghan had begun molesting boys in his first assignment after his 1962 ordination.) In fact, Law moved him to new parishes where the priest sexually assaulted new crops of boys, their parents unaware of the serial child rapist in their midst. It took the cardinal 14 years and an untold number of victims before he sought to remove Geoghan from the priesthood.

Law hadn't acted differently than other Catholic bishops. He had done as he was trained to do: deal with scandals in-house and keep them, at any cost, out of the public eye. What he didn't realize was that by 2002, modernity had caught up to the Catholic Church. No longer could the civil authorities be influenced into inaction and the media bullied or ignored. For once, the story wasn't going to flare up for a moment and then go quietly away. When the *Globe* attempted to get a comment from Law for the Geoghan story, his spokeswoman not only declined comment but said the archdiocese "had no interest in knowing what the *Globe's* questions would be." They thought the controversy would blow over, as it had done many times before.

The newspaper's initial series in January 2002 was a remarkable piece of reporting in part because it cracked open the wall of secrecy that church officials had hid behind for decades. *Globe* reporters combed the 84 civil lawsuits still pending against Geoghan for any facts they could use to construct the story, though they couldn't gain access to the evidence gathered in those suits because church attorneys got a judge to seal it. (After a motion by the *Globe*, a judge finally ordered the records unsealed on January 26, 2002.) Still, the bare facts of the cases, supplemented by moving interviews with Geoghan's now-grown victims, allowed the journalists to put together a chilling tale.

Knowing the *Globe* was working on a major investigation, Cardinal Law tried to do everything in his power to stop the story. His lawyer threatened legal sanctions against the *Globe* if it published any information taken from confidential records in the lawsuits. The newspaper also reported that Law's attorney "warned that he would seek court-imposed sanctions even if *Globe* reporters asked questions of clergy involved in the case."

The *Globe* stories were a pumped-up version of our own "Father Hollywood" story: they detailed how the Catholic Church protected a predatory priest and ignored his victims. My convenient theory—that Harris was an isolated case—started to crumble.

I was a member of the Religion Newswriters Association, a group of professional journalists who cover the faith beat for media outlets across the United States. As soon as the *Globe* published the first of its stories, a buzz swirled among religion reporters. We recognized that the story had the potential to leap across the fire line of the Archdiocese of Boston and spread to other dioceses. And sure enough, when a Boston judge released 30,000 pages of internal church documents later in the month, the scandal broke wide open.

The Boston church file—spanning the decades of the late 20th century—revealed the pattern for how the church handled nearly every case of clergy sexual abuse: first, move the offending priest to a new, unsuspecting parish or, in extreme cases, another diocese or country; second, lie or intimidate the victims and their families. The police were never called to investigate these felonies; no one in the new parishes was warned of a potential problem.

Notes from Law and his aides turned the stomachs of Boston parishioners and Catholics across the country. They included a warm note from Law to Geoghan in 1996 after the priest was forced to step down.

"Yours has been an effective life of ministry, sadly impaired by illness," the cardinal wrote. "On behalf of those you have served well, and in my own name, I would like to thank you. I understand yours is a painful situation. The Passion we share can indeed seem unbearable and unrelenting."

In referencing the Passion, Law apparently saw a parallel between the suffering experienced by Christ on the cross with Geoghan's compulsion to rape children.

The cardinal sent a similar letter of appreciation when Father Robert M. Burns, another serial molester, was forced out of ministry in 1991. "It would have been better were things to have ended differently, but such was not the case," Law wrote. "Nevertheless I still feel that it is important to express my gratitude to you for the care you have given to the people of the Archdiocese of Boston . . . I am certain that during this time you have been a generous instrument of the Lord's love in the lives of most people you served."

In the documents, the cardinal euphemistically labeled the molestations "inappropriate activity," "boundary violations" and "inappropriate affection." Inappropriate affection? He gave a high recommendation to one particular priest who was being considered for a new assignment in California, even though the cleric had *publicly* advocated for man–boy sexual relations.

Similar stories, including Father Hollywood's, had arisen occasionally during the previous two decades, but they hadn't jumped the local firewalls. Yet in 2002, the church could no longer contain the controversy. Church officials had always relied on Catholic-friendly police officers, district attorneys, judges and media to keep clergy sexual abuse out of the public eye, but this Old Boy's Network had broken down. Credit for the new era of openness belonged to the advent of the Internet, which provided wide and instant dissemination of the news, sparking the media to launch similar investigations in other dioceses. The Internet also became a clearinghouse of information for abuse victims, allowing them to track their molesters, to find out whether they had been accused before and to gain strength from other survivors. For many, it was the first time they had realized they were not alone and that they had power. The Internet tore away the veil of secrecy the church hid behind, and the sins of the Archdiocese of Boston echoed across the country.

In just the first two months of the Catholic sex scandal, nearly 100 priests in 11 states were accused of molestation by previously silent victims or by reporters' investigations. And that was just the start. It soon seemed the Catholic Church was projectile vomiting decades of cases of sexual abuse that had been covered up and had caused great sickness within the institution. In a report released by United States bishops in February 2004, they found that 4,392 priests—4 percent of all clerics—had allegedly abused as many as 10,000 minors since 1950. Because the bishops compiled the report themselves—and many victims never step forward—the numbers in the report, as large as they were, underreported the scope of the scandal. For me, the most revealing statistic was this: only *2 percent* of the molesting clerics had received prison sentences. It gives you some idea of the power of the church and the extent of the successful cover-up.

The priests and their bishops hadn't taken Jesus at His word when He told His disciples, "But if anyone causes one of these little ones who believe in me to sin, it would be better for him to have a large millstone hung around his neck and to be drowned in the depths of the sea." (Matthew 18:6)

Though I continued to work other religion stories, my editors wanted my primary focus to be the Catholic sex scandal. I began to live a dual life. By day, I investigated the local dioceses, dug up documents in courthouses, talked with a seemingly endless string of victims and interviewed bishops, their aides, attorneys and priests. In my off-hours, I put in my final months of training to become a Catholic.

I learned a lot from my Rite of Christian Initiation for Adults classes. I knew that the Immaculate Conception referred to Mary herself being born without sin, not to her getting pregnant without intercourse. I could correct the misconceptions about the doctrine of papal infallibility, which had been invoked only once since it was established in 1870; Pope Pius XII declared it in 1950 to include the assumption of Mary as an article of faith. I liked knowing that embedded in most altars is a small box that holds a relic, or bone, of at least one saint, often the person after which the church is named. I discovered the beauty of walking through the 14 Stations of the Cross—reliefs or paintings in Catholic churches that depict the final hours of Jesus' life. Mediating and praying in front of each piece of art allows you to be an eyewitness to the Passion, from the moment Jesus was condemned to death to when He rises from His tomb. I couldn't wait to go through my last rite of initiation into the church on March 30, 2002—on Easter Vigil, or Easter eve—little more than two months away.

As I wrote about the clergy sexual abuse scandal during the day and went to church at night and on weekends, I had no idea that

I had placed my Christian beliefs in mortal danger. I believed in Jesus and the church; the institution might be rotten, perhaps, but its purpose was pure.

One evening, Father Vincent addressed the scandal head-on. He warned us Catholics-to-be not to be poisoned by a relatively few bad clerics. He said the priests who molested children could be rightfully convicted of committing spiritual murder on their victims. But, Father Vincent warned, if we let their actions kill our faith, that would be spiritual suicide. His words resonated with me, and I vowed never to take that road.

Yet I would eventually find Father Vincent's assumption wrong. Spiritual suicide infers that people make a conscious decision to abandon their faith. Yet it isn't simply a matter of will. Many people want desperately to believe, but just can't. They may feel tortured that their faith has evaporated, but they can't will it back into existence. If an autopsy could be done on their spiritual life, the cause of death wouldn't be murder or suicide. It would be natural causes—the organic death of a belief system that collapsed under the weight of experience and reason.

But in early 2002, I still felt that believing in God and in Jesus was a choice, and I had made mine. I loved the passage in the Hebrew Scriptures in which Joshua lays out his faith plainly for his fellow Jews, whose belief in one God was unsteady at best:

> *But if serving the Lord seems undesirable to you, then choose for yourselves this day whom you will serve, whether the gods your forefathers served beyond the River, or the gods of the Amorites, in whose land you are living. But as for me and my household, we will serve the Lord.*

> —JOSHUA 24:15

I was with Joshua. I felt sad for those around me who didn't choose to serve the Lord. It wasn't because I thought they would end up in hell; I believed a loving God would be merciful to all His children, no matter how far they strayed. But I did think they were missing out on a deeper, more satisfying, more significant life—a life I had found and wasn't going to give up. For someone with a faith as deep as mine, it would take more than corruption within the Catholic Church to turn me away from the Lord.

It was clear to me that the real story wasn't about the molesting priests, but rather the bishops who covered up for them and caused thousands of additional children to be sodomized, orally copulated, raped and masturbated. Even today, most of these bishops are still in office; some have been promoted and all are revered by the faithful who deferentially call them "shepherds" and, in the case of a cardinal, "Your Eminence." Cardinal Law, who was run out of Boston by his parishioners and priests, is now the archpriest of St. Mary Major Basilica in Rome and celebrated one of Pope John Paul II's funeral masses.

Pope Benedict XVI has said that less than 1 percent of priests are molesters and that the Catholic sex scandal in America was an "intentional, manipulated . . . desire to discredit the church" by the media.

Larry Drivon, an attorney from Northern California who represents victims of clergy sexual abuse, uses an analogy to explain why the scandal was about the bishops, not the priests or sex: If a man-eating tiger eats a zoo patron, is it the tiger's fault or is the zookeeper who knowingly left open the cage responsible? These bishops knew they had predators working for them, but they let them continue to roam free.

When it comes to the sex scandal, there is, for now, an unbridgeable disconnect between the vast majority of the Catholic clergy and the rest of society. Because of their training and culture, transparency and sharing of authority are foreign concepts. For 2,000 years, the church has policed itself and rarely answered to anyone. Despite words crafted by the bishops' public relations people, this mindset hasn't changed overnight—and won't for the foreseeable future. To many in the clergy, the public scrutiny during the sex scandal seemed like an attack on the church, which they believed was the sole possessor of the truth. I think that's why the bishops and church's attorneys attacked the victims who came forward in the past with disproportional viciousness. The victims threatened to bring scandal to the church, and therefore could diminish the holiness of Catholicism in the eyes of some. They weren't just plaintiffs, but enemies who needed to be vanquished in such a way as to repel even the thought of future attacks. If a child fell down some stairs at a parish and became quadriplegic, church attorneys might argue that the church was not responsible for the fall, but they wouldn't personally attack the kid in the wheelchair.

Just as many in the clergy see the journalists' reporting and the public's outrage as basically Catholic bashing, most of society simply can't comprehend how people of God failed to protect children in their care. The opening paragraphs of a 2005 Philadelphia Grand Jury (which included several practicing Catholics) summed it up succinctly:

> *This report contains the findings of the Grand Jury: how dozens of priests sexually abused hundreds of children; how Philadelphia Archdiocese officials—including Cardinal Bevilacqua and Cardinal Krol—excused and enabled the abuse; and how the law must be changed so that it doesn't happen again. Some may be tempted to describe these events*

as tragic. Tragedies such as tidal waves, however, are out-side human control. What we found were not acts of God, but of men who acted in His name and defiled it.

But the biggest crime of all this is: it worked. The abuser priests, by choosing children as targets and trafficking on their trust, were able to prevent or delay reports of their sexual assaults, to the point where applicable statutes of limitation expired. And Archdiocese officials, by burying those reports they did receive and covering up the conduct, similarly managed to outlast any statutes of limitation. As a result, these priests and officials will necessarily escape criminal prosecution. We surely would have charged them if we could have done so.

. . . Sexually abusive priests were either left quietly in place or "recycled" to unsuspecting new parishes—vastly expanding the number of children who were abused. It didn't have to be this way. Prompt action and a climate of compassion for the child victims could have significantly limited the damage done.

Philadelphia's lead investigator, a veteran assistant district attorney named Will Spade, would later tell the *National Catholic Reporter* that interviewing the scores of victims affected him like no other case in his career.

"It was like working in a factory," Spade said. "And in this factory was a conveyer belt of damaged people. Every day it was another damaged person.

"There would be times when I would come home after a par-ticularly bad day," he continued, "and I would lie down on the couch with my head in my wife's lap and cry, uncontrollably cry."

As a reporter, the victims got to me, too. Nearly every day I heard from at least one more victim, and each story was simply heartbreaking. It made it worse that I was the father of four boys; I could easily imagine the devastation to our family if a trusted priest sodomized one or more of my kids. I couldn't get the victims' stories or the bishops' lies—many of them written on their own stationery, undeniable and permanent—out of my head. I had been in journalism more than two decades and had dealt with murders, rapes and other violent crimes, senseless deaths and tragedies. But this was different—the children were so innocent, their parents so faithful, the priests so sick and bishops so corrupt.

The only thing that quieted the victims' voices for me was alcohol. Since my born-again turnaround I hadn't been a big drinker, and it was rare when I had more than a beer on a weeknight, but now I found myself coming home and pouring several stiff drinks. I started to look forward to the end of the evening, usually after the kids had gone to bed, when I could feel the buzz of the tequila or rum working its magic to numb my emotions. It troubled me that I needed this self-medication; it wasn't good for my health and I hadn't earned the right to the pain. I had only listened to the stories of the real victims. I kept my pain and drinking a secret, except from my wife. With her, I shared the stories I had heard. This turned out to save our marriage. Our talks insured that we were traveling down the same spiritual path, no matter where it led.

Unbeknownst to us, it was leading toward skepticism. We would find, in fact, a deep connection between faith in the church and faith in God. The Catholic Church presents an extreme case of institutional deference, which helps explain the success of the cover-up of abuse for so many decades. Members of the laity aren't supposed to question their "fathers." This is more than just a simile to faith in God, which involves a leap beyond question. There's a reason why atheists and agnostics used to be called free-thinkers.

I don't think Greer and I could have lived happily in our marriage with one of us devoutly religious and the other a nonbeliever. The gap in worldviews would have been too large to bridge or ignore.

As I was collecting pain, many of the victims were shedding some of theirs. The scandal had given them a voice at last. It was liberating, freeing an explosion from below. I wrote about it on March 21, 2002:

> *After years of being disdained, dismissed or simply ignored, longtime crusaders against sexual abuse by priests suddenly have entered a kind of promised land. It's an unfamiliar place where Catholic bishops apologize, prosecutors and politicians listen, and a friendly media army helps fight their battles.*
>
> *And, perhaps most soothing to the victims' scarred souls, people finally believe them.*
>
> *"I'd never thought I'd see this day," said David Clohessy, national director of the St. Louis–based Survivors Network of Those Abused by Priests, known as SNAP, one of the nation's two largest such groups, with 3,500 members. "We've been crying from the rooftops for someone to notice what's going on for so long."*

The sex scandal provided fertile ground for stories. The unfolding drama—with its secret documents, lies, tragedies, lawsuits, villains, heroes and million-dollar payouts—provided me with the raw material for many high-profile pieces of journalism that began to get national attention. I felt like a television reporter in the eye of a hurricane, speaking to the camera while tied to a palm tree. By March other *Times* reporters, who normally could care less about religion coverage, asked to be put on the team. They could smell the blood in the water.

I now was within a few weeks of my Catholic conversion. I still viewed the scandal as a necessary evil that would give the institution a badly needed cleansing. I believed my own reporting, in small part, would contribute to the movement that would force the United States bishops to enact reforms to protect the parishioners' children and to bring back holiness to the Catholic Church. I saw the process as anything but anti-Catholic. The church was on a corrective course that would bring it much closer to the principles of Jesus than those of a corporation.

I studied my church history. Catholicism had strayed before from the path blazed by Jesus, only to be placed back on the straight and narrow by a reformer—someone who bucked the establishment, was hated for it, but usually ended up a saint. Many students of history know about the corruption of the Renaissance, when popes and their underlings fathered children and lived licentiously. But sexual abuse has an even older history. In the fourth century, St. Basil of Caesarea got so fed up with sexual abuse that he set up a detailed system of punishment to deal with clerics at his monastery who molested boys. Perpetrators were to be flogged and put in chains for six months; they were never again allowed unsupervised interaction with minors. In the 11th century, St. Peter Damian, a Benedictine monk, wrote a treatise called the *Book of Gomorrah* that he gave to Pope Leo IX circa 1050, pleading for him to get serious about stopping clergy sexual abuse, including the molestation of minors.

"Unless the [Catholic Church] intervenes as soon as possible, there is no doubt but that this unbridled wickedness, even though it should wish to be restrained, will be unable to stop on its headlong course," St. Peter Damian wrote.

In a return letter, the pope praised Damian for addressing the subject and wrote that clerics would be removed from the priesthood if for a long period of time (or a short period of time with many) they "have defiled themselves by either of the two kinds of filthiness which you have described, or, which is horrible to hear or speak of, have sunk to the level of anal intercourse."

Leo IX also warned: "For he who does not attack vice, but deals with it lightly, is rightly judged to be guilty of his death, along with the one who dies in sin."

I and other reporters covering the story were called Catholic-bashers by some, including many in the clergy. Others—especially the hard-core believers on either end of the Catholic spectrum—called to encourage more reporting. They didn't care whether the cost of the thousands of sexual abuse cases bankrupted the church. In the process, they thought that Catholicism would be purified.

Doubt. It seemed to have sneaked up on me. The closer I approached the rite of initiation into the church, the more I became aware of this new sensation. It had nothing to do with God (I thought), but I did begin to waver. Was this the right time to be accepted into the church? If I went through the rite, would it be a slap in the face to the survivors who had courageously stepped forward? Converting to the Catholic faith was something that I kept quiet. No victims would know that I had entered the church. But *I* would know. And it started to feel, deep in my gut, like it might be the wrong thing to do.

Still, I firmly believed the institution would emerge from the scandal reformed and humbled, and I took some advice from a friend who said, "Keep your eye on the person on the cross and not the men behind the altar." This was God's church, not man's. And it was never going to be perfect, given the sinfulness of man.

That the church was flawed shouldn't stop me from joining other faithful Catholic for worship, Communion and a fulfilling spiritual life.

I sought solace in the belief that a church's heart was in the pews, not the pulpits or its administrative offices. I loved the Catholics and soon-to-be Catholics in my conversion class. I'd rarely been around a nicer group of people. They had showered me with love and even gifts—CDs featuring Gregorian chant and rosary beads from Our Lady of Lourdes in France. I was certain that the people reading about the scandal would recoil and, in the end, recapture God's house. I pushed aside my doubts about becoming a Catholic.

·ELEVEN·

A Gentle Whisper Silenced

After the earthquake came a fire, but the Lord was not in the fire. And after the fire came a gentle whisper.

— 1 KINGS 19:12

ON THE FIRST weekend in March 2002, I received two great story tips. The first one: Cardinal Roger Mahony of Los Angeles had quietly dismissed somewhere between six and 12 priests with credible allegations of sexual abuse in their past. Included in the dismissals were two *convicted* child molesters still in ministry and another priest who had admitted to the cardinal some years earlier that he had molested two boys—and had gone on to abuse others.

The second: Bishop Tod D. Brown of Orange had ordered an admitted pedophile removed from ministry, and that priest, Michael Pecharich, would be announcing his resignation at Sunday services at San Francisco Solano Church in Rancho Santa Margarita. Diocesan officials told me that in the spirit of openness, I was welcome to attend a service and the "healing" session afterward with parishioners.

I had wrongly assumed that the dioceses of Los Angeles and Orange had no priests left in ministry who had sexually abused children. Cardinal Mahony and Bishop Brown had agreed to get rid of them more than six months earlier as part of the $5.2 million Ryan DiMaria settlement. My assumption was naïve. It was more than curious that the prelates had gotten around to dumping the molesting priests just as the national sex scandal arrived at the doorsteps of their dioceses. With more victims coming forward each day, the dioceses felt forced to clear out their rosters of any pedophiles before a survivor or journalist exposed them for violating the terms of their settlement by keeping a molester in ministry. I should have been more skeptical, something I'd unfortunately have to learn many times covering religion.

On March 3, 2002, a warm and sunny Southern California day, I drove to South Orange County to the elegant Spanish mission–style church in Rancho Santa Margarita to see how the Diocese of Orange would rid itself of Father Michael Pecharich.

In a packed sanctuary that held hundreds, Father Mike, as he was known, stood before the congregation he had led for a dozen years. Reading from a statement, he told them that 19 years ago he had "transgressed the personal boundaries of an adolescent." (Only later would it emerge that the diocese knew he, in fact, had been accused of sexual misconduct with several other children.) With the diocese's zero-tolerance policy now in place, he said he was being forced to step down. The tone of his statement made him sound like a martyr—someone who had been kicked out of ministry for a single mistake, a simple boundary violation—nearly two decades ago. As he read his short statement, the parishioners sat in stunned silence. Some women fished in their purses for tissues to wipe away their tears. As Father Mike walked out of the church, the congregation rose and gave him a standing ovation.

It took me a while to understand that these people had been victimized, too. Father Mike was their spiritual leader, someone who had presided over their confirmations, marriages, baptisms and funerals. He had counseled them and heard their confessions. They had invited him into their homes. And now, they couldn't process the disconnect between the Father Mike they knew and the admitted child molester.

When the applause started, my first reaction was disbelief. A standing ovation? Though the language softened the act, I had just heard this priest admit that he had molested a minor. Diocesan officials had kept the information secret from the parishioners of San Francisco Solano, who until now would never have thought twice about leaving their children in the pastor's charge. As a parent, my response was outrage and disgust. Imagine that a beloved schoolteacher who had taught your children had admitted to once sexually molesting a child but the school district never called the police, kicked him out or bothered to tell the parents. Would you rally around the teacher? Or would you be angry that a predator was left in a position of great trust with easy access to children— without your knowledge? I'd guess that the school superintendent would be forced to resign under pressure from parents—and face criminal charges for aiding and abetting a criminal.

After the service, I walked with church members to a newly completed parish hall, where diocesan officials held a "healing session" to answer questions and allow people to vent. I took a seat in the back. Some parishioners trembled with rage as they peppered the church officials with questions that centered around why their pastor was being penalized now for something he did 19 years ago and that church officials had known about since 1996. Their rage was aimed at his removal, not his sin. Some demanded to know how church officials even knew the sex crime had happened. The response: Father Mike had admitted it.

Soon, the conversation turned to finding a way to honor Father Mike. Someone hit upon the idea of naming the new parish hall after him. Others seconded the proposal. I scanned the room to see whether anyone aside from me thought this was crazy. My eyes locked on a man who stood near a side door. He had the muscular build and close-cropped haircut of a military man or a police officer. With his jaw tightened, he glared at the parishioners who were lobbying to christen the building the Father Michael Pecharich Parish Hall. I could see the veins start to stick out of his neck. He finally yelled, "Don't put this man on a pedestal!" With the parishioners silenced, he explained in a biting tone that he worked as a sheriff's deputy and handled many child molestation cases. These molesters, he said, almost never have just one victim. And why, he continued, wasn't anyone else angry that they hadn't been told about Father Mike's past before now? He had left his children at church many times, unaware that a child molester was in charge. How dare the parents not be told! He ended his speech by asking why no one had said anything in support of the victim. Why all this compassion for the perpetrator of a crime? With that, he abruptly walked out.

I wanted to see whether he'd agree to be quoted for the newspaper, so I stuffed my notebook in my back pocket and started to rise. That's when a woman in the front row stood up and bellowed, "There's an even more important question here." I thought, oh, boy, this just keeps getting better. I stood waiting for it. But then she turned around and pointed at me. "What's an *L.A. Times* reporter doing in our midst?"

I had no idea how she knew I was there, but the entire angry mob of parishioners—with nowhere else to vent their feelings—turned on me, pointing fingers and snarling. I spoke quickly, saying that I'd be glad to tell them why I was here and who invited me, but first I needed to talk to the gentleman who'd just spoken. After that, I'd come back.

I walked briskly out the door and caught up with the deputy in the courtyard. He politely explained that he couldn't talk to me because of his job. When I turned to go back inside the hall, I found my path blocked by a half-circle of fuming Catholics. They started screaming at me. I had no business being there, they spat; I told them the bishop had invited me. They yelled that this wasn't a news story; I answered that this Catholic parish, with more than 4,000 families, was probably the largest and most influential organization in town, and Father Mike was one of the most recognized figures in Rancho Santa Margarita—it was news by any definition. They shouted that I would ruin Father Mike's life if the story were published; I told them that Father Mike had ruined his own life when he molested a boy. They argued that they were positive that he had molested only once and he had lived an exemplary life for the past two decades.

"I believe that's what makes us so passionate about the departure of Father Mike, the fact that the crime he is guilty of took place 19 years ago," one parishioner told me. "In my eyes, he has done a noteworthy job of changing his life and becoming someone we could feel safe to have our children around."

I said that I hoped she was right, but in my experience, molesters didn't abuse just one child and I'd bet anyone that my phone would ring tomorrow after the story ran with another victim coming forward. That's what usually occurs, I said. Indeed, it happened the next day.

We talked until everyone was talked out. By the time we were done, sadness—not anger—was the primary emotion. And I drove back to the office with a huge headache and many questions. How was the church ever going to reform if parishioners instinctively threw their allegiance behind molesting priests and not their victims? San Francisco Solano's reaction was typical. I've talked with victims of clergy sexual abuse whose parents blamed them for "seducing" the priest. I've watched Catholics yell at and even spit on victims who picketed outside a parish. I've seen congregants offer molesting priests jobs and even raise their bail. I've read letters from parishioners and priests who wrote glowing testimonies to bishops and judges about a convicted priest sex offender, pleading for leniency.

A colleague of one priest convicted on 46 counts of sexual abuse wrote to a judge that "our work brings us into intimate contact with people's lives. In a time when the exchange of simple affection within the most intimate of circles has become a rare commodity, our associations with others run the grave risk of being misunderstood by all parties including perhaps the priest himself." Jaime Soto, the priest who penned the letter of support, is now bishop of Sacramento and a rising star in the Catholic Church.

The parishioners' responses in these situations underscore how desperately we all crave spiritual leadership. We want to invest our trust in good men (and women, in most faiths) whom we can look up to—and even idolize. It is comforting to believe that there are people who are holier than ourselves, who we know and can follow. God is just the most extreme example. But viewed in the light of the scandal, this devotion appears sick.

With little more than a week before Easter, I didn't know what I was going to do. I had invested a year into becoming a Catholic. I was brimming with knowledge and love for the church. But could I join this church at this moment? After all the revelations?

I probably should have discussed my doubts with Father Vincent or my sponsor, but I worried about disappointing them—and also casting a pall over what was the holiest week of the Christian year. Everyone in our class was gearing up for the big evening, which would include celebratory dinners, parties and gifts, and I didn't want to throw a shadow over the group. Besides, I could predict their response—I was confusing man's sinfulness with God's church—and I had reached the point where that answer didn't suffice. I just didn't want to join an organization that was run by leaders so out of touch with the modern world that they never picked up the phone to turn in child rapists—something most of us would do automatically, even if the perpetrator were a member of our own family.

For counsel, I turned to a veteran reporter with the *National Catholic Reporter*, a weekly newspaper. I had admired his work as a journalist, and through his writings, I knew him to be a devout Catholic and gentle soul. I had exchanged some e-mails with him since I landed on the religion beat. With nowhere else to turn, I imposed on our fledgling friendship. I sent him an e-mail describing my feelings and thoughts while standing at the precipice of Catholicism amidst the buffeting winds of the scandal. I told him I didn't know what to do and asked for his advice. The next day, he wrote back:

> *I'm sorry your heart was heavy.*
>
> *Sometimes I wonder why the heck I bother with it all . . . All churches, but certainly this one, are magnets for good people who deserve protection from institutional corruptions—the standard corruptions that exist in every institution.*
>
> *And if they are not being corrupted, then the people*

who [make up] the institution we call church, and who together form church, radiate little bits of good through themselves and their actions that somehow are anchored in what Jesus came from and God wants of us.

In pressing for reform, I occasionally liken us all in these generations to those generations of Quakers who fought against slavery and lived and died in the fight never knowing whether slavery would be abolished or not. It was sufficient to fight for it.

And I suppose that's my basic tenet.

Christians aren't asked to succeed. They're only asked to "do." The sin is not "doing." Success is up to God.

. . . I realize that's all terribly simplistic. But then I have a peasant's faith rather than an intellectual's!

Meanwhile, don't worry about not doing anything at Easter, or future Easters. The things of your soul are sufficient to the day. And to God.

The rest is the joyous part of formality, and communion. And that will happen as and when it should.

His counsel put me at ease. I still had about a week to decide, and I would do what my heart told me was right. Whatever happened, there would be other Easters. On Good Friday, I decided I couldn't go through with the conversion. Converting to Catholicism during the height of a horrific scandal felt like an endorsement of the establishment. Worse, it felt like at least symbolically that I was turning against the people who were victimized by the church—horribly wounded people who said, to the person, that the church's betrayal was worse than what their priest did to them.

I had always imagined the rite of initiation to be a serious but joyous ceremony—like a wedding, which it basically was. If I was going to be married to the Catholic Church, I wanted to enter the relationship with no doubts or misgivings.

I told my wife. She said she understood. I called my sponsor and broke the news. He sounded disappointed but said he understood, too. I was a big admirer of his and hoped he didn't feel as though he had somehow failed in bringing me into the church. I don't think he did. I told him—and I really believed—that I would be back. I said that as soon as I felt excited again about the church, I'd become a member. Maybe during next year's Easter vigil. But now, the timing was wrong, and my heart said no.

It was the first of many agonizing choices on my journey away from God. They would each come down to picking sides. Do I side with what I wish to be true? Or do I go with what I know to be true? I didn't realize it at the time, but not becoming a Catholic was the first tangible sign that I was losing my faith. But the thought was so scary, so unwanted and so profound that it would be a long time before I actually admitted it, even to myself.

A few days later, I spent Easter at home for the first time in a dozen years.

Several months later, I stopped attending church on a regular basis. At first, I told myself it was because of my busy work and family schedules. But that wasn't it. Before, attending church had been the number-one priority of my week. Now it was something I did if nothing else came up. Most weeks I just couldn't muster the motivation to go. I needed my weekends to escape from the subject I was reporting on for 40-plus hours during the week.

The kids didn't mind having their Saturday nights or Sunday mornings free, though my teenagers still attended popular week-night youth programs at St. Andrew's Presbyterian Church (I suspected mostly because of the large number of girls present). My wife was struggling to reconcile the idealized vision of the Catholic Church of her youth with the institution portrayed in my stories. She welcomed the weeks off, too.

Soon, I found myself not going at all. In truth, I had sunk into a depression. My long honeymoon with Christianity had ended, and I wondered what was next. I still prayed and read the Bible each day, but I didn't do it eagerly—I had to force myself. I started to go to therapy twice a week. Religion wasn't the only problem in my life at the time. At the 14-year mark, my marriage had hit a particularly rough patch. Part of my motivation for going into the Catholic Church was so Greer and I could be married "in God's eyes." Now, Greer said she didn't want to marry me again, even if I became Catholic. In fact, she wanted a divorce. She couldn't repress any longer the unresolved issues of our relationship, especially its rocky beginning. We were learning the same lesson that the Catholic Church was: you can't hide the truth forever. Eventually, it will come out. Greer and I informally separated but because neither of us would leave the children, we both stayed in the house, occupying separate bedrooms. Without kids, we would have been finished. But neither of us could face a life without living full-time with our boys. We decided to do whatever it took to save our relationship. Christianity can be a form of self-help, but now we started to see that we could also help ourselves. It took months and months and much of our savings to pay for counseling, but the marital seas began to calm down, thanks especially to a wonderful psychotherapist.

My faith was another story. As soon as I'd beat back one doubt, two more would pop up. I felt angry with God for making faith such a guessing game. I didn't treat my sons as God treated me. I gave them clear direction, quick answers, steady discipline and plenty of love. There was little mystery in our relationship; they didn't have to strain to hear my "gentle whisper." How to hear God, love Him and best serve Him shouldn't be so open to interpretation. It shouldn't be that hard.

It started to bother me greatly that God's institutions—ones He was supposed to be guiding—were often more corrupt than their secular counterparts. If these churches were infused and guided by the Holy Spirit, shouldn't it follow that they would function in a morally superior fashion than a corporation or government entity? In general, I was finding this wasn't the case. I started to see that religious institutions are *more* susceptible to corruption than their secular counterparts because of their reliance on God, and not human checks and balances, for governance. The answers to prayer or God's desires, whether in a hierarchical structure such as the Catholic Church or the more representational form of governance in many Protestant churches, are prone to human interpretation that can be easily twisted for selfish and sinful needs. This is reflected in the lack of Christian unity, often described as the faith's largest scandal.

Shortly before his death, Jesus prayed that all Christians "may be one, Father, just as you are in me and I am in you. May they also be in us so that the world may believe that you have sent me. I have given them the glory that you gave me, that they may be one as we are one: I in them and you in me. May they be brought to complete unity to let the world know that you sent me and have loved them even as you have loved me." (John 17:21–23)

The Roman Catholic Church's College of Cardinals, after intense prayer and guided by the Holy Spirit, has selected popes for nearly a millennium. Some Holy Fathers have turned out to be saints; others became murderers (Pope John XII), torturers (Pope Urban VI) and adulterers (too many to name). Less reliance on faith and more, for example, on a democratized search for a pope might have kept the more notorious ones from office. And certainly a more practical belief that God had not ordained every pope to lead the church would have led to the quick firing of the most corrupt ones.

In the Protestant world, corruption often seeps into institutions under the cover of God's will—or the belief by the congregation or the board of elders that pastors have a special connection to God. Only a relatively few churches decide God's guidance is not enough and have put into place strict but commonsense rules to cut down on the potential for scandal.

Up until now, I had, as a Christian, been able to quickly repel doubts about my faith, whether by study or prayer, or simply by ignoring them. Now, doubts were hitting me from all angles and sticking to me like Velcro. I couldn't free myself of them.

·TWELVE·

"Rebuild My Church"

Now about spiritual gifts, brothers, I do not want you to be ignorant . . . There are different kinds of gifts, but the same Spirit. There are different kinds of service, but the same Lord . . . Now to each one the manifestation of the Spirit is given for the common good.

—1 CORINTHIANS 12:1–7

WITH MY NEW set of doubts, I started to obsess about hell, worrying that I would wind up there if I tumbled into disbelief. I didn't think of hell as a fiery pit, but something closer to C. S. Lewis's vision of it in *The Great Divorce*—a place of unending blandness far from the pleasures of God:

I had been wandering for hours in similar mean streets, always in the rain and always in the evening twilight. Time seemed to have paused on that dismal moment when only a few shops have lit up and it is not yet dark enough for their windows to look cheering. And just as the evening

never advanced to night, so my walking had never brought
me to the better parts of the town.

Except for the right-wing fringe of Christianity, I didn't see many other people worried about hell; it was as if the place was never mentioned in the Bible. In covering the Catholic sex scandal, I often wondered: Did these people truly believe in hell? It's an important part of their doctrine, but no one seemed concerned about eternal damnation. I saw that the Catholic bishops believed deeply in their institution and their office—enough so that they routinely lied, violated secular laws or put children in harm's way to protect the church. Their actions show that they had dedicated their lives not to the Gospel, but to a Roman system that valued loyalty and obedience to superiors and punished those who brought scandal. It was easy for the bishops to appear to be holy when celebrating a Mass or tending to the sick; it was much more difficult when they actually had to sacrifice something—such as the derailment of their careers by the Vatican if they turned in a molesting priest to civil authorities and created a scandal, rather than dealing with the matter internally and making it neatly disappear. As a reporter, I couldn't find the maverick bishop who stood up to the institution and protected the children in his charge. And I could find only a relative handful of priests who tried to buck the system—most of whom paid the price for turning in a brother priest with their careers.

I met one of them, Father John Conley, in San Francisco. In November 1997, the priest came home early one evening to his parish, only to find his pastor wrestling in the dark with a young boy. Conley, a federal prosecutor before becoming a priest, believed he had witnessed an act of sexual abuse. According to depositions and other legal documents, he reported the incident to San Francisco archdiocesan officials and told them he was going to file a report with civil authorities, as required by law. Conley said one official asked him, "Now, are you sure you want to do this?"

The archdiocese backed the priest suspected by Conley of molesting the boy, and Conley was soon removed from active ministry (church officials said his demotion was unrelated to his whistle-blowing). Eventually, the accused priest admitted that he had sexually abused several boys, and Conley filed a whistle-blower lawsuit against the Archdiocese of San Francisco, winning a large settlement in 2002. William Levada, now a top official at the Vatican, was then the archbishop of San Francisco.

In his deposition, an angry Conley said he asked the vicar of clergy to relay a message to the archbishop: "The message was to tell the archbishop to grow some balls and start acting like a man."

Conley explained his anger by saying it was "because I felt this was a very serious matter involving child abuse and that they were hiding their heads in the sand, refusing to deal with it."

I wondered: Shouldn't faith, if you truly had it, give you the strength to grow some balls and do the right thing, no matter the consequences? According to Christian tradition, the apostles suffered martyrs' deaths because they refused to renounce their belief, after the Resurrection, that Jesus was the Messiah. Christian apologetics use this as a key piece of evidence to prove Christ's divinity; if the apostles hadn't witnessed the resurrected Jesus and had simply been promoting a lie, they certainly would have recanted in the face of death.

The Catholic bishops, facing only the potential death of their careers, ignored the teachings of Christ—and the laws of the land. It's impossible even to skim the pages of the Gospels and not see the importance Jesus placed on children and their protection. If the Bible were true, many bishops would have been better off placing millstones around their necks and jumping into the ocean than behaving the way they did. According to Scriptures, they face a hellish future.

Hell has a fundamental role in Christianity. The Scriptures tells us that God sent His Son to Earth to die for our sins and if we believed in Jesus, we could avoid hell and eternal separation from the Lord and be ushered into heaven. The Bible doesn't mess around when describing hell. It's a dreadful place where souls languish in unspeakable pain for eternity. Jesus calls hell the "outer darkness" consumed by "everlasting fire." The book of Revelation warns that sinners will be "thrown into the lake of fire." Matthew's Gospel offers a soundtrack: the "weeping and gnashing of teeth." In the New Testament, hell is also described as "everlasting destruction," "blackest darkness" and a place where people are "tormented day and night for ever and ever."

During the Middle Ages and the Renaissance, a lurid image of hell was firmly cemented in people's minds by the church and many faithful thinkers. Dante wrote that within the seventh circle of hell runs "the river of blood, within which boiling is/Whoe'er by violence doth injure others." Artist Hieronymus Bosch depicted naked souls being devoured by a birdlike creature, pierced by spears and tormented by half-human demons.

Today, it's rare to hear about hell from a member of the clergy. The Catholic Church, the original promoters of a Dante-esque hell, has softened its view quite a bit. In 1999, Pope John Paul II made headlines by saying that hell should be seen not as a fiery underworld but as "the state of those who freely and definitively separate themselves from God, the source of all life and joy."

Evangelical pulpits have banished hell as well. Log onto www.pastors.com, the website run by Saddleback Church, whose senior pastor, Rick Warren, says the Bible's teachings on hell guide his ministry. Scan the scores of sermons available for free and for sale. There are messages on abortion, addiction and ambition. Laughter, leadership and love. War, work and worry—but nothing on hell.

Six months into my reporting on the sex scandal, I teamed up with colleague Mike Anton for a story on the state of hell within American Christianity. I was startled to find that the subject was rarely brought up in church these days. Though 71 percent of Americans claim they still believe that hell exists, the concept is simply ignored by most pastors, even conservative ones. Many of them fear a backlash from their congregants, who don't want to hear such unpleasantness on their Sunday mornings. In short, hell has been frozen out mostly because of consumer desires, not theological concerns. Pastors are unwilling to risk market share by tackling an unpopular topic.

Robert H. Schuller, the *Hour of Power* televangelist and founder of the Crystal Cathedral in Garden Grove, California, stopped preaching on the subject 40 years ago, moving on to a theology that stresses individual success in such books as *If It's Going to Be, It's Up to Me!*

"I don't ever want people to become Christian to escape hell," Schuller told my colleague. He added that people shouldn't be threatened with God's stick when dangling a carrot is enough to close the deal.

One measure of hell's continued decline can be found in the changed attitude of the Reverend Billy Graham, who came to prominence in the 1940s as a fire-and-brimstone Gospel preacher. His depiction of hell was unequivocal, an unpleasant address for unrepentant sinners. Now he's not so sure.

Graham told an interviewer in 1991: ". . . I believe that hell is essentially separation from God. That we are separated from God, so we can have hell in this life and hell in the life to come . . . But to describe hell in vivid terms like I might have done 30 or 40 years ago, I'm not at liberty to do that because . . . whether there is actually fire in hell or not, I do not know."

We found that traditional denominations also have pushed hell to the margins. The Presbyterian Church (USA)'s first catechism, approved in 1998, mentions hell only once. George Hunsinger, a professor at Princeton Theological Seminary and the catechism's principal author, would have liked the document to address hell more directly and "talk about divine judgment in a responsible way." But the committee rejected the idea without much debate.

"It's a failure of nerve by churches that are not wanting to take on a non-popular stance," Hunsinger told us.

The pastors who speak regularly about hell are, for the most part, far-right preachers who are viewed as wacky by most of Christianity. Mike talked with Pastor Ray Comfort, who believes hell is as real and as bad as advertised in the New Testament. The New Zealand transplant crisscrosses the country to preach at churches that still embrace the old-fashioned concept of hell. He warns that churches that sugarcoat or ignore the Bible's warning about hell will become irrelevant. "God will remove his spirit, his power from them, and they will become just like social clubs," he said.

It's possible that 71 percent of us really do believe hell is real, but just don't want to hear about it, leading to a theology of market denial. Or possibly, many of us say one thing to a pollster—not wanting to appear so cocky as to be beyond the reach of godly justice—and another thing to themselves—not really being so sure after all. But most of us commit lesser sins. We're occasionally thoughtless or mean, or we cheat on our taxes. We stop short of rape, molestation and covering up such evil. Seeing so many priests do what they did, and so many bishops cover for them, I wondered whether hell frightened them at all. Or maybe they were so far beyond reality, they didn't think of their behavior as sinful.

Hell has always been a stumbling block for me as a Christian. Anger welled up inside me when evangelicals talked about how sad it was that people who didn't believe in Christ would be sent to hell. I could never imagine banishing one of my sons to eternal damnation because he walked away from me. That wasn't unconditional love. I had faith that He wouldn't send my own two brothers and sister—who are my moral superiors though not believers—to hell for even one second, much less an eternity. But I chalked it up to one of the mysteries of faith I wouldn't solve in this lifetime. Soon enough, I believed, God would make it clear for me what hell was about and who, if any, were banished there. It wasn't a satisfying answer, but at the time, it was enough.

I did feel my lack of certainty about hell was a shortcoming as a Christian. With the Bible's rather straightforward language about hell, it was difficult to wave it off as unknowable. But as for those pastors who said they believed in hell, why in heaven's name would they skirt the issue so completely in public? After all, it's a teaching with eternal consequences. To banish hell from the pulpit was to avoid talking about an elephant in the room. Even if I personally didn't want to believe in that elephant, it was there.

The thought of hell haunted me. I had hopscotched from an evangelical church to a Presbyterian congregation and finally to a Catholic parish. During that time, I never considered my soul in danger, because I still believed in Jesus. He was my Savior and my insurance policy. If I was wrong about hell (and it did exist) but right about Jesus, I was still safe. Believers use the term "Savior" for Jesus, and all it really means is "saved from hell." If there is no hell, the term is meaningless. As doubts about faith crept into my mind, hell—even just the remote possibility of hell—was a great motivator for me to redouble my spiritual efforts.

Though I questioned the existence of hell, I did accept the notion that evil, or Satan, operated in the world and was trying to lure us away from God. I believed this was done in mostly subtle ways that we don't recognize until it is too late. He works through the flirty co-worker who creates lustful thoughts. He amplifies your unrelenting desire for a tropical vacation, pushing you into taking a trip that puts you deep into credit card debt. He uses your envy of your wealthy neighbor to make you feel miserable about your own life. I believed Satan was tempting me at every vulnerable part of my life, expertly manipulating my fears, desires and weaknesses. C. S. Lewis said that each action you take either brings you closer to or farther away from God. I was easily led away from holiness. I often looked up from my daily travels only to discover I was far from God.

By the internal logic of Christian belief, there are other ways of looking at hell's disappearance from the pulpit beyond denial and disbelief. Perhaps Satan has done a remarkable job of convincing pastors and their followers to soft-pedal hell. Maybe the Bible—though divinely inspired—is a flawed document that should be interpreted liberally. Or perhaps the Bible and hell are works of fiction, something some believers may sense, and fear, deep in their souls, allowing them to ignore one of its essential teachings.

For a dozen years, I had been blessed with an unshakable faith that seemed to get deeper with each passing year. Now, my backstage pass to the world of religion had become a curse. I no longer gathered information about my faith from carefully written books, inspiring sermons, classes taught by and filled with fellow Christians, and well-choreographed church services. Starting with the Catholic Church scandal, I began to cover much less bright, shiny stories. I began to look behind the front of many bright, shiny facades. I didn't like what I saw, and I didn't like the questions that continued to surface within me because of it. Why did I keep circling back to these stories about corruption and hypocrisy within the Body of Christ? I couldn't figure out an answer until I read a biography of St. Francis of Assisi (my third or fourth) and began to think my calling from God had shifted. Maybe the Lord wanted me, as he did St. Francis, to "rebuild His church"—in my case, not in some grand way that would lead to sainthood but by simply reporting on the corruption within any and all churches. This thought—which I believed came from God—gave me great comfort. It gave me something to hold on to, something that made sense of what I was going through. The Body of Christ was sick. My investigative reporting skills could help uncover the infection and promote the healing. I was sure this had been part of the Lord's plan for me all along. Maybe I, like St. Francis, just didn't understand Him at first. When St. Francis heard God's voice commanding him to rebuild His church, he initially took the Lord quite literally and began fixing up a chapel that had fallen into ruin near his home. Only later did Francis understand that God wanted him to reform the church.

I thought I had heard God's voice loud and clear. But as with most everything else about working the religion beat, it didn't turn out as I had planned.

·THIRTEEN·

Heal Thyself

The idols speak deceit,
diviners see visions that lie;
they tell dreams that are false,
they give comfort in vain.
Therefore the people wander like sheep
oppressed for lack of a shepherd.

— ZECHARIAH 10:2

As I gazed down at the frail man in his bed, I thought: there's no way this can be Ole E. Anthony, the scourge of some of the world's richest and most powerful televangelists, a man so despised that preachers have labeled him "Ole Antichrist." The then 64-year-old didn't look like much of a threat to anyone. The lingering effects of a near-fatal electrocution 23 years earlier had left him severely disabled and in crippling pain generated from thousands of burned nerve endings.

It was November 2003. I was looking at a modern St. Francis, someone who was trying to rebuild the Body of Christ from within. He had plenty of work to do; he specialized in taking down televangelists.

As I watched, Ole gave himself a shot of the painkiller Nubain in his left thigh. Six electrodes were attached to his legs, pumping small electrical currents through his nervous system. Tan-tinted prescription bottles of Nalbuphine, Zanaflex, Acetamin and Skelaxin sat on his bed stand. A cabinet across the room was filled with bottles containing vitamins, amino acids and other concoctions. He wore a cervical collar. A walker and canes were scattered throughout his bedroom, which was thick with the smell of pipe tobacco and so small there was barely room for my chair.

A radical believer, Ole founded the Trinity Foundation to serve the poor. His group comprises some 400 Christians, 100 of whom live communally in a poor section of Dallas, attempting to emulate the practices of the first-century church—right down to its poverty. Each Trinity employee, including Ole, earns about $50 per week, after room and board. Trinity's annual budget is about $500,000, a sum that some of the nation's most popular televangelists routinely raise in a single day. Foundation members hold Bible studies and church services in their houses and apartments, and run a small school and a restaurant serving hearty dinners for under $5. The organization's primary mission is to house the homeless, not in dedicated shelters, but in the bedrooms and living rooms of Trinity members.

It was by serving the poor that Ole came to oversee a national spy operation dedicated to rooting out fraud and excess among some of America's biggest TV pastors. Many of the destitute who took refuge at Trinity told him that they had given their last dollars to televangelists who had promised the gullible and often desperate believers a huge return on their faith-inspired giving. Televangelism in America is a massive operation based on a fraud that can't be challenged in court. It's called the Prosperity Gospel, and it's preached over the airwaves to generate money for the televangelists' ministries. A twisted piece of theology, the Prosperity Gospel claims that if you perform an act of faith for God (for instance, contribute money to a televangelist), He will shower you with untold riches and good health.

Despite being mostly confined to bed, Ole directs some half-dozen investigators who expose the worst of the televangelists. The tax-free, unregulated industry of televangelism generates at least $1 billion each year through its roughly 2,000 electronic preachers, including about 100 nationally syndicated television pastors. Trinity's forces dig through trash bins, search computer databases and go undercover with hidden cameras. They run a hotline for victims and informants. They enlist double agents, usually Christians of conscience who can't stand what they are seeing.

Ole became something of a legend in 1991 when he went undercover with a hidden camera to expose the operations of Robert Tilton, a televangelist now based in Fort Lauderdale, Florida. At the height of his success, Tilton appeared in every television market in the United States, sometimes as often as six times a day. Ole simply posed as himself, president of the Trinity Foundation, a religious organization, saying he was interested in using Tilton's direct-mail provider for his own ministry. Ole's video footage documented the ugly details behind Tilton's well-oiled direct-mail operation, which was raking in an estimated $380,000 *a day*.

Part of the investigation focused on how the mail was processed: Trinity alleged that Tilton's organization put checks and cash in one pile and dumped the accompanying prayer requests into the trash—an accusation still hotly disputed by Tilton supporters. The video and documents obtained by Trinity became the basis of an ABC *PrimeTime Live* exposé by Diane Sawyer that crippled Tilton's huge ministry. The hour-long broadcast also exposed two other televangelists, one of whom, W. V. Grant, spent 16 months in jail for tax fraud after Trinity's investigation.

"I do enjoy the hunt," Ole told me. "But I'd much rather be out of a job . . . It's a perverted theology that tells people they'll get a return on their investment. They're told they'll get a hundredfold blessing for their money. They are told to write hot checks, take out loans. These televangelists have got to know what they're doing."

When Ole talks about televangelists, his face often reddens with anger. He sees them as putting an ugly stain on the Body of Christ.

"The people on [Christian television] are living the lifestyle of fabulous wealth on the backs of the poorest and most desperate people in our society," Ole told me. "People have lost their faith in God because they believe they weren't worthy after not receiving their financial blessing."

The Trinity Foundation's community of believers isn't utopia. To begin with, Ole can be a cantankerous and dominating figure, despite his frailties. Some former members describe the organization as a cult, pointing to Ole's heavy-handedness and Trinity's former practice of putting members on "the hot seat," where they publicly revealed their deepest faults and secrets to the members.

"It could get pretty intense," Pete Evans, a longtime member, told me. "We want to see ourselves as God sees us: stripped down and naked with whatever sins we've got laid on the table. That honesty is what knitted us close together." The sessions stopped mostly because of Ole's failing health.

In my two weeks at the Trinity Foundation, I didn't witness any cultlike behavior, though I imagine everyone could have been putting up a front for a visiting journalist. I did see people who had given up comfortable lives to follow Jesus, a decision they told me had provided them with a sense of serenity and purpose.

My trip to Dallas was part of an investigation into televangelism that would become a two-year project. Ole's undercover work and the earlier scandals from the 1980s had brought down some of the country's top televangelists, including Jim and Tammy Bakker and Jimmy Swaggert. Yet the Prosperity Gospel as a whole was flourishing, and two of the world's most successful operators in the world of televangelism were headquartered in Southern California, within a short drive of my office at *The Times*'s Orange County bureau: the Trinity Broadcasting Network (TBN), the world's largest religious broadcaster, and Benny Hinn, the world's most financially successful "faith healer."

Ole's community offered a stark contrast to the lifestyles and spiritual focus of the televangelists. Ole and his motley band of Christians tried to live, in their own flawed way, godly lives in a run-down section of Dallas. Meanwhile some of the world's most successful and revered pastors on television acted like spiritual carnies, amassing huge piles of earthly treasure by conning worshipful and desperate viewers out of what little money they had. Ole's world was a monastery. Theirs was Sodom and Gomorrah.

Trying to penetrate TBN, I starting looking into its biggest star, Pastor Benny Hinn. Meeting Hinn was like being in the presence of a rock star. He pulled up to the Four Seasons hotel in Newport Beach in a new Mercedes SUV. Two beefy bodyguards jumped out of the car to flank him, scanning the entrance for any threats. In the marbled lobby, two associates and two public relations men joined the entourage, their dress shoes clicking on the polished stone floor. All this for an interview with me.

Hinn, the flamboyant, self-proclaimed "faith healer," is a familiar figure to casual channel surfers: he speaks with a thick Middle

Eastern accent, wears white Nehru jackets and sports a swirl of salt-and-pepper hair that has been described as a soufflé. He is perhaps most famous for the seeming ability to send believers fainting backward with a flick of his hand as they are "slain" by the Holy Spirit. His physical appearance and showmanship, displayed an hour each day on his television program, *This Is Your Day!*, were mimicked by Steve Martin in the 1994 movie *Leap of Faith*.

Hinn claims to be a healing tool of the Lord. His viewers and "Miracle Crusade" attendees are told that if they have enough faith—measured by the size of their donation—God will heal them. It's clear his ministry has made him a wealthy man. It's less certain whether anyone has been healed. And it's known that a number of people have died after mistakenly thinking they had been cured, stopping their medicines and avoiding the doctor.

I was excited to talk with Hinn, who normally didn't grant audiences with the media. For months he had refused to speak with me, even by phone. But apparently I had gathered enough unflattering information about him and his ministry that he decided cooperation might blunt my coming story. For spin assistance, he hired A. Larry Ross, a six-foot-eight giant with the thickness of a retired NFL lineman. Ross is one of the country's leading Christian PR consultants, with a client list that includes superstar pastors Billy Graham, Rick Warren and T. D. Jakes. Ross brought his top lieutenant with him from Dallas for the interview.

I had known Ross from other stories I had worked on and always found him to be highly professional and competent. He portrayed himself as a man with deep Christian convictions who represented only the best clients within the Body of Christ. Ross's two premiere clients, Billy Graham and Rick Warren, are inspiring preachers whose ministries do awe-inspiring work for the sick, poor and lonely. The worst a cynic could say about them is that they encourage belief in things that might not be true. Even a critic would have to concede that they inspire a lot of good works. But Hinn?

Investigating Hinn wasn't easy. He calls his tax-exempt television ministry a "church," freeing him from filing public tax documents. He forbids anyone in his ministry to talk to the media. He lives behind gates in an oceanfront mansion in Dana Point worth in the vicinity of $20 million. Even the names of his board of directors are a closely guarded secret. Hinn's ministry is nearly impenetrable.

Aside from the occasional investigation by the secular media, few people care to expose Hinn and his ministry. While legions of vulnerable viewers are being told that generous donations to Hinn's ministry will lead to a miraculous healing, most Christian leaders are content to pass by on the other side of the street, their eyes averted—like the rabbi in the story of the good Samaritan.

Ole Anthony is among the notable exceptions. For years, he has been the premiere Hinn watchdog, which explains why I went to Dallas to comb through the dusty archives of Trinity Foundation.

For Ole's operatives, the most productive investigative work is frequently the dirtiest: making "trash runs" behind the televangelists' headquarters, their banks, accountants' and attorneys' offices, direct-mail houses and homes. (Trash is public property, though going through Dumpsters on private property is trespassing.) Under the cover of night, Ole's troops jump into trash bins wearing old clothes and latex gloves. They sort through spoiled food, leaky soda cans and soggy coffee grounds in search of pay dirt: a memo, minutes of a meeting, a bank statement, an airline ticket, a staff roster. Those scraps of information, collected over years, can piece together a bigger story.

In looking into Hinn's ministry, they had struck pay dirt in a south Florida Dumpster behind a travel agency used by the pastor. They found a travel itinerary for Hinn that included first-class tickets on the Concorde from New York to London ($8,850 each) and reservations for presidential suites at pricey European hotels ($2,200 a night). A news story, including footage of Hinn and his associates boarding the jet, ran on CNN. In addition, property records and videos supplied by Trinity investigators led to CNN and *Dallas Morning News* coverage of another Hinn controversy: fund-raising for an alleged $30 million healing center in Dallas that was never built.

I came away from Dallas with a treasure trove of information on Hinn, including video of the faith healer making bizarre theological statements:

- "Adam was a super-being when God created him. I don't know whether people know this, but he was the first superman that really ever lived. . . . Adam not only flew, he flew to space. With one thought he would be on the moon."
- "You're going to have people raised from the dead watching [the Trinity Broadcasting Network, on which his show appears]. I see rows of caskets lining up in front of this TV set . . . and I see actual loved ones picking up the hands of the dead and letting them touch the screen and people are getting raised."

From Trinity, I received copies of documents smuggled out by employees sickened by what they saw within the ministry: invoices and other papers unearthed in the ministry's Dumpsters and contact numbers of current and former employees, as well as people whose faith in the ministry had not been rewarded.

I also met Justin Peters, a freshly minted Southern Baptist minister from Mississippi. He appeared during my stay to do some research of his own about Hinn. Justin's arms and legs, in the clutches of cerebral palsy, were twisted and spastic. He told me why he became a pastor and had dedicated his life to exposing charlatan faith healers.

As a teenager, his parents drove him hundreds of miles to see a faith healer, hoping God would cure their son and allow him to finally be able to run and play like other kids. Despite his initial skepticism, Justin's hopes for a cure rose as he entered the venue for the faith healer's performance. At the service, Justin watched as a poor elderly man in a wheelchair next to him emptied his wallet into the offering bucket, a move that caught the eye of the preacher. Justin recalled the pastor pointing to the man, telling the audience about the generous donation and saying, "Brother, before this night is over, you're going to walk out of here!"

At the end of the service, Justin looked over at the man, still in the wheelchair. There was anguish in his eyes.

"It was something you see and never forget," Justin said.

Why did Christianity produce so few people like Justin and so many others like Christian public relations guru Larry Ross, who, though wildly talented and professing a deep Christian belief, have no problem promoting a charlatan like Hinn?

Shortly after my trip to Dallas, I saw similar scenes played out at a Benny Hinn Miracle Crusade in Anaheim. Hinn's public relations handlers kept me in a confined area on the arena floor and never left my side. Yet they couldn't shield me from the simple logic of Hinn's operations: raise false hope, and extract money.

A Benny Hinn Miracle Crusade is one of the greatest shows on Earth. The free event usually draws capacity crowds at sports arenas and stadiums in the United States and abroad. It's easy to see why millions of people—especially those with crippling or terminal illnesses—get swept away by the promises of the charismatic pastor.

Hinn's healing service is a sophisticated, choreographed production that lasts nearly four hours. It includes a long warm-up featuring robed choirs from local churches, hip videos on giant screens and audience members shaking violently and speaking in tongues, overcome by the Holy Spirit. Everything is captured on television equipment that Hinn brings to each crusade along with his own production crew, using seven cameras and a staff of as many as 100.

In Anaheim, Hinn made his entrance during a rendition of "How Great Thou Art," stepping triumphantly onstage in a dramatic spotlight, dressed in a dazzling white suit. He could have been an angel sent down from heaven.

He started by asking anyone to come forward who wanted to believe in Christ. Hundreds of people, many already in tears, walked down the arena's aisles to the stage, heard a prayer from Hinn and were handed literature that included a list of nearby churches.

Next, volunteer ushers handed buckets to worshipers, who passed them throughout the arena, filling them with cash and checks—signs of faith, Hinn told them, that they believe in God's healing power. Hinn's ministry collects enough money at crusades and on television to generate about $100 million annually, roughly the same as Billy Graham's organization. (Hinn reportedly earns more than $1 million a year, lives in an oceanfront mansion, drives the latest luxury cars and travels by private jet, the Concorde no longer being an option. As part of my investigation, a former associate of Hinn's slipped me two notebooks full of copies of ministry expenses, including massive American

Express bills and pages of unexplained cash withdrawals for the faith healer and his family.)

After more music, Hinn started ticking off the healings that were taking place throughout the arena at that very moment. Within a ten-minute span, the pastor proclaimed that people in the arena had just been cured of asthma, cancerous tumors, arthritis, leukemia, emphysema and 22 other ailments. And believers lined up on both sides of the stage to tell the pastor that they had been healed of heart conditions, knee problems, osteoporosis, breast cancer, deafness and more. Hinn applied his touch to their foreheads, scattering them like bowling pins across the stage.

The real drama happened after the pastor left the stage and the music stopped. Terminally ill people remained, just as sick as before. There were folks with Parkinson's disease whose limbs were still twisted and shaking. There were quadriplegics who couldn't move any muscle below their neck. These people—and there were hundreds, maybe thousands of them at each crusade—sat in their chairs, bewildered and crushed that God hadn't healed them; their caretakers tried to offer some comforting words.

Brian Darby has worked for more than two decades with severely handicapped people in Northern California and often has experienced the disappointment left in the wake of a Miracle Crusade. Over the years, he told me many of his clients have attended the events, where they were swept up in a wave of excitement, thinking they were about to walk for the first time or have their limbs straightened.

"You can't minimize the impact of *not* being healed on the person, the family, the extended family," Darby told me. "They have a sense of euphoria at the crusade and then crash down. [Hinn is not] around to pick up the pieces."

Many people believe, as Hinn preaches, that God fails to heal them because their faith isn't strong enough. Maybe they didn't give enough money to Hinn's ministry. Or maybe they just didn't *believe* enough.

In Anaheim, Jordie Gibson, then 21, wanted God to know how much he believed. Before the crusade, he stopped kidney dialysis as an act of faith before he flew to Southern California from Calgary, Canada.

"When I told my doctors, they said they could make arrangements for me to do dialysis" in Orange County, Jordie told me. "But I was going to be healed, so it didn't matter. I needed to step out in faith."

A volunteer usher at the event, Jordie pushed up the sleeve of his shirt to show the shunt in his arm used for dialysis. He survived "stepping out in faith," but had to go back on dialysis once he returned to Canada. He told me that blood work showed his kidneys were functioning better after the event. "Whatever the Bible says is true," he added. "And it says God can heal you. It's true. All you need to do is ask."

There is a great deal of medical research on the placebo effect, the idea that the body responds to the mind if the mind is duped. The extent of the placebo effect varies greatly depending on how and when it's used, but studies show up to 75 percent of patients who take sugar pills have a measurable response to them. You could argue that Hinn is a placebo provider, and this does some good. But what of all those who go off their meds? CNN and the Australian version of *60 Minutes* have aired interviews with relatives whose family members died after they allegedly stopped medical treatment because Hinn had told them they were cured of their terminal cancer.

Sitting with me for the interview at the Four Seasons, the pastor seemed like an entirely different man from the faith healer I'd seen onstage the night before. He dressed casually in black, with designer sunglasses, leather jacket and black shoes. His trademark hair had been brushed forward, bangs hanging over his forehead like Caesar. Hinn fiddled with his cell phone, which sported a Mercedes logo. The fingers that allegedly heal people were delicate, with manicured and polished nails. A gold wedding band, so wide it covered the bottom of his left ring finger from knuckle to knuckle like a piece of copper pipe, bore the insignia of his church: a dove, symbolizing the Holy Spirit, sparkling with a cluster of diamonds.

"I know me, and those close to me know me," he said. "But sadly, the outside world thinks I'm some kind of a crook. I think it's time for me to change that."

He was quiet, charming, humble and introspective. We talked for three hours. I asked him a series of questions delving into his ministry's finances, his lavish salary and perks and the inability to prove that his "healings" lasted after the euphoria of the event was over.

He admitted that even one of his daughters, then 11, had a difficult time figuring him out: "One day she asked me a question that absolutely blew me away—from my own child! 'Daddy, who are you? That man up there [onstage], I don't know.' If my own child is asking that, surely the whole world is asking that."

He told me he had a heart condition that God hadn't cured, and his parents had suffered serious medical problems.

"That is a very difficult thing for me because I told my daddy to believe," Hinn said. "But he died. Now I don't know why . . . My mom has diabetes, my daddy died with cancer. That's life."

The way Hinn portrayed it, being a faith healer was a terrible burden placed on him by God. If not for the divine calling, Hinn said he would walk away from the job in an instant. I couldn't look into Hinn's soul, but from where I sat, I saw a gifted actor who parlayed his theatrical skills and feel for the human condition into the material life of a movie star. I didn't think for a moment he believed a word of what he preached—or that he was bothered that people who didn't get their miracle cure had died. I imagined him behind the doors of his cliff-top Dana Point mansion, giggling to himself at his good fortune as he looked out the floor-to-ceiling windows at the 180-degree view of the Pacific with surfers bobbing in the waves, dolphins swimming just outside the surf line and sailboats dotting the horizon. He had hit the lottery, his actions protected from the law by the First Amendment.

Most people would discern this simply by watching his show. I had the added advantage of meeting people such as William Vandenkolk. He was a nine-year-old boy living in Las Vegas with his aunt and uncle, who were raising him. Unbeknownst to his guardians, a babysitter took the legally blind boy to a Miracle Crusade in hopes of regaining his eyesight. She managed to get William onstage, and Hinn bent down and placed his hands on the child's face. "Look at these tears," said Hinn, peering into the child's eyes. "William, baby, can you see me?"

Before more than 15,000 people in a Las Vegas arena, William nodded. In a small voice, the boy said: "As soon as God healed me, I could see better." Hinn, an arm wrapped around William, told the audience that God had just instructed him to pay the child's medical expenses and education. People wept. The video clip was shown repeatedly on Hinn's television show, a tear-producing, faith-inspiring fund-raising tool.

Two years later, William was still legally blind. He told me his sight never improved and that his onstage comments were the wishful thinking of a little boy not wanting to disappoint God and the thousands of people who were watching him.

"It's pretty sad when you mess with a little boy's mind," said

Randy Melthratter, William's uncle and guardian. It took two years, a series of phone calls and my inquiry before his family was told that a $10,000 fund had been set up in William's name. Randy still couldn't get any details on how to access the account until a second story appeared about William.

When my piece on Benny Hinn was published, I thought his donations would dip at least a little. I even hoped it would prompt him to clean up his act. I was wrong on both counts. His supporters had been indoctrinated in the belief that the mainstream media was a tool of the devil designed to bring down great ministries and men of God. If I had caught Benny in bed with a dead woman or live boy, it wouldn't have made a difference. CNN, HBO and NBC's *Dateline* have done devastating reports on Benny Hinn and his ministry, and Pastor Benny's career has kept sailing along. My article didn't stand a chance. Today, he continues to be, by far, the most financially successful "faith healer" in the world.

Besides a handful of secular media outlets and a few fringe Christian organizations, no one is bothered enough by Hinn's antics and the harm he does to people and the Body of Christ to call him out. Many fear the tight relationship between Hinn and the leaders of the Trinity Broadcasting Network—coming out against the faith healer would mean incurring the wrath of the world's largest religious broadcaster. The Christian media, whose voice could make a difference with believers, have shied away from most criticism as well. In general, the Christian media is extremely hesitant to undertake investigative reporting on Christian organizations, no matter how corrupt. Controversy—and the resulting loss of advertisers and readers—scares them. Several freelancers have come to me with their unpublished stories after Christian magazines rejected the material as too controversial. I started to wonder why my faith had so few people of principle.

. . .

My story about Benny Hinn was part of a larger investigation into the Trinity Broadcasting Network. From time to time I had received e-mails making allegations about the leadership of TBN. Often the anonymous messages came with details about sexual impropriety, lavish spending and questionable use of donor money. But no proof was offered, and the senders rarely responded to my questions. Then I wrote a small, straightforward news story that involved TBN. Twenty-four hours later, a flurry of e-mails arrived in my inbox accusing TBN and its founders, televangelists Paul and Jan Crouch, of various misdeeds. I decided that where there was smoke, there might be fire.

TBN was the Fort Knox of Christian organizations. No reporter had completely penetrated it; the network operated with a level of secrecy that the CIA would envy. The ministry is valued at more than $2 billion, generates about $200 million annually and beams its programming from dozens of satellites into every country on Earth. If a pastor can get a show on TBN (the waiting list is long), money pours in. What went on behind the scenes was a closely guarded secret. The network's founders didn't give media interviews, and their employees were told not to talk to the press.

Channel surfers probably know TBN by the image of Jan Crouch, who wears heavy makeup, long false lashes and champagne-colored wigs piled high on her head. She speaks in a singsong voice and lets her tears flow freely, whether reading a viewer's letter or recalling how God resurrected her pet chicken when she was a child.

Her husband, Paul, with his silver hair, mustache and bifocals, comes across as a grandfatherly sort. What he calls his "German temper" can rise quickly, however. He often punctuates a point by shaking a finger at the camera.

"Get out of God's way," he said once, referring to TBN's detractors. "Quit blocking God's bridges or God is going to shoot you, if I don't."

The Crouches' eldest son, Paul Crouch Jr., a thick man with bushy graying hair and a 1970s-style mustache, has taken the reins of the television empire from his aging parents and is trying to modernize it. Already under the leadership of PJ, as he is known, the studio sets have gone from gold and gaudy to chic. The programming is tilting rapidly away from big-haired Southern preachers to Christianized versions of secular fare, including an *American Idol*-style reality show featuring gospel singers.

Together, the three Crouches make up TBN's entire board of directors, giving the ministry little outside oversight. Like a miner looking at rock formations, a journalist can survey the ground before him and see the potential for a good story: secrecy, concentrated power and lack of oversight. But digging beneath the surface isn't easy. Over the next two years, while juggling other stories, I traveled back and forth across the country several times to meet with sources, stake out houses, knock on doors late at night, comb courthouses for documents and even sift through piles of trash others had collected in order to produce a portrait of the TBN empire and Paul and Jan Crouch.

I received threatening phone calls. A man with a menacing voice asked if I would be driving my usual way home that night and warned me to watch my back. Another caller said that a private investigator had discovered an illicit affair I was having with a male newsroom colleague (not true). A pastor in Riverside, California launched a website devoted to "bringing me down" because I was doing Satan's work. He posted a series of lies about me (such as that my editors had kicked me off the story) along with personal information about my family and me. He solicited donations so he could hire a private investigator to dig up dirt.

I didn't think I was in physical danger. My sources, however, felt their lives were at risk. I talked with hundreds of people for the story, and more than a few believed that their phones had been bugged and that they were being followed. This was undoubtedly just paranoia, but some of it was bred by the culture at TBN—an us-against-them mindset. Either you were with TBN and Jan and Paul Crouch or you were working for Satan. (The bunker mentality filtered right down to TBN viewers. I called fans of TBN, looking for their positive take on the ministry and what it meant to their lives. Inevitably the first question they would ask was, "Did Jan and Paul say it was okay if I talked with you?" I was able to talk to many of them only after Paul Crouch Jr. announced on the air that it was okay.)

I spoke with many former TBN employees and current and former associates who said that as Christians, they wanted to blow the whistle on what they believed was abuse of donor money and immoral behavior, but they just couldn't. It would be too risky, they said, even if I withheld their names. Several were so scared that they reported our conversation to TBN officials. I grew increasingly frustrated by this nearly uniform lack of courage by people who claimed to be devout Christians. I'd often find myself quoting Scripture to them to see how they justified silence when they claimed to know about abuses within God's ministry.

"What do you think Jesus meant when he told his disciples, 'If anyone wishes to come after Me, he must deny himself, and take up his cross and follow Me'?" I would ask. "Didn't Jesus warn repeatedly that the Christian life would involve sacrifice?"

But TBN provided a gravy train for producers, pastors, singers and filmmakers. Rank-and-file employees needed a paycheck. Almost no one wanted to risk what he had, even when I'd ask about Jesus' promise that "everyone who has left houses or brothers or sisters or father or mother or children or fields for my sake will receive a hundred times as much and will inherit eternal life."

There were some wonderful exceptions. A few workers had been concerned enough about how donations were being used to smuggle out documents showing lavish spending by the Crouches. And I did find several brave souls who felt it was their Christian duty to talk about what was happening inside TBN. First among them was a quiet, unassuming woman with a soft Southern accent named Kelly Whitmore. She had seen a lot as Jan Crouch's personal assistant for several years; she told me she fled the ministry in the middle of the night, fed up with the hypocrisy.

TBN officials painted Whitmore, then 46, as a disgruntled former employee, but that just didn't fit. She was sweet, polite, naïve, and had an unwavering sense of right and wrong. Her accounts were straightforward and filled with telling details. Other witnesses and documents corroborated much of her information. I talked with Kelly for hours, and she seemed to have only one primary motive: to shed a light onto what was happening within TBN. (She had retained an agent and talked about selling her story to Hollywood, but that seemed to be pushed more by her friends than by Kelly.) A lot of her information ended up in my story, but even more was left out, because in many cases I couldn't get anyone on the record to back her up out of fear of retribution. People didn't even want to be used as anonymous sources. Kelly and a few others stood alone, but they—along with hundreds of documents—were enough.

By September 2004, when my series of stories was published, I thought I had gathered information devastating enough to TBN and the Crouches that the ministry would be forced to reform itself. I had discovered, for instance, that TBN's patriarch, Pastor Paul Crouch, had secretly paid $425,000 to keep allegations of a homosexual tryst with one of his employees under wraps. TBN viewers often heard about the evils of homosexuality and how to battle the "scourge." In 1990, Pastor Benny Hinn prophesied on TBN: "The Lord also tells me to tell you in the mid '90s, about '94 to '95, no later than that, God will destroy the homosexual community of America. [The audience applauded.] But He will not destroy it with what many minds have thought [He would use], He will destroy it with fire. And many will turn and be saved, and many will rebel and be destroyed."

Lonnie Ford, a former TBN employee, claimed that he was forced to have sex with Paul Crouch during a weekend stay at the ministry's cabin in Lake Arrowhead. Through his attorney, Crouch denied the allegations and said he paid a settlement to avoid a sensational trial and massive legal bills. TBN officials pointed out that Ford was a drug addict and felon. Still, Ford's story couldn't be easily dismissed.

Working as a mortgage salesman at the time of my story, Ford had been hired in 1992 to work in TBN's telephone bank in Orange County. Crouch took an interest in him. Within four years, Ford said, he was doing special assignments for the pastor. One such job was to drive Crouch to Hollywood and take publicity photos for TBN at a Christian nightclub. Ford said he and others in the ministry were surprised at the assignment because he wasn't a photographer.

"They had to show me—and I'm not kidding—how to work a camera," Ford told me. Crouch told him not to worry about it.

After visiting the nightclub, Ford said Crouch took him to dinner at the Regent Beverly Wilshire Hotel in Beverly Hills. Shortly after that, in October 1996, Ford said he and Crouch spent two nights at the same hotel in separate rooms. Ford said they worked out together at the hotel gym and ate expensive meals with bottles of wine and after-dinner drinks. "I knew what he was doing," Ford said. "He was seducing me." Ford was an openly gay man.

After checking out of the hotel, Ford said, Crouch took him to a TBN-owned cabin near Lake Arrowhead. It was there, Ford said, that Crouch first had sex with him. "I did it because I didn't know if this man is going to throw me straight out of that cabin," Ford said. "And I didn't want to lose my job. I was going to be in trouble if I said no."

The next morning, Ford said, Crouch read a Bible passage (Proverbs 6:16–19) to him in an attempt to reassure him about the night before.

> There are six things the LORD hates,
> seven that are detestable to him:
> haughty eyes,
> a lying tongue,
> hands that shed innocent blood,
> a heart that devises wicked schemes,
> feet that are quick to rush into evil,
> a false witness who pours out lies
> and a man who stirs up dissension among brothers.

Crouch told him that because homosexuality wasn't listed among the sins, the Lord wasn't worried about what they had done. Still, Ford said, Crouch warned him to keep the encounter quiet "because people wouldn't understand."

Ford said Crouch told him the ministry would pay his debts—about $17,000—and offered him a rent-free apartment at TBN's Tustin studios. He believed Crouch was trying to pay him off. Ministry officials confirmed that TBN paid at least some of Ford's debts around that time. They said it was an act of Christian charity that TBN performs regularly for employees.

Within weeks of the alleged Arrowhead encounter, Ford—on probation for drug-related offenses—tested positive for cocaine and marijuana. He was arrested in the fall of 1996 and sent to a drug treatment center in the state prison system. After he was released in early 1998, TBN officials refused to rehire him. Ford threatened to file a lawsuit alleging wrongful termination and sexual harassment and quietly settled for $425,000.

Though I had been on the religion beat for six years at this point, I still possessed some level of naïveté. I thought when the news broke that Paul Crouch had paid nearly a half-million dollars to keep quiet allegations of a homosexual tryst, the TBN faithful would get in an uproar, demanding more information from Crouch and maybe even his resignation. Instead, there was mostly silence. Donations streamed in unabated. Then came my two-part series that detailed the Crouches' lavish spending, Paul Crouch's drinking (a Pentecostal no-no), their strained marriage, their ministry-owned mansions, ranch and dozens of homes across the country and the rest of their earthly treasures. This information didn't jar the fans of TBN, either.

In fact, my stories were used as fund-raising tools—evidence that TBN was doing God's work and that the devil (that is, yours truly) was trying to stop it. Of course, one way to fight this satanic attack was to give money to TBN, allowing the network to continue to spread the Gospel to the ends of the Earth, as Jesus commanded. In 2004, the year my stories were published, TBN raised $188 million in tax-free money, a slight increase over the prior year. Its profit: $69 million.

The stories weren't ignored just by TBN's fan base. Top-name pastors such as Billy and Franklin Graham, Robert H. Schuller, Joel

Osteen and Greg Laurie continued to air their programs on TBN. Politicians, including Senator John McCain, still used the network as one of their media platforms. And B-list celebrities, including Chuck Norris, Kirk Cameron, MC Hammer and Gavin MacLeod, never stopped using TBN as a way to stay in the spotlight.

In the Gospels, Jesus warns that what you didn't do for the "least" among us, you "did not do for me." (Matthew 25:45) That's pretty sobering news, whether you're passing by a homeless person on the street or watching idly as the poor and desperate are manipulated by pastors on TBN to send in what little money they have in hopes of a financial windfall. TBN pastors even recommend that those with massive credit card debt put their donation on a credit card—showing God an ultimate act of faith that will result in that credit card balance being paid off within a month.

I walked away from the TBN stories doubting God's call for me was to report on corruption within the church. It just didn't make a difference. Many believers couldn't be bothered with any bad news that could break the fantasy of their belief. They held a blind allegiance to their favorite Christian leader—whether it was a priest, a Mormon prophet or a faith healer. Those who could help clean up messes like Benny Hinn and TBN— such as the big-name ministers who appeared on the network or Christian journalists—turned a blind eye. This allowed a handful of pastors and the network to keep flourishing, and caused millions of viewers to keep waiting patiently for their financial blessing or miracle cure.

I didn't know what to call the arrangement, but it wasn't Christianity. Or if it was, I didn't want to be a part of it. I had lost my way.

· FOURTEEN ·

The Dark Night of the Soul

As the deer pants for streams of water,
so my soul pants for you, O God.
My soul thirsts for God, for the living God.
When can I go and meet with God?
My tears have been my food
day and night,
while men say to me all day long,
"Where is your God?"

— PSALM 42:1–3

IN CHRISTIAN CIRCLES, the book *The Case for Christ: A Journalist's Personal Investigation of the Evidence for Jesus* became an instant classic when it was published in 1998. Written by Lee Strobel, a respected legal reporter with the *Chicago Tribune*, the book chronicles the author's spiritual journey from skeptic to devout evangelical as he investigates the scientific and historical evidence of Christianity.

Inspired by Strobel's work, I thought I, too, could use my investigative skills to bolster my waning faith. I wanted to find evidence that what the Apostle Paul told the Corinthians was true: that a person would be transformed by his belief in Christ.

"And [Jesus] died for all, that those who live should no longer live for themselves but for him who died for them and was raised again," Paul wrote (1 Corinthians 5:15–20). "Therefore, if anyone is in Christ, he is a new creation; the old has gone, the new has come! . . . We are therefore Christ's ambassadors, as though God were making his appeal through us."

If the Gospels were true, then shouldn't I be able to find plenty of data that showed Christians acted differently—superior in their morals and ethics—from the rest of society? I wanted to see that people were changed in fundamental ways by their belief in Christ. This was a new tack for me. For years, my assumption was that Christianity was true, and my studies and readings focused on shoring up that belief. I used the historical record, the Bible, anecdotal evidence and arguments by theologians and apologists to back up my position. Now, I wanted to take a step back and test my assumption about the truth of Christianity itself by examining how Christians behaved, looking at their actions, not their words.

I wasn't worried about what I would find. I viewed my own doubts as a symptom of my failings as a Christian, and not that something was fundamentally wrong with Christianity. I did feel a growing distance between God and me, but I knew this wasn't an unusual condition for people of faith. I took solace in reading about St. John of the Cross, the 16th-century Spanish mystic who felt abandoned by God and experienced a crisis of faith, a period of time he referred to as the "dark night of the soul."

"The soul perceives itself to be so unclean and miserable that it seems as if God had set Himself against it," he wrote. The separation from God nearly drove St. John mad—that's how badly the Spaniard wanted a relationship with the Lord.

I also identified with another beloved saint, St. Therese of Lisieux. Born in the 18th century, the sickly Carmelite nun known as the "Little Flower of Jesus" successfully petitioned the pope to allow her to enter a convent early, at age 15. She died after nine years of cloistered life, virtually unknown outside the gates of the small, anonymous convent of Lisieux in northern France. She wrote a spiritual memoir there called *Story of a Soul*, in which she described the "Little Way" by which she strived for holiness— through small acts of kindness, patience and understanding that she believed pleased the Lord.

"Love proves itself by deeds, so how am I to show my love?" she wrote. "Great deeds are forbidden me. The only way I can prove my love is by scattering flowers and these flowers are every little sacrifice, every glance and word, and the doing of the least actions for love."

The memoir, not written with the public in mind and published posthumously, became one of the best-selling religious books of the 20th century. St. Therese's writings revealed in honest detail the spiritual crises she had gone through despite her great faith. "Jesus isn't doing much to keep the conversation going," she once said of her prayers. She also wrote about her uncertainty about the afterlife: "If you only knew what darkness I am plunged into."

The doubts of St. John of the Cross and St. Therese were something that even Jesus experienced. While on the cross, he stunned witnesses and Christians through the centuries by shouting, "My God, my God, why have you forsaken me?"

The doubts of holy men and women continue today. Mother Teresa was one of the most revered religious persons of our time, symbolizing for millions the beauty of Christian devotion, sacrifice, holiness and works. Yet she suffered excruciating doubt. Recently published letters in *Come By My Light* reveal that she felt absent from God for the last 50 years of her life. Not five days or five months or five years, but *five decades*. Frustrated, ashamed and sometimes in doubt about God's existence, Mother Teresa kept her spiritual crisis a secret from everyone but a few spiritual mentors.

"Please pray specially for me that I may not spoil His work and that Our Lord may show Himself—for there is such terrible darkness within me, as if everything was dead," she wrote in 1953.

In another letter, she wrote: "I spoke as if my very heart was in love with God—tender, personal love. If you were [there], you would have said, 'What hypocrisy.' "

"Jesus has a very special love for you," she assured one mentor in 1979. "[But] as for me, the silence and the emptiness is so great, that I look and do not see,—Listen and do not hear—the tongue moves [in prayer] but does not speak . . . I want you to pray for me—that I let Him have [a] free hand."

These saints had struggled with faith just as I was now wrestling with it. I found comfort in reading about them, because honest discussions of doubt were rare commodities in the modern church. Today, many Christians—especially evangelicals—express doubt in catch phrases: "I'm in the desert right now," "I'm going through a dry patch," "I'm not walking with God these days." Their doubts are treated with pat prescriptions: more prayer, more church, more Bible study and more bromides: "If you're at the end of your rope, tie a knot of faith and hang on," "Stop running away from God so He can catch up," "You just need to turn toward God and He'll be there."

I often heard a story called "Footsteps in the Sand," in which Jesus shows someone who recently died how He had walked with him throughout his life, symbolized by two sets of footsteps side by side in the sand. But the follower of Christ points to a particularly rough time in his life when there was only one set of footprints.

"Jesus, why did you abandon me when I really needed you most?"

"I didn't abandon you, my son. I was carrying you."

Most Christians keep any deep spiritual crisis under wraps. I felt I was failing as a Christian because I was experiencing such feelings. Somehow I had let Satan disrupt my spiritual life. Maybe it was because I had stopped attending church. Or quit going to Bible study. Perhaps I wasn't praying enough. It could be that the pat prescriptions were correct. Whatever the reason, I was sure it was my fault. God hadn't moved away from me; I had moved away from Him. I refused to consider that my faith was evaporating.

Few people were comfortable talking about the subject, and many just didn't understand what was happening to someone whose faith was slipping away. I wouldn't have understood it myself a few years earlier. Like addiction or mental illness, it's something that is difficult to have empathy for until you've gone through it yourself.

I wondered whether I was being tested like Job in the Hebrew Scriptures. The Book of Job is the only biblical story in which the curtain is pulled back to reveal the machinations of God's world. The Lord tells Satan that Job will always stay faithful to Him. The devil responds that if enough were taken away from the prosperous Job, the once-faithful servant would turn on God. The Lord accepts Satan's challenge and the game is on, with poor Job the unwitting pawn. In rapid succession, he suffers the deaths of his sons, daughters and servants, the loss of his fortune and the infliction of boils all over his body. But not once does Job forsake God. I identified more with Job's wife, who witnesses all this and says to her husband (as he stoically scrapes off his boils with a shard of pottery): "Are you still holding on to your integrity? Curse God and die!" Her position seems more reasonable than Job's.

During one of our Monday-morning runs along Newport's Back Bay, I confided to my best friend, Hugh, that I had entered a spiritual wasteland. I expected a heavy conversation, perhaps some disappointment and a mild rebuke for allowing myself to fall away from God. But Hugh, the eternal optimist, didn't think much of it.

"It happens all the time, Billy," he said. "It will come back, don't worry. You can't lose God. He'll always be there for you."

He advised me to get my butt back to church and to attend an upcoming men's retreat run by his church. He reminded me that it had been more than a decade since my born-again mountaintop experience, and I hadn't gone on a retreat with him for the past couple of years. He said it would be the perfect chance to recharge my spiritual batteries. I wanted to say no; a retreat with a bunch of gung-ho Christians wasn't very appealing at the moment. But I knew Hugh wouldn't let it rest until I agreed to go. He can be very annoying that way. I said yes.

On the second half of the run, we prayed, as usual. Hugh asked for the usual things: world peace, protection for his family, comfort and healing for those who are sick or in need. He always thanked God for my friendship, which made me feel good. Hugh also asked the Lord to strengthen my faith and reveal His perfect love for me. When it came my turn, what had felt as natural as breathing in years' past now seemed awkward and tense. As the words came of my mouth, it no longer felt as if I was talking to my heavenly father who loved me unconditionally. Instead, I was talking to myself, and felt stupid doing it. It occurred to me that maybe this was again Satan's work—or even a Job-like test from God—so I continued in prayer, but kept it short. My dialogue with God had changed. What had seemed like a two-way conversation had turned into a monologue. Now when I prayed, I started to feel a bit like a mental patient, babbling to myself.

The men's retreat in the San Bernardino Mountains didn't bring me closer to God. The difference between my first retreat and this one was striking. I wasn't swept away by the music, the testimonies, the sermons and the small-group sharing. I felt like an outsider, watching the rituals of a foreign tribe whose language I didn't understand. Anger unexpectedly welled up inside me at my brothers in Christ. Was it that easy for them? Were they just sheep? Didn't anyone else feel the way I did? Why in the world would God make it so hard to follow Him? What was with all the mystery? It was depressing. When it came time to meet in small groups or participate in other retreat events, I snuck back to my cabin and read a book or slept. I wanted it all to go away. I couldn't wait to get off that mountain.

On the drive home, Hugh and I talked about ways to rekindle my faith. I thought about using some accrued vacation time to head to Europe and walk the 1,000-mile "Way of St. James"—*El Camino de Santiago*. Millions of pilgrims had been making the journey to the cathedral in Santiago, Spain, for more than 1,000 years to visit what was said to be the tomb of St. James. I had read many stories of pilgrims who talked about the transformative experiences they had on the trail, particularly when they met other Christians along the way. It seemed like a wonderful way to unplug from the world, spend time with God and other Christians and pump up my faith.

My other idea was to go on a month-long retreat to a monastery that taught the Spiritual Exercises of St. Ignatius. The founder of the Society of Jesus, or Jesuits, developed rigorous spiritual exercises that involve deep meditation on specific verses of Scripture, visualizing oneself with Jesus during his three-year ministry. Ignatius used his imagination to place himself in the biblical scenes of Jesus, either as an unseen witness or as one of the characters. I talked with people who participated in the exercises. They said they felt as though they had experienced life with Jesus. They reported smelling the fish being caught on the Sea of Galilee, hearing Jesus' words during the Sermon on the Mount and tasting the bread and wine at the Last Supper.

Ignatius was a late convert to Catholicism, so I always had been attracted to him. Born in 1491, he grew up in a wealthy family in Spain. He was ambitious, romantic, conceited and free-spirited—anything but religious. But at age 30 he suffered a leg wound in a battle against the French at Pamplona. While convalescing in the castle of Loyola, Ignatius had only two texts to read: a four-volume life of Christ and a book on the saints. The books left him with a sense of peace and tranquility, a marked contrast to the depression and emptiness he felt after reading his favorite books of romance and chivalry. The reflections helped ignite a conversion that led Ignatius to develop a systematic method of prayer, and to eventually found the Society of Jesus, in 1539. I thought Ignatius's 500-year-old program could help me.

Hugh said both ideas, if I could afford the time and money, had promise. I thought so, too. But before I made the investment, I decided it wise to collect some evidence that showed me Christians were measurably different from others. Otherwise, a pilgrimage or retreat was just an extension of a fantasy.

It was discouragingly easy—though incredibly surprising—to find out that Christians, as a group, acted no differently than anyone else, including atheists. Sometimes they performed a little better; other times a little worse. But the Body of Christ didn't stand out as morally superior. Some of my data came from secular institutions such as the Pew Research Center and the Gallup Poll, but the most devastating information was collected by the Barna Group, a respected research company run by an evangelical Christian worried about the health of Christianity in America. For years, George Barna has studied more than 70 moral behaviors of believers and nonbelievers. His conclusion: the faith of Christians has grown fat and flabby. He contends that statistically, the difference between behaviors of Christians and others has been erased. According to his data and other studies, Christians divorce at about the same rate as or even at a slightly higher rate than atheists. White evangelical Christians are more racist than others. Evangelicals take antidepressants at about the same rate (7 percent) as others. Non-Christians are more likely to give money to a homeless or poor person in any given year (34 percent) than are born-again Christians (24 percent). Born-again Christians are taught to give 10 percent of their money to the church or charity, but 95 percent of them decline to do so. The percentage of Christian youth infected with sexually transmitted diseases is virtually the same as the rate among their non-Christian counterparts. Ronald J. Sider, a professor at Palmer Theological Seminary and an evangelical, covers a lot of these statistics and more in his 2007 book, *The Scandal of the Evangelical Conscience.*

"Whether the issue is divorce, materialism, sexual promiscuity, racism, physical abuse in marriage, or neglect of a biblical worldview, the polling data point to widespread, blatant disobedience of clear biblical moral demands on the part of the people who allegedly are evangelical, born-again Christians," Sider writes. "The statistics are devastating."

George Barna doesn't see the data as casting doubt upon faith. "The issue isn't whether Jesus or Christianity is real," Barna says. "The issue is, are Americans willing to put Christ first in their lives?"

But okay, I thought, let's assume for a moment that the Body of Christ has fallen off the straight and narrow path because of man's insatiable need for sin. After all, the Bible is filled with characters who receive clear directions from God and proceed to transgress them, starting with Adam and Eve. Every apostle, except perhaps Judas, expressed doubt at one time that Jesus was the Messiah. The most remarkable for me is Peter, who Jesus proclaims as the "rock" upon which His church will be built. Peter spent several years by the side of Jesus, witnessing His miracles and absorbing His teachings. No one could have been better prepared to defend Jesus against his enemies, proclaiming Him the Messiah. But on the night before His death, Jesus tells Peter that the disciple will deny that he knew Him three times before "the rooster crows" at sunrise. Peter looks at Jesus and says, "Even if I have to die with you, I will never disown you." (Mark 14:31)

After Jesus is arrested, the Roman authorities set out to find His accomplices. Three times Peter is asked if he knew Jesus, and three times he says no. As the rooster crows, Peter remembers his Lord's prediction and weeps "bitterly." If Peter—an eyewitness—couldn't get it straight, how are we supposed to 2,000 years later?

And I already knew that the majority of Catholics ignored some of the church's basic teachings. A recent poll co-sponsored by the *National Catholic Reporter* found that the majority American Catholics believed they did not have to obey church doctrine on abortion, birth control, divorce, remarriage or weekly attendance at Mass to be "good Catholics." Catholic women have about the same rate of abortion as the rest of society, according to a 2002 study by Perspectives on Sexual and Reproductive Health. And 98 percent of sexually active Catholic women have used a modern method of contraception, according to a 2002 national survey by the Centers for Disease Control and Prevention.

I just couldn't find any evidence within Protestantism or Catholicism that the actions of Christians, in general, showed that they took their faith seriously or that their religion made them morally or ethically better than even atheists.

But what about prayer, I thought? We Christians believe in the power of prayer. We pray in church, in the morning and at night, before our meals. We hold prayer meetings and prayer vigils. We pray 24 hours straight on the official Day of Prayer. Those of us who have a special knack for it are called "prayer warriors," and given lists of people who need something from the Lord—a biopsy to come back negative, a teenager to get off drugs, a laid-off worker to find a job, a pregnant woman to have a healthy baby, a cancer patient to be cured. Every day, millions upon millions of believers utter prayers to the Lord. Surely I could find some scientific evidence that prayer works.

I couldn't.

There aren't many quality scientific studies on the efficacy of intercessory prayer. The best are double-blind studies where patients with medical conditions are unknowingly prayed for by others. A 2001 study by Columbia University did show that women undergoing in-vitro fertilization treatments benefited from the prayers of others, getting pregnant at twice the rate of those who weren't prayed for. In the following months, however, skeptics found fatal flaws in the research methods and discovered that one of the researchers had been accused (and later convicted) of fraud. After an internal investigation, Columbia officials admitted to problems with the study and pulled it off their website. Of course, even today, Christians cite this study as proof that prayer works. As Mark Twain said, "A lie can travel halfway around the world while the truth is putting its shoes on." Other double-blind studies failed to show any benefit to intercessory prayer.

In 2006, a few years after my investigation, Harvard researchers published a comprehensive study on 1) whether intercessory prayer works and 2) whether the knowledge of receiving it influences a patient's recovery after heart bypass surgery. The study found that prayer didn't have an effect on patients who were unaware of it. Patients who knew they were being prayed for actually had *more* complications than another group who received prayer unknowingly. Atheists trumpeted the news that not only didn't prayer work, but in some cases it actually worsened the condition of patients. Those who believed in the power of prayer criticized various aspects of the study. The more sophisticated argument, I thought, was that it was nearly impossible, at least today, to conduct a valid study on the efficacy of prayer. For example, should the prayers be the same? Should the people saying the prayers and the people prayed for be of the same faith? The same denomination? And as Richard Dawkins in *The God Delusion* and Christian theologians argue, would God even consent to be a participant in a study about prayer?

"The Oxford theologian Richard Swinburne . . . objected to [a study on the effects of prayer] on the grounds that God answers prayers only if they are offered up for good reasons," Dawkins writes. "Praying for somebody rather than somebody else, simply because of the fall of the dice in the design of a double-blind experiment, does not constitute a good reason. God would see through it."

I did find one study that, because of its simplicity, seemed to answer the question. In the first scientific study of its kind, Sir Francis Galton in 1872 tested a very simple premise: Since every churchgoer in England prayed for good health for the royal family, shouldn't British royalty live longer than other affluent classes in England?

It turned out that monarchs had the shortest life span of his sample, finishing just ahead of the clergy (who also had many people praying for them). Kings and queens and pastors, on average, died sooner than lawyers, doctors, aristocrats, officers in the Royal navy and artists.

"I show that the divines are not specially favoured in those worldly matters for which they naturally pray, but rather the contrary, a fact which I ascribe in part to their having, as a class, indifferent constitutional vigour," wrote Galton, a half-cousin to Charles Darwin.

As for the clerics' shorter life spans, Galton wrote, "Prayers of the clergy for protection against the perils and dangers of the night, for protection during the day, and for recovery from sickness, appear to be futile in result."

I found one other simple argument that trumped the double-blind studies. I discovered it on a website called "Why Does God Hate Amputees?" In a straightforward manner, the website's authors pose some uncomfortable questions for those who believe in the healing power of prayer. They set up their argument by showing that those who believe in the Bible should expect their prayers to be answered. They click off many passages where Jesus promises this.

> *"If you believe, you will receive whatever you ask for in prayer." (Matthew 21:21)*
>
> *"If you ask anything in my name, I will do it." (John 14:14)*
>
> *"Ask, and it will be given you." (Matthew 7:7)*
>
> *"Nothing will be impossible to you." (Matthew 17:20)*
>
> *"Believe that you have received it, and it will be yours." (Mark 11:24)*

The website shows how "miracle" cures for cancer and other terrible diseases are often used by Christians as proof of God's all-powerful and all-loving nature. But, it then asks, what about amputees? Why doesn't God regenerate the limbs of amputees—including the heroic young men and women in the armed forces who sacrificed a body part for their country?

"No matter how many people pray, no matter how often they pray, no matter how sincere they are, no matter how much they believe, no matter how deserving the amputee, what we know is that prayers do not inspire God to regenerate amputated legs," the website states. "It would appear, to an unbiased observer, that God is singling out amputees and purposefully ignoring them."

Of course, there is a simpler explanation, more elegant, though it's deeply dispiriting. The most logical answer to why God won't heal amputees is that either God doesn't care or doesn't exist. This would also explain the lack of miraculous healings for people with Lou Gehrig's disease, long-term quadriplegics, untreated AIDS patients and those with Parkinson's disease, mental retardation, Down syndrome and a host of other maladies. Christian apologists offer different explanations to try to make sense of why bad things happen to good people. Among their explanations for why people who have lost limbs are never made whole by God (also detailed on the "Why Does God Hate Amputees?" website): healings for amputees aren't part of God's plan; the Lord sometimes answers prayers by saying "No"; God needs to remain hidden, and regenerating a limb would display the Lord's miraculous powers too openly; God has a special purpose for amputees—just the way they are; and God answers the prayers of amputees by having scientists develop artificial limbs.

These explanations remind me of my parents' answers when I started to question whether Santa Claus was real. How does he get down our chimney when he's so fat? He can squeeze himself down to fit. How can he deliver presents to every child in the whole entire world in one night? He moves faster than we can imagine. How big does his bag need to get to carry all the presents? It's a magic, bottomless bag. How can he eat cookies and milk in so many homes? He just does. My parents' valiant but ultimately weak explanations held off the truth for a year, but eventually, like all children, I had to face the truth.

I was starting to feel the same way about Christianity and God. And now that my eyes were opening to a different reality, the evidence against the likelihood of God seemed to be found at every turn. Even suppressed doubts started to surface. I began to realize that God may not be that perfect father I longed to believe in—and be loved by. In fact, He may not even exist. Sigmund Freud put it this way, writing in 1910:

> *The roots of the need for religion are in the parental complex; the almighty and just God, and kindly Nature, appear to us as grand sublimations of father and mother, or rather, as revivals and restorations of the young child's idea of them ... when at a later date he perceives how truly forlorn and weak he is when confronted with the great forces of life, he feels his condition as he did in childhood, and attempts to deny his own despondency by a regressive revival of the forces which protected his infancy.*

The flaws in my belief system started to overwhelm me. I obsessed about why God received praise no matter what He did— or did not do. If a young girl is cured of cancer, "Praise God for answering our prayers!" If a young girl dies of cancer, "Praise God. Our prayers got answered, but not in the way we expected or even wanted. We don't know His plans, but we will someday and this will all make sense. It looks like He needed her in heaven more than on Earth. She's with Him now."

This kind of reasoning was always on display during natural disasters. When a tsunami wiped out more than 225,000 people in Indonesia in 2004, the media featured several survivors who claimed God had miraculously answered their prayers and saved them. It made me want to scream. If He answered their prayers, why did He sit by and allow the killing of nearly a quarter-million people—many who were praying, too, as they were being washed away? It made no sense. Where were the people crying out, "Why would God let this happen? What kind of God would allow so many people to die, and create so much heartbreak and so much misery?" Why save a random person or two? Why not everyone? Or everyone *but* a random person or two—preferably atheists?

I had flashbacks to the Benny Hinn Miracle Crusade, and those scores of people who sat in the wheelchairs at the back of the arena floor. I knew they wouldn't be cured that night; so did Benny Hinn. Only the afflicted themselves believed that they would walk home that night healthy and whole. They didn't. But why wouldn't God heal them, if He so willingly healed others afflicted with apparently more convenient maladies?

Could it be that a God who took a personal interest in me and the rest of humanity simply didn't exist? I felt I was quickly approaching a turning point in my life. Admitting mistakes hadn't been a problem for me. I have screwed up my relationship with my wife several times over 20 years. I consider myself a good father, but I have messed up many times in raising my kids. I could list each friend I betrayed or failed to stand up for. I could probably tell you every big mistake I've made in my journalism career—if you had enough time. James Joyce believed that "mistakes are the portals of discovery." That's how I've come to see them. My mistakes, though plentiful and painful, have made me a better person, wiser and more mature.

But I couldn't yet admit I had made a mistake about the truth of Christianity. I was hoping for some sort of miracle that would restore my faith. Being an atheist in America—or even within my own family—was appalling to me. About 98 percent of Americans say they believe in God. I wasn't anxious to be part of a 2 percent minority, especially knowing the passions of the majority. Besides, what if I were wrong? It wasn't the most positive incentive, but the specter of hell did keep me clinging to religion; facing an eternity in Hades was a big price to pay if I were wrong. And if I admitted to my disbelief, what would I tell my kids? It was one thing to send myself to hell; it would be unthinkable to guide my children along that path.

Christians often talk about Pascal's Wager, which argues that it's a good bet to believe in Christ. If you're right, you'll spend eternity in heaven. If you're wrong, you'll just be dead like everyone else. But it seems to me that to indulge in Pascal's Wager, you actually have to believe in Christ. The Lord would know if you were faking. I could no longer fake it. It was time to be honest about where I was in my faith.

As principles go, Occam's Razor seemed like a better bet. It basically says that all things being equal, the simplest solution is most likely the correct one. It was becoming harder and harder for me to fit my idea of a loving, personal God into the reality of the world in which I lived. The simplest explanation kept boomeranging back to me: there was no God.

FIFTEEN

At the Edge of the Earth

Let those who love the LORD hate evil,
for he guards the lives of his faithful ones
and delivers them from the hand of the wicked.

— PSALM 97:10

IF YOU ARE having doubts about God, you don't want to
find yourself on St. Michael Island, Alaska, where a single Catholic missionary raped an entire generation of Alaska Native boys.
Unless you meet Peter "Packy" Kobuk, one of the victims who,
despite it all, remains a believer himself. My encounter with him
would show me the limits of my faith, measured against the stubbornness of his.

I first heard about the story from John Manly, the Newport
Beach attorney who had represented Ryan DiMaria and hundreds of victims of clergy sexual abuse since 2001. Manly had
just returned from a trip to the Alaskan island when I sat down
for lunch with him. Since we both had been engulfed in the lives
of sexual abuse victims, we usually used gallows humor to deal

with the heartache and tragedy we saw. But at lunch, John wasn't in a joking mood. In fact, he looked like someone close to him had died.

"What's wrong with you?" I asked.

"Dude, you wouldn't believe what I saw in this Eskimo village," John said, his eyes staring vacantly ahead. "I can't even put it into words."

Already a prosperous real-estate attorney, Manly stumbled into the field of clergy sexual abuse litigation with the Ryan DiMaria case— despite the fact that many of his colleagues and friends advised him and his then partner, Katherine K. Freberg, not to take it. Whether it was providence, fate or just coincidence, Manly had an advantage working the case because he was a cradle Catholic, a former altar boy and the product of parochial schools. He knew better than most the Catholic system and Catholic thinking. Over the next few years, he expanded on that expertise by hiring former Catholic insiders to do battle against the church's hierarchy.

He brought onboard Patrick Wall, a former Benedictine monk who had heard Manly interviewed on the radio and called to volunteer his expertise. Wall, a former lineman for the St. John's University football team in Collegeville, Minnesota, had gained a reputation as a fix-it priest for the Catholic Church. His first four assignments out of the seminary were to straighten out parishes tainted by molestation and financial scandal. In 1999, a half-dozen years into his vocation, he walked away from the priesthood— largely because he had grown weary of watching the church hierarchy put its desire to avoid scandal ahead of the needs of sexual abuse victims. He had grown tired of seeing innocent people run over by what he described as "the Roman machine coming down the tracks in all its glory."

Wall still saw himself as a fix-it man for the Catholic Church—only now he worked for the good guys. As Manly's expert in church, or canon, law and church practices, Wall—in his late 30s—helped the lawyers interpret church documents and understand church structure, finances and culture. He had firsthand experience in how the church hierarchy processes molestation claims. He knew where critical information was hidden. He thought like the bishops thought. He could read Greek, Hebrew, Latin and Italian—the latter two languages essential to understanding documents produced by the Vatican and not meant for plaintiff's attorneys.

"We're now on equal footing with the church," Wall told me, "and we can deal with the cases on their merits." He added that the job with Manly served as a way to redeem his shortcomings as a priest. "The biggest thing I failed in doing [as a priest] was to stand up to our leaders. We all maintained the silence. This is something I can concretely do—helping the church refocus on the poorest and weakest among us. That's who the victims are."

Manly also hired his former client Ryan DiMaria, who passed the California bar exam after being awarded a $5.2 million clergy sexual abuse settlement. DiMaria brought a survivor's point of view to the law firm, giving him instant rapport with other victims. He also brought a thirst for justice that only a victim of abuse could have.

"I'm really grateful for what my attorneys did for me in my case," DiMaria told me. "My fate was in their hands. It made me want to work on these kinds of cases and do the same for other people."

Victims of clergy sexual abuse loved having DiMaria for their attorney. As one told me: "He's not just a lawyer trying to get money. He's a lawyer trying to make things right. He has a cause. He's been through it. He understands."

Manly also regularly consulted with Richard Sipe, who had

spent 18 years as a monk in a Benedictine monastery before becoming a psychotherapist specializing in counseling clergy. Sipe, author of several books on sexuality and the priesthood, believes mandatory celibacy has failed spectacularly. He estimates about 50 percent of the clergy have sexual partners at any one time, and 80 to 90 percent of them masturbate—a violation of the vow of celibacy. His research shows about 6 percent of Catholic priests molest minors. (His 6 percent estimate had been dismissed as preposterous by church officials until the sex scandal broke in 2002.) Manly's other insider was Tom Doyle, the priest who warned bishops in the United States in 1985 that a Catholic sex scandal could sweep the nation—and cost the church $1 billion (a low estimate, it turned out)—if the problem wasn't addressed.

All in all, Manly had brought together a law firm's version of Murderer's Row to take on the Catholic Church. It was a line-up that Catholic officials feared. The story was probably apocryphal, but one church official told me that "Mad Dog Manly" was the attorney's nickname inside the Diocese of Orange. You could see the meaning of that name by reviewing some of Manly's depositions of church officials. Often, his rage and contempt at how bishops and their lieutenants failed to protect children from pedophile priests spilled out in his questions. (Manly's masterful deposition of serial child rapist Father Oliver O'Grady was the basis for *Deliver Us From Evil*, a 2007 Academy Award–nominated documentary by Amy Berg.)

For instance, in the Alaska cases, Manly talked about the Jesuit order's "Manifestation of Conscience" tradition, where a priest gives an accounting of his spiritual journey of the past year. Jesuit superiors had taken the legal position that the Manifestation of Conscience was privileged communication—like a confession—that needn't be revealed to outside authorities. Manly and others—

including some Jesuits—say the Manifestation of Conscience was used as a human resources tool, and not a sacred communication between a priest and his superior. In this 2005 deposition of Father Frank Case, a top-ranking Jesuit in North America, Manly explored the issue:

> MANLY: *Now, if somebody manifested to you that they had chopped off the head of an eight-year-old little girl, raped her, and buried her body and you knew, Father, that the parents were out looking for that child's body, would you tell anybody?*

> CASE: *I would be obligated with the same level of confidentiality as I would have in confessional.*

> MANLY: *So, is it your testimony, Father, that you wouldn't tell anyone?*

> CASE: *I wouldn't tell anyone.*

Father Stephen Sundborg, former chief of the Oregon Province, expressed a similar view in his 2005 deposition with Manly:

> MANLY: *If a priest, while you were provincial, manifested to you that he had raped a seven- or eight-year-old little girl on the day of her First Communion, he chopped her head off after the rape, buried her body, had sex with her body after he chopped her head off and was hiding it, and you knew that the parents and the police were looking for that child, would you alert the authorities?*

SUNDBORG: *Okay. There is nothing that is said or that I would learn in a Manifestation of Conscience that I would reveal to another person.*

MANLY: *So you wouldn't tell the police in that situation?*

SUNDBORG: *I would not.*

Sundborg, the president of Seattle University, also told Manly that he would not report crimes of rape perpetrated against students at the university if he had learned of them during a Manifestation of Conscience.

MANLY: *If a priest at Seattle U manifested to you that he was serially raping students . . . , would you have alerted the head of security at Seattle University?*

SUNDBORG: *I would have immediately removed him from Seattle University and restricted him from all ministry.*

MANLY: *Okay. Would you have alerted the authorities, either at Seattle University or the Seattle police department?*

SUNDBORG: *No.*

In a later deposition with Sundborg that touched on Manifestation of Conscience, Manly finally lost it. "It is beyond me that you would take a beautiful thing like Ignatius's order and the spiritual exercises and pervert it to hide perverts," Manly said.

In a deposition of Father William "Lom" Loyens, former head of the Jesuits in Alaska, you can sense Manly's anger. Loyens testified that childhood sexual abuse didn't affect Eskimos as badly as others because of the Alaska natives' "loose" sexual mores.

MANLY: *I'm interested in your observations as somebody who understands native people as to the impact being molested by a priest would have on one of those men, those boys. Can you address that for me?*

LOYENS: *Well, in the Athabascan culture, they were fairly loose on sexual matters. And let's say, generally speaking, American culture, being very heavily influenced by Protestantism, was much more uptight over all these things than the native people were; in this case, the Athabascans. So—I give you an example. I have spoken a number of times with ladies that talk to me on the path, or whatever, that had a baby, a male baby, in one arm while they were playing with his testicles and the little boy was enjoying this immensely. There was a different attitude for sexual matters, in terms of older boys breaking in younger girls and older girls breaking in younger boys, and so forth. It's just considerably different. And we could say "loose," but as an anthropologist, I say that is just the culture.*

MANLY: *I guess what I'm asking you, Father, is do you have a personal opinion, either as a priest or an anthropologist, of the impact, whether positive or negative, of Father Convert molesting these boys would have had generally?*

LOYENS: *Well, see, the word "molesting," what are we talking about?*

MANLY: *I'll tell you what we're talking about. "Come and spend the night. You're going to serve Mass in the morning. I'm going to stick my hands in your pants, grab your testicles and your penis, possibly make you ejaculate when you're ten years old or eight years old or six years old or twelve years old; making you take a bath the night before while I bathe you as a priest feeling the priest's erection in your back as you're an eight- or ten-year-old little boy." That's what I'm talking about, Father.*

LOYENS: *Okay. Well, now at least we know what we're talking about because till now—*

MANLY: *I'm happy to share it with you in all its glorious detail. So what do you think the impact of that would be?*

LOYENS: *In the Athabascan culture 40 years ago or 30 years ago, whenever it was, since there are no years attached to it here, that would be less impressive than it would be for, say, somebody in Fairbanks or Spokane.*

The passion of Manly—along with the team of experts he assembled—earned survivors of clergy sexual abuse and his law firm millions of dollars in settlements. But the price for Manly has been high.

"Imagine every day your job is to go and pick up intestines that have spilled out of people's guts," Manly says. "You stuff them back in, and sew them up and try to find the person with the knife who did this. The clergy sexual abuse cases are like that, except it's emotional guts you're dealing with and you're trying to put these people back together. Though they are adults, you're really dealing with that child who got hurt.

"In my personal life, I was spiraling downward, and I kept thinking, how can the priest and bishops go on with their lives as if nothing happened? The priest wielded the knife, and the bishops cleaned it off and put it back where the priest could find it again—and you have to be one depraved motherfucker to do that. They are cold and calculating. How can these guys not do anything about it? And at the moment of consecration [during the Eucharist], these people are supposed to be *in persona Christi,* or 'in the person of Christ'?"

During first five years of the new millennium, Manly's blood pressure rose to dangerous levels, and he packed on more than 75 pounds to his six-foot frame. When he couldn't sleep late at night, he'd sit down with his "old friend, Jack Daniels." Manly's seething anger and depression nearly ruined his seemingly idyllic family life in the seaside town of Corona del Mar. His stunning wife, a former college basketball player who knew several languages and used to work for the State Department, threatened divorce, and his relationship with his four children, especially his two older teenage girls, turned rocky.

"I was so angry and upset that anything would set me off," Manly says. "It got so bad that when I went on vacation to Italy, I wasn't able to get out of bed. It was that bleak."

On a drive one day down Pacific Coast Highway near San Clemente, he contemplated exactly how he would kill himself with a .45-calibre Glock. The thought scared Manly into an intense multi-year counseling program that he now credits with saving his marriage, bettering his relationship with his girls and relieving him of the oppressive anger.

One thing counseling couldn't give Manly back was his faith. He realized he first started to lose his religion during a 2001 deposition with retired Bishop of Orange Norman McFarland, a key witness in the Ryan DiMaria case. When the bishop entered the conference room, he set down a rosary and a prayer book in front of him. Manly's mother regularly used a similar rosary and prayer book set, and the pages of her devotional had become torn and tattered. To Manly's eyes, McFarland's prayer book appeared unused.

"I realized that the rosary and prayer book were just props," Manly says, adding that his suspicions were reinforced by this exchange with the bishop, who admitted that a "precocious" 15-year-old girl could prove to be quite a temptation for a priest:

> MANLY: *Does it make any difference to you in terms of how you handle priest matters [whether] the priest abused a three-year-old or sexually abused a seventeen-year-old?*
>
> MCFARLAND: *Yes, there is a difference.*
>
> MANLY: *What is the difference?*
>
> MCFARLAND: *From what I have learned the experts say that pedophilia, I don't think, is [curable].*
>
> MANLY: *How about a fifteen-year-old girl?*
>
> MCFARLAND: *Well, that is also very wrong. But I think there is more a chance [of that] being an isolated incident . . . I can understand the temptation of that more. It can't even occur to me with a child or baby. Does one make a distinction [between] 15 or 17? She may be very, very precocious or adult-looking, and there would be temptation there.*

By the time the Alaska cases surfaced in 2003, Manly knew his faith was lost. "When I started this, I thought clergy sexual abuse was a holiness problem involving a few priests," Manly says. "But I've found no one in the clergy, in all my cases, who did the right thing. Some of them weren't bad people, but they didn't have the courage to do what was right.

"As a Catholic, you are raised into thinking the priest is like Jesus and you're a sinner, and you're so tough on yourself as a young person. Now I realize that you're just a fucking tool—a pod for them to grow and get money from. They use 'we'll get your soul into heaven' as a guise. When the reality of it hits you in the face, it really knocks you on your ass."

One morning in 2006, Manly took off his neck a well-worn Miraculous Medal, a popular symbol among Catholics, said to be created by St. Catherine Laboure in the 18th century at the request of the Virgin Mary. "All who wear them will receive great graces," Mary reportedly said. Manly received his Miraculous Medal as a second-grader on his First Communion. On the back were the words "I'm a Catholic. Please call a priest." He had worn it every day of his life since the age of seven.

"It was part of me," Manly said. "Taking it off was the final sign that I was really done. I felt very sad, but it was the beginning of real freedom—emotionally and spiritually. I couldn't do it anymore."

Journalists always walk a tightrope between professional and personal friendships. During the Catholic sex scandal, I developed several close professional relationships with people on both sides of the controversy, but I never crossed the line to share my own views. (I did develop one personal friendship within the church, told my editors and stopped reporting on that person.) I knew a little about John's loss of faith. Only later, after I left the beat, did I discover that we had traveled such a similar path, one filled with difficult emotions, marital challenges, disillusionment, therapy and, ultimately, a loss of faith.

But back in 2004, when I sat across from Manly at the restaurant, he was a source. I knew him as the fearless and sometimes bull-headed scourge of the church. Yet there he was, barely able to talk to me at lunch about what he had seen in Alaska. Before the meal was over, I knew it was a story I wanted to cover. A few months later, I headed up to western Alaska with *Los Angeles Times* photographer Damon Winter to see for myself what had happened. I knew it would make for a riveting tale, but I also felt compelled to do it because it represented the last major, untold story about the Catholic sex scandal—molesting priests had invaded even some of the world's most remote outposts. So despite a healthy fear of flying in bush planes and only a hooded sweatshirt for cold weather, I found myself onboard an Alaska Airlines flight from Orange County to Anchorage in late January 2005, the start of the first of two trips to the villages.

My first stop in Anchorage was the REI store to pick up $1,500 worth of arctic gear. I then met up with John Manly, his associate Patrick Wall and Ken Roosa, an attorney based in Anchorage who represented scores of Alaska Natives who had been sexually abused by Catholic priests and missionaries. A former state sex crimes and federal prosecutor, Roosa—a soft-spoken man with a love of the outdoors—had fallen into the business of suing the Catholic Church quite by accident.

When he left the government for private practice, he was looking for clients for his new law firm and was handed a file that another attorney didn't have time to check out. An Alaska Native said he had been abused as a child by a Catholic priest, an allegation that intrigued Roosa because of his background in prosecuting sex crimes. That case ultimately yielded another seven victims of the same priest. The Diocese of Fairbanks offered $10,000 to each Alaska

Native. The average clergy sexual abuse settlement in Los Angeles was $1.6 million; the Catholic Church initially estimated the life of a Yu'pik was worth about 1 percent of an Angeleno's. Eventually, Roosa accepted a multimillion-dollar offer from the church to settle those cases. Within the small world of Alaska attorneys, he became known as the guy who handled clergy sexual abuse claims. More victims started coming forward, first in a trickle, and then a deluge. As the numbers grew, Roosa called Manly, an attorney he had read about on the Internet, and asked for his assistance.

Together, all of us hopped a flight to Nome, the last town before the Alaska Native villages. At the tiny Nome airport, we climbed into a small prop plane for a noisy 90-minute flight to St. Michael Island. Our bush pilot had a wild gray beard and old-fashioned leather flying helmet. I took an Ativan to calm my nerves and tried not to hyperventilate. With the midday winter sun hugging the horizon, I looked down and saw the frozen Bering Sea spread like a bumpy white blanket in all directions. I had done some research about the history of the Catholic Church in Alaska, and it came alive for me as our plane headed to the frozen edge of civilization.

In 1886, the Jesuits established their first mission in western Alaska. Making converts in this unforgiving corner of the world proved difficult at first. For thousands of years, Eskimo hunters and gatherers had been ruled by *Yuuyaaraq*, or "the way of the human being." Yu'pik people believed that their elaborate oral traditions and spiritual beliefs helped ward off bad weather, famine and illness. It wasn't until an influenza epidemic in 1900 wiped out more than 60 percent of Alaska's native population that the Jesuits began to make headway. The Eskimo shamans were no match for the deadly virus. Entire villages converted to the new religion virtually overnight.

Today, the Roman Catholic Diocese of Fairbanks stretches across the upper two-thirds of Alaska, a rugged chunk of territory bigger than Texas but with only 41 churches and 24 priests. Jesuits, who still staff the diocese, call the villages "the world's toughest missionary field!" in advertisements that use photos of darling Alaska Native children to raise funds for the religious order.

In our plane, we circled the wind-swept island and set down on a small landing strip a few miles from the village of St. Michael and its 370 residents. An elder of the village, Tommy Cheemuk, was waiting for us in a battered and rusted Ford pickup truck with no reverse gear. We piled into the uncovered bed of the truck and huddled together for warmth as Tommy drove us to his village. As I watched the barren landscape go by on that impossibly cold afternoon, I immediately could see why Manly told me that this was the perfect setting for a molesting missionary. Just 200 miles below the Arctic Circle, St. Michael and its neighboring village, Stebbins, sit on a rugged section of coast where the tundra meets the Bering Sea. They are accessible only by small plane or, when the ice melts on Norton Sound, by boat. In the 1960s and 1970s, when most of the molestations took place, the villages had no police officers and only a few phones. (During my trip there, they still didn't have running water.) The most respected man in the villages was whoever the Jesuits sent to run the parishes. For such a man, it was a pedophile's paradise.

Though the Jesuits deny it, there's evidence to suggest that the villages of western Alaska served as a dumping ground for molesting priests.

"It's like the French Foreign Legion—you join rather than go to prison," says Richard Sipe, the former Benedictine monk. "I was absolutely convinced this happened in Alaska."

Since the Catholic sex scandal broke in 2002, more than 110

Alaska Natives from 15 villages have stepped forward to say they had been molested by Jesuits. These victims also contend, with tears streaming down their face, that many others—cut off for decades from legal and emotional help—have committed suicide to end their pain.

Packy Kobuk has to walk past the Catholic church of St. Michael to get almost anywhere. To fill a drum of heating oil. To take his children to school. To wash his clothes at the only Laundromat in his village.

"I think about burning it down, but I have to block that out," Kobuk, then 46, told me on that trip. "It all comes back to me right away each time I have to see it."

Even after 30 years, he and his fellow victims couldn't shake their memories of the late Joseph Lundowski, a volunteer Catholic missionary who arrived in their village in 1968. Staffing remote village parishes with full-time priests had proved impossible, which was why Lundowski and other volunteers played a key role in these ministries. The devoutly Catholic village elders welcomed Lundowski warmly, as they did all men of the cloth. But the children soon grew to fear and despise him.

Now grown, they claim that over a seven-year period "Deacon Joe" molested nearly every boy in St. Michael and the neighboring settlement of Stebbins, villages connected by a winding 12-mile dirt road. The alleged victims, now in their 40s and 50s, secretly carried this burden until 2004—not even talking about it with each other. Only after watching the Catholic sexual abuse scandal unfold across the nation on satellite television did 28 men from the two villages decide to break their silence. The numbers of those raped by Lundowski would eventually rise to 70 natives in six villages. Correspondence from early in the missionary's career in Alaska shows that his superiors knew that he had a serious problem but did nothing to stop him.

"No one would believe us," Kobuk told me. "[Lundowski] worked for God, and I was just an Eskimo child."

On my first trip to St. Michael Island, I spent five days in the villages interviewing the men who had been abused. It was the first time most of them talked in depth about these experiences. Few had told their wives, fearful that they would be thought of as homosexuals. Most of them wanted to talk with me away from their homes. Usually stoic, many broke down, shaking and crying. Their faces contorted. They begged to somehow be freed of the unending pain. The scene was simply indescribable in words, but *Times* photographer Damon Winter was able to capture enough of it to become a Pulitzer prize finalist for his work. His photos showed the anguish of Tommy Cheemuk, crying as his wife tried to comfort him. Of John Lockwood, a broken man in a tattered shirt, sitting on a bucket, one hand covering his eyes, the other holding a lighted cigarette. Of another Alaska Native who has believed for years that a salmon bone was stuck in his throat, ready to kill him at any moment. He became housebound, too afraid to venture far from the phone in case the bone broke away and punctured an artery or his heart. Multiple tests by doctors failed to reveal any bone. I thought it more likely that he was experiencing a psychosomatic response to being forced to have oral sex with Lundowski. I had seen similar symptoms before.

Upon hearing the abuse claims, the Jesuits did the usual duck and cover. They offered no help to the Yu'piks. They denied that Lundowski had ever worked in the villages or for them, a claim easily disproved by documents in their own files. Finally, in 2007, the Jesuit order of the Roman Catholic Church agreed to pay $50 million to 110 Eskimos to settle their claims.

During my two trips to St. Michael, as odd as this may sound, I felt satisfaction for the first time about my religious doubts. What had happened to helpless boys at the edge of the world made a lot more sense if there were no God. Confronted with evil, whether man-made or satanic, our task is always to fight it. But it helps to try to understand it, too—and I found it refreshing to focus entirely on the fight, knowing that one bad man and one corrupt institution had been purely self-interested. I did not have to worry about God's role anymore.

I attended a Sunday service at the St. Michael parish on a bitterly cold morning. I was secretly delighted to see only a handful of elderly Alaska Natives and one younger family show up to a Mass that once drew the entire village. The residents knew what the church had done to their children, and they no longer wanted any part of it. It was hard to worship a God that let this kind of thing happen, in a church run by the men who looked the other way—and even now, 40 years later and in a more enlightened age, refuse to help.

And yet. (There is always an "and yet.") How to explain Packy Kobuk? On my return home from my winter trip to Alaska, I stopped by Nome's Anvil Mountain Correction Center, where Packy was serving three months for assault. Sitting in a tiny visitor's room, I studied Packy's round face. In St. Michael, the Yu'piks lived in many ways just as their ancestors did 10,000 years ago. They harpooned whales, tracked herds of caribou migrating across the tundra and hunted walruses sleeping on icebergs in the Bering Sea. In midsummer they gathered wild berries, a key ingredient in Eskimo ice cream—a frozen and oddly tasty concoction of lard, fish, sugar and berries. Smells of the outdoor life hung heavy in the village: the salt air, the strips of salmon drying on racks, the seaweed washed up on the beach.

For now, Packy could smell only the disinfectants used to scrub the jail's concrete floors. Alcohol and a violent temper had put him here often in his 46 years. As a child-abuse victim, who can blame him?

Wearing navy-blue prison clothes, the short, powerfully built man folded his callused hands on the table between us. A home-made Rosary hung from his neck, the blue beads held together by string from one of his village's fishing nets. All of the now-grown Eskimos I had interviewed over the past week had lost their faith—except Packy.

He had been sodomized for years by Lundowski, who had also forced him to perform sex acts with other children. It began when Packy was 12. In exchange, Lundowski gave Packy coins from the collection box and cakes and casseroles made by villagers. These gifts raised his family's standard of living in a place where poverty was of the Third World variety.

After eight years of abuse, Lundowski left St. Michael suddenly one morning on a hastily arranged flight with a bush pilot, report-edly chased from the village by angry parents who had finally uncovered the truth. No one in the village ever talked about what happened—except Packy. He had asked for help over the years from at least two bishops, five priests and village elders. Everyone told him to keep quiet and stop stirring up trouble.

Following the death in 1999 of a priest who served in St. Michael and Stebbins, Kobuk was asked by a Jesuit superior to take more than 16 loads of documents, notepads, books and trash from the two parishes to the villages' dumps in his four-wheel ATV and trailer.

Kobuk said he brought along 15 gallons of stove oil because the priest said the trash needed to be burned. He said the priest fed the documents and books into the flames, eliminating any evidence of wrongdoing that happened in the parishes over the years. (Jesuit officials claim it was a routine housecleaning and that nothing important was destroyed.)

"He made sure these would burn to ashes and made sure there was no trace," Packy said. "He was reading a lot of them, too, before he threw them in."

I pointed to the Rosary.

"Why do you still believe?"

"It's not God's work what happened to me," he said softly, running his fingers along the Rosary beads. He spoke in clipped words whose cadence matched the Yu'pik language he no longer understood. "They were breaking God's commandments—even the people who didn't help. They weren't loving their neighbors as themselves."

I didn't tell Packy about my own doubts about faith. Listening to him filled me with shame. My faith had collapsed. He had been through much worse than anything I could imagine—raped for years by a man he believed was Christ's representative on Earth. Told to keep quiet by bishops, priests and village elders. And his belief never wavered.

I asked him to tell me more. He told me that he regularly got down on his knees in his jail cell to pray, an act that brought ridicule from other inmates.

"A lot of people make fun of me, asking if the Virgin Mary is going to rescue me," Packy said. "Well, I've gotten help more times from the Virgin Mary through intercession than from anyone else. I won't stop. My children need my prayers."

In the late spring, I met Packy again, this time at his home in St. Michael. He told me he had recently followed the fresh tracks that a grizzly bear had made in the gray sand of a deserted beach.

Packy said he could never commit suicide because it was against his beliefs, but he had hoped the grizzly would eat him and end his misery. But then, approaching some bushes where he was sure the bear has hiding, Packy had a change of heart. As he ran back down the beach, he prayed to Jesus to rescue him.

Packy's heart aches for the church in St. Michael. Until recently, he couldn't bring himself to set foot in it. Instead, on Sundays, Packy walked through his dilapidated village, reciting prayers and parts of the Catholic liturgy that he had learned from Lundowski. Packy included a prayer for his molester, who died in 1995. The Alaska Native asks God to accept his molester into heaven.

"I pray for Lundowski, for this soul," Packy says. "I just want to heal."

SIXTEEN

Letting Go of God

It would be very nice if there were a God who created the
world and was a benevolent providence, and if there were
a moral order in the universe and an after-life; but it is a
very striking fact that all this is exactly as we are bound to
wish it to be.

— SIGMUND FREUD, *THE FUTURE OF AN ILLUSION*

AFTER MY TRIP to Alaska, my head finally had to admit to
what had happened in my heart three years before, when I had
stopped attending church. I no longer believed in God—at least
not a personal one who lovingly looked over me and answered my
prayers. But before I officially surrendered my faith, I made one
last stab at trying to recover it.

I turned to John Huffman, my pastor at St. Andrew's Presbyterian Church in Newport Beach. He had always been a spiritual
Superman to me—and not because of the national reputation that
landed him on the board of directors for evangelical powerhouse
organizations such as World Vision and *Christianity Today*. It was

because he had lost a wonderful 23-year-old daughter to cancer at the height of his very public ministry and handled the tragedy with incredible grace—a gift, he would tell you in his booming baritone voice, that came from God. He had been through life's cruelest moment, tested like few had, and his faith remained steadfast.

I also liked John because of his approachability. Though a first-rate intellectual who had earned a PhD, he also was a weekend athlete and a huge sports fan, and had a good sense of humor that allowed him to poke fun even at his own tendency to drop names. It was an attractive combination. I took John to dinner and told him about my crisis of faith. I asked him if I could e-mail him some tough questions about Christianity. He agreed without hesitation. Rock solid in his faith, I think he welcomed the challenge.

My questions were basic, verging on the clichéd, but I desperately wanted some solid answers I could grasp so I could climb back up into my faith. Why do bad things happen to good people? Why does God get credit for answered prayers but no blame for unanswered ones? Why do we believe in the miraculous healing power of God when He's never been able to regenerate a limb or heal a severed spinal chord? Here is our exchange:

Bill: "Okay, John. I've been holding off until I think of the perfect question to begin. Since that hasn't happened, let's just start here. Does it bother you that God seems to get a pass no matter how a prayer turns out? If the prayer is answered (and someone recovers from a grave illness, for example), then God is said to be a loving Lord who cares about His children's wishes. They asked and they received.

"But then when the prayer doesn't get answered (the person

dies, for example), the Christian will say: Well, it's God's will. Or the prayer was answered, but not in the way we expected. Or we simply can't know the Lord's mysterious ways.

"The bottom line is: God seems to be praised, or at least still believed in, no matter how the prayers turn out. Is that just too convenient?"

John: "I know what you mean. I must admit that I get a bit ticked off myself at the insensitivity and even narcissism of people who seem to blithely dismiss life's tragedies, exempting God from any responsibility while they grandly praise Him for everything good that happens.

"I remember how hurt I was when my daughter Suzanne died of cancer at age 23, while I heard some Christians praising God for His goodness on matters as small as getting a parking space to items as big as the fact that their child diagnosed with terminal cancer was finally healed.

"At the same time, I'd have to admit that I probably fall into the category somewhat similar to those you've described, as I find myself troubled with those people who wouldn't think for a moment to express gratitude to God for the good they experience but are quick to damn Him for anything that goes wrong.

"Genuine gratitude can transform one's life. The capacity to thank God for the blessings and also praise Him in difficult times, in my estimation, is a sign of maturing faith. As much as I hated losing my precious daughter, every so often someone would come to me and say, 'Why in the world would God allow your daughter to die, given all the good you do as a pastor?' My genuine response would be, 'Why shouldn't I experience this pain? Why should I be any more exempt from loss than anyone else?'

"I don't think that God is in the business of zapping people indiscriminately. He didn't create sin. He didn't create disease. He didn't create spousal abuse. The buildup of sludge from all of our centuries of human disobedience to God takes its toll.

"But ultimately, I may end up sounding just like the persons who give you trouble. My ultimate affirmation is let God be God and acknowledge that He is in charge. He knows what I don't know. And frankly, if I'm totally honest with you, a life of gratitude is one that bows before the Sovereign God arguing with Him on those things that trouble me, lamenting the losses of life, but ultimately saying, 'Thank you for your blessings and help me handle the painful losses, because I know that You know what I don't know. You, God, are infinite; I'm human and finite. Right now, I only see in part from my human perspective. You see the big picture. Thank you for the blessings and thank you for giving me the strength to handle life's tragedies and even to voluntarily involve myself in the pain of others, helping them in a way in which I allow my heart to be broken by the very things that break the heart of God.' "

Bill: "So the seeming randomness of God's blessing and intervention isn't random at all, but we can only understand the bigger picture after death? In the meantime, the crooked, atheist businessman prospers and the child of devout Christian parents dies. Why would a loving God make this impossible for us to understand? What's the point of that?"

John: "I guess I'd have to accept your observation that the randomness of God's blessing and intervention isn't random at all and that perhaps we can only understand the bigger picture after death.

"But I'm not prepared to quite leave it at that.

"I am a rational person, like you, and I do want left-brain answers to just about everything.

"I've discovered that there are some good answers to some of my questions in life, like 'Will we have a wreck if I irresponsibly take a left turn into oncoming fast-moving traffic?' The answer is quite easy for me to see. It's my own error, stupidity, mental lapse or selfishness that causes tragedy and may kill me and my loved ones. For such activity on my part, if I survive, I must face the consequences.

"However, I doubt that what is an answer for me, as the one who caused the accident, is an adequate answer for the family of those in the oncoming car who lose a spouse and a couple of children. They may be forever in this life screaming out to God with the question, 'Why?'

"Yes, at times to me God's apparent random blessing and intervention or apparent absence of involvement seems quite arbitrary and even whimsical from my limited perspective.

"The Bible does address the very question you raise about the crooked atheist businessman, the age-old question, 'Why do the wicked prosper and the righteous go wanting?' The Bible declares that 'The rain falls on the just and the unjust alike.'

"I don't think it is that the loving God intentionally makes it impossible for us to understand. I don't think that that is the point. I think the point is that I am human, finite, and God is supernatural, above-human. God is infinite. The fact is that He has not chosen to reveal everything to us. I can whine and complain that He hasn't, demanding that God make it possible for me to understand everything. But when I do that, I'm getting pretty close to self-worship, lifting myself to the position of God, or perhaps even to a position superior to God, demanding that God function on my ground rules instead of me, humbly in worship, functioning on His.

"Perhaps as you suggest, we will understand all this when we die. It's also possible that, by then, it will be irrelevant. The Bible says, 'By then we will know as we are known.' Our whole perspective will be different.

"The bottom line for me is that right now I choose to trust God. That's faith.

"Job, who innocently lost everything, declared in faith that 'though He kill me, I will trust Him!' That's faith, the very essence of my existence as a believer in Jesus Christ. But even in the process of trusting Him, I am free to talk with Him, argue with Him in prayer, lament the unfairness and raise questions directly to Him about the apparent random nature of evil and good. But at the end of the day, I thank Him for His blessings, and I am determined to love and trust Him for what I simply don't understand.

"In all honesty, to be human is to not know it all. To be divine is to know it all. I in my not-know-it-all-ness would rather bow in worship before the One who does know it all and trust Him rather than to demand all the answers. God is good enough even though I don't understand everything, including the death of my daughter and other of my more private, painful realities. Instead of lashing out in destructive anger toward God, if there is a God, and the unfairness of life, I am prepared to trust Him in those areas that are a mystery and may remain so all through this life."

Reading John's words, I was glad I picked him to answer my questions. From a Christian perspective, his answers were nearly perfect. He was giving me the best Christianity had to offer, but I just didn't believe it anymore. I replied to John that though I appreciated his response, it was frustrating because I had seen too many innocent people live out lives full of tragedy and pain.

Bill: "The only way I can make sense of these tragedies (if God allowed them to happen) is if I measure the length of a tortured life (a sexual abuse victim, a severely handicapped child) against that of eternity.

"Do you think along those lines? That even the worst life on Earth will be like a pinprick compared to eternity?"

John: "Thanks for not backing off from the toughest of questions. I can feel your frustration. I believe that what you have described breaks the heart of God. In fact, this is why God came in the Person of Jesus Christ to make possible a new beginning in this life, not only in the life to come.

"Yes, even the worst of life on earth will be like a pinprick compared to eternity. That's not a good enough answer for me. I believe in a literal heaven in which all of us who repent of sin will be healed persons, experiencing a wholeness of life beyond anything possible here on earth.

"But as a minister of the gospel of Jesus Christ, mine is to not give blithe promises of 'pie in the sky by and by.' I say that not to minimize the reality of God's promises for the life beyond this life but to comment on the possibility of 'eternal life,' a God-quality life right here in this life as well as in the life to come.

"That's what Jesus was talking about when he said, 'For God so loved the world that He gave His only begotten Son that whosoever believeth in Him should not perish but have eternal life.' He was describing not just 'everlasting life,' He was describing a God-quality life available to every one of us, no matter how horrendous our circumstances are both in this life and in the life to come.

"Bill, you and I both are traumatized by our professional experience. You as an investigative reporter see the rotten underbelly of human experience and the unfairness of life, the consequences of sin, heartbreaking emptiness of the abuser and devastation of the abused. I as a pastor join you in this professional hazard of seeing the worst of life on a regular basis. When I pastored in Pittsburgh, one of my members, a pediatric neurosurgeon, came to me in a faith crisis. All he saw day after day was innocent little children rendered para- or quadriplegic by accidents or whose lives were threatened by malignancies of the brain. He came very close to an emotional/spiritual breakdown, wondering how a good God could allow such human tragedies. People like the three of us see life at its very worst and can sometimes forget that even the most tragic victim of life's unfairness can have good days, experience joy and be grateful for life's tender mercies.

"We also can forget that often the abuser was once abused. There is no ultimate healing until we recognize that all of us are fallen men and women in a fallen and broken world in which each of us needs both to offer forgiveness to others and to experience God's forgiveness of us.

"The only way I can handle the tough kinds of questions you're asking is not to just delay them all to be solved in the life beyond this life. But I need also for this life to know that God is walking alongside each of us as our friend, even the most broken and hurting.

"This is a little bit longer response than I expected to give. Let me conclude by mentioning a German theologian by the name of Juergen Multmann, who wrote a classic work titled *The Crucified God*. In it, he notes the biblical statement that no human being is capable of looking into the face of God. Traditionally, that is thought to mean that the glory of God is such a blinding light of beauty and grandeur we could not exist in His presence. He toys with the idea that the reverse may be true. It's possible that the very God of all creation so identifies with us in the worst of our pain, bearing our sins on the cross, the weight of humankind's inhumanity, that His very face is so distorted in anguish for us that we cannot stand looking at such a grotesque sight.

"The only way I'm able to handle the kinds of tough questions you're raising is to get there and identify with this gruesome underbelly of human existence and, with God's help, have some small role in bringing His healing. There's no greater joy than to sense the gratitude of one you are able to genuinely help, if only by simply being there for them.

"I know this response isn't that of a neat little answer perfectly packaged with a bow on it. I'm not prepared to crumble in total despair. I have yet to see a person who, when push comes to shove, will not acknowledge their many blessings even in the most tragic of circumstances."

No matter how good his responses, I felt like I was wasting John's time and stopped the e-mail exchanges. He was an excellent pastor, but he couldn't reach me. He was a stubborn optimist, facing all the same challenges to logic and emotion and believing in spite of them. He wasn't falling back on an impersonal, transcendent God in the background; he was insisting on a God who could intervene and often chose not to stop pain. It all sounded so empty to me, even as I admired him. For years now, I had tried to push away doubts and reconcile an all-powerful and infinitely loving God with what I had seen, but the battle was lost. I couldn't keep ignoring reality. I couldn't believe in Christianity any more than I could believe two plus two equals five. My worldview had shifted. There was no time machine that could send me back to a more comfortable period when believing in God was natural and automatic.

I started to see that the miracles of my Christian life had rational explanations. My born-again experience at the mountain retreat had been about fatigue, spiritual longing and emotional vulnerability, not about being touched by Jesus. My old boss gave me the $45,000 because he felt it was the right thing to do, not because I had asked God for it. I began to attribute my personal and professional turnaround to maturity, not to guidance from God. Landing the religion writing job at *The Times* was a product of years of hard work and persistence, not divine intervention.

I had changed in another way. I saw now that belief in God, no matter how grounded in logic and reason, requires a leap of faith. Either you have the gift of faith or you don't. It's not a choice. I used to think that you simply made a decision: to believe in Jesus or not. Collect the facts and then decide for yourself. But it's not that simple. Faith is something that is triggered deep within your soul—influenced by upbringing, family, friends, experiences and desires. It's not like registering to vote, checking a box to signal that you are a Democrat, Republican or Independent. Christians often talk to those who have fallen away from the faith as if they had made a choice to turn away from God. But as deeply as I missed my faith, as hard as I tried to keep it, my head could not command my gut. I know now that it was wishful thinking, not truth. I just didn't believe in God anymore, despite my best attempts to hold on to my beliefs. Faith can't be willed into existence. There's no faking it if you're honest about the state of your soul.

This new honesty made me feel quite alone—and scared. I revealed the extent of my disbelief only to Hugh and to my wife, Greer. Hugh believed that I was misinterpreting what was happening to me. He was confident that I was still a Christian, but just experiencing a dark night of the soul. He was sure that I'd be back in church sooner or later. I had been saved, and that was forever.

"God won't let you get away, Billy," he said.

Greer, who had admitted to her loss of faith earlier, was a different story. She is one of the most disciplined people on Earth. She rises early each morning to work out, cares for our four boys, runs a thriving web-based business called GreersOC.com that reports on the latest in Orange County fashion, dining and trends, and volunteers for the Orange County Juvenile Diabetes Research Foundation, a cause she joined when our second son, Tristan, was diagnosed with Type 1 diabetes at age 14. In her spare time, she's run a dozen marathons.

She brings that same kind of tenacity to other pursuits, whether it's reading some of the most challenging classic literature at night or searching for the truth about God. I don't know whether I should take credit or blame, but her loss of religion was sparked by our talks after I got home from work. I would tell her about my day, and she would listen, as flabbergasted by what I had seen as I was. The never-ending supply of stories ignited long-dormant doubts about her faith and caused her to see her Catholic experiences in a new light. For years, she said she had been "judged up the gazinga" by priests during confession and counseling sessions, making her feel guilty and worthless. Now she was finding out that these same priests had been covering up for their molesting brethren, or that they themselves had unconfessed sins far greater than hers. She came to see Catholic priests as regular people who belonged to an all-male club that absurdly believed its members held special powers—like turning bread and wine into the literal body and blood of Christ—that set them apart of the rest of humanity. From there, her faith fell rapidly, and Greer quick-marched to the anger phase of the grieving process. She couldn't believe how the faithful showed automatic, deep reverence to priests simply because they had been ordained by the church. She was angry that she had been barred from Communion—she was an adulterer in the priests' eyes—because she had not married in the Catholic Church. She found it sad and amusing that parishioners took seriously the garments worn by priests or the skullcaps and miters worn by bishops, cardinals and the pope, when they were just costumes from the Roman era. It bothered her that Catholics refer to a cardinal as "Your Eminence" or the pope as "Your Holiness," as if they deserved titles that bordered on idolatry.

"I'm sorry it took me until I was 42 to figure it out," Greer said. "But I feel free now. I don't have one doubt."

If I had still been a believer, I would have argued that her criticism was focused on human and institutional flaws. They didn't reflect the underlying truth about God. But I had passed through that phase myself, and kept right on falling through the deeper logical underpinnings of belief. Yet I was still in the mourning stage over my loss of faith. I felt envious of people who had it. To me, their life was simpler—not tortured by doubt, and with a road map that put them on the path to eternal bliss.

Without God, I had a whole new set of problems. There was no almighty supernatural power that had my back. I didn't have the comfort of a church home, where the music, the sermons and the fellowship could inspire me. Most significantly, I had to accept the fact that there was no perfect father out there, ready to sweep me up into his arms and love me no matter what I did. In many ways, I had to accept the fact that I was alone in this world. I didn't want to join up with the atheists, who could be as arrogant and cocksure of their beliefs as fundamentalist Christians. And attending the inclusive Unitarian Church—which had Christians, Jews, Buddhists, agnostics, atheists and others inside its big tent—was to me like drinking non-alcoholic beer. What was the point?

My new disbelief affected smaller parts of my life as well. I suddenly felt awkward when I heard about someone who had been laid off, had fallen ill or experienced a death in the family. It didn't feel right to use the comforting "You're in my thoughts and prayers," as I had done for years. Even the simpler "You're in my thoughts" sounded a little empty. I felt helpless and even negligent that I couldn't pray for divine intervention—despite knowing that prayer didn't work. I settled on sending "positive thoughts" their way. Now I know that the best thing to do is offer to help, and the next best is simply to make contact. Human intervention isn't miraculous, but I think it beats silent prayer.

My biggest challenge was death. Never the most comfortable subject, it now terrified me. I no longer believed in an eternal life in heaven. Jesus said that He would prepare a room especially for me in His Father's House, and I always imagined that room as a little kid might—filled with my favorite things, including my best friends, favorite foods, wide-screen TV with an endless supply of great sports events and movies, a swimming pool, workout equipment and easy access to the beach and waves. At some level, I assumed the truth about heaven was more sublime—time spent with the Lord—but the heavenly fun house was the symbolic shorthand that I had often used. Now, without the Bible as a guide, my afterlife was an abyss. Assuming, that is, I didn't end up in hell because I rejected God.

One day, Greer read a nice review in *The Times* about a one-woman play called *Letting Go of God*. Intrigued, she bought two tickets, and we soon found ourselves sitting in a small theater in Hollywood, waiting for Julia Sweeney to take the stage.

Best known for her androgynous character "Pat" on *Saturday Night Live*, Sweeney had written and was starring in a play based on her own religious experiences. As she moved into her monologue, I could feel my pulse quicken. I scooted to the edge of my chair. As she told the story of her spiritual journey—from Catholic to happy atheist—I had goose bumps. Though the details varied, it was my story, too. Using humor, insight, sensitivity and reason, she seemed to be talking directly to me, *for* me. It felt so good to know I had company—not among wild-eyed atheists and cynical nonbelievers, but with someone who had taken her faith seriously and sought to shore up her beliefs when they started to crumble.

A cradle Catholic, Sweeney told the audience that the beginning of her doubt came when she signed up for a Bible study class at her parish and began to read the Good Book straight through, beginning at Genesis and ending at Revelation:

> *I knew the Bible had nutty stories but I guess I thought they'd be wedged in amongst an ocean of inspiration and history. But instead the stories just got darker and more convoluted, like when God asked Abraham to murder his son, Isaac. As a kid we were taught to admire it. I caught my breath reading it. We were taught to admire it? What kind of sadistic test of loyalty is that, to ask someone to kill his or her own child? And isn't the proper answer, "No, I will not kill my child, or any child"?*

I had the same problems. I had always believed that it was silly to take the Bible literally—I never could get past the story of Noah and the Ark. How could every species on Earth fit into a single boat? How did the animals get fed—and who cleaned up after them? How could Noah live to be 950 years old? God could make anything happen, I thought, but this story had the smell of a man-made fable, not His inerrant word. The Bible is filled with these kinds of tales. It also portrays God as merciful and merciless, vengeful and forgiving, angry and kind, patient and impatient, unpredictable and unchanging. You could get whiplash trying to keep track of his moods. Sweeney talked about other surprises she found:

Even if you leave aside the creepy sacrifice-your-own-off-spring stories, the laws of the Old Testament were really hard to take. Leviticus and Deuteronomy are filled with archaic, just hard-to-imagine laws. Like if a man has sex with an animal, both the man and the animal should be killed. Which I could almost understand for the man, but the animal? Because the animal was a willing participant? Because now the animals had the taste of human sex and won't be satisfied without it?

The New Testament didn't get any better for Sweeney, who found Jesus to be "much angrier than I had expected . . . and very impatient." I suppressed the urge to shout, "Preach it, sister!"

I have to say, that for me, the most deeply upsetting thing about Jesus is his family values. Which is amazing when you think how there's so many groups out there who say they base their family values on the Bible. I mean he seems to have no real close ties to his parents. He puts his mother off cruelly, over and over again. At the wedding feast, he says to her, "Woman, what have I to do with you?" And once, while he was speaking to a crowd, Mary waited patiently off to the side to talk to him, and Jesus said to the disciples, "Send her away, you are my family now." . . . Jesus discourages any contact his converts have with their own families. As we know, he himself does not marry or have children and he explicitly tells his followers not to have families as well, and if they do, they should just abandon them.

She detailed how she tried desperately to retain her faith, despite seeing its deep flaws. She eventually looked for God in

Eastern religions, nature and love—the refuge of impersonal transcendentalists. She said she finally had to accept "what was true over what I wished were true." This was, for me, the most profound moment in the play. I had been wishing Christianity were true, as if I wished hard enough, I could turn fantasy into reality.

Sweeney's description of her atheist life was quite comforting to me. Right up front, she tackled the subject of death, saying that she believes our consciousness dies along with our other organs. This made sense to me: before I was born, I had no consciousness; after I die, I will have no consciousness. There will be nothing. The revelation had an instant and curious effect. The intense squeeze of time—the difference between eternity and one lifetime— made my life, and my time on Earth, much more precious. Sweeney put it like this:

> *I suddenly felt very deeply that I was alive: Alive with my own particular thoughts, with my own particular story, in this itty-bitty splash of time. And in that splash of time, I get to think about things and do stuff and wonder about the world and love people, and drink my coffee if I want to. And then that's it.*

Driving home from the play, adrenaline raced through my body. It felt as if I had made a discovery that made sense of my life and gave my mind some rest. For me, the play was the key I had been missing in my new worldview. I could now open the door to a new life—one without God. It didn't feel too scary; it felt more like something new and exciting. Like exploring a new home.

In college I had earned money working as a lifeguard on the sands of Huntington Beach, California. It was the perfect summer job—guarding the waters of one of the world's best and most dangerous beaches. I made about 1,500 rescues during my four summers there. Most of the swimmers I helped were caught in rip currents—rivers that form in the surf and pull people out to sea. Rips themselves are harmless. They don't yank people under, they aren't very wide and they dissipate outside the surf line. But inexperienced swimmers don't know this. All they sense is that they are being pulled quickly out to sea. Panicking, they claw at the water, fighting in vain to get back to the beach. They tire, choke on water and go down. No swimmer can make headway against a strong rip current. But someone with ocean experience can get out of a rip easily, simply by swimming to its side. Or she can just relax and let it carry her beyond the surf, where it will quickly dissipate.

At first, experiencing doubts about my faith, I acted like one of those frightened beachgoers who swim madly against the current, trying to get back to what I thought was the safety of Christianity. But the current of truth had me and wasn't going to let me go. When I decided to stop fighting it, I felt relief—even serenity. I decided to ride it out past the surf line and see where it would take me.

SEVENTEEN

One Story Too Many

The church is always trying to get other people to reform;
it might not be a bad idea to reform itself a little, by way
of example.

— MARK TWAIN, *A TRAMP ABROAD*

I WAS NOW a godless journalist on the religion beat. The problem that loomed before me wasn't lack of objectivity—I knew I could still produce fair and balanced stories—but burnout. Like a homicide detective, I had seen too much. A cop friend of mine says his job is hard because he is always dealing with the worst people or people at their worst. That was me on the religion beat. And because I had developed a reputation for a certain kind of story, I kept getting great tips about unsavory people within religion. Some of the best stories never made print: the semi-famous pastor under investigation for hiring a hit man to kill his former gay lover, or the nationally known conservative preacher who took a wide variety of illegal drugs deep into each night and was a serial adulterer. Sometimes prosecutors never filed charges. Other times I couldn't get additional sources to back up the story.

My body of work nevertheless continued to improve, earning me national awards each year. But I had developed a cynicism I didn't like. I tried to focus on more positive stories about faith, but even that didn't help. I had lost the reporting mojo that made the religion beat—even at its darkest—a journalistic rush. Since I now believed that God hadn't called me to this job, I no longer felt bound to stay on the beat. The end was near.

It came in the summer of 2005, in a courtroom in Multnomah County, Oregon. Just as there is a large network of clergy sexual abuse survivors, there are also several national support groups for women whose children were conceived by Catholic priests. Most of the priests have spurned their children. Their superiors generally offer little support—morally or financially—for these kids. One of my sources had called me with a tip, and that's how I ended up in the Portland courtroom. I was reporting on a story about an unemployed mother who had been impregnated by a seminary student 13 years earlier. She had gone to court trying to get increased child support for her sickly 12-year-old son.

Father Arturo Uribe, 47, took the witness stand. The priest had never seen nor talked with his son. He even had trouble properly pronouncing the boy's name. On the stand, Uribe looked relaxed. He wore a white button-down shirt, gray slacks, blue blazer with a small gold cross on the lapel and an easy smile. In a thick Spanish accent, Uribe confidently offered the court a simple reason as to why he couldn't pay more than $323 a month in child support for his ailing 12-year-old son. He simply had neither money nor income.

"The only thing I own are my clothes," he told a Portland judge.

His defense—orchestrated by a razor-sharp attorney paid for

by Uribe's religious order—boiled down to this: I'm a Roman Catholic priest, I've taken a vow of poverty and child-support laws can't touch me.

The boy's mother, Stephanie, couldn't afford a lawyer. Unemployed, she lived rent-free in the basement of a friend's home in a run-down section of Portland. The dank housing exacerbated their son's chronic asthma and allergies, which had been kept under control by 28 prescriptions over the past year. She had joined a food donation program so she and her boy would have enough to eat.

Uribe's "having success, moving up the ladder, and we're just stuck here, struggling," Stephanie told me before the hearing. "My situation is not ambiguous. I've got DNA walking around that proves he and [his religion order] have responsibility. They are so morally corrupt."

In court, Stephanie was flummoxed by the legal proceedings, stumbling badly as she acted as her own attorney. Many times, the judge helped her along. On legal points that didn't matter, even Uribe's attorney helped. But on any argument of consequence, the opposing lawyer shut her down mercilessly with rapid-fire objections. It went on, painfully, for three hours. The judge ruled almost apologetically in favor of Uribe, who was serving as the pastor of a large parish in Whittier, California. The fact was, the priest had no income or significant possessions. It didn't matter that his order had plenty of resources; it wasn't the boy's father. There was nothing the law could do.

"It didn't look that great," Stephanie said afterward, wiping tears from her eyes. "It didn't sound that great . . . but at least I stood up for myself."

It wasn't the first time Stephanie had been savaged by the Catholic Church. A dozen years earlier she had filed suit against the Archdiocese of Portland, hoping to get child support for her son. Then-Archbishop of Portland William Joseph Levada, now a cardinal in the Vatican and close advisor to Pope Benedict XVI, argued in a motion that the "birth of the plaintiff's child and the resultant expenses . . . are the result of the plaintiff's own negligence," specifically because she engaged in "unprotected intercourse." The church's attorney later told me that he was using every available legal argument to be an advocate for his client. Legal documents filed on behalf of Levada, one of the top Catholic leaders in the world, argued that Stephanie was negligent because she had *not* used birth control—even though birth control is a mortal sin in Catholicism.

At first, Uribe's religious order agreed to pay Stephanie $215 a month, a sum that was raised by $108 a few years later. But as her son's medical and other expenses grew, neither Uribe nor his order would pay more. Uribe summed up his position in a statement he sent to me before my story was published, which had a distinctly lawyerly, not a fatherly, tone to it:

> *The leadership of the order agreed to assume my obligations for child support. The order has continued to do so and has provided or offered more support than I have been [legally] obligated to pay. . . . I will continue keeping my son and his mom in my prayers.*

Stephanie said that Uribe had never attempted to contact his son—even after the boy sent him an album filled with photographs of himself and tried to interview him for an elementary school journalism project after the death of Pope John Paul II. Stephanie's son sat by the phone each afternoon for days, waiting for the call from his dad that would never come.

"It is unclear to me just who Arturo is praying to on our behalf," she said. "Certainly the God of my faith has no tolerance for a father shunning his own child."

During Stephanie's latest courtroom battle, the only spectators, besides myself, were her sister and brother-in-law. When the hearing was adjourned, I stood outside the courtroom doors, waiting to get a comment from the priest or his attorney. As the triumphant pair walked out, smiles on their faces, I introduced myself as a reporter with the *Los Angeles Times* and started to ask Uribe a question.

"He has no comment!" the startled attorney said. "No comment!"

"Do you want to comment, Father?" I asked.

"No comment," she said for him.

The two stalked off and disappeared into an elevator, angry that a reporter from Los Angeles had crashed the hearing. A few minutes later, the elevator doors opened again and out they came. The attorney marched back into the courtroom and tried to get the judge to put the public hearing under seal, a request he denied.

If it weren't so sad, it would have been funny. I could see why the Catholic Church would try to cover up the case. When my story ran, even the most faithful parishioners were shocked at how callously the church dealt with a priest's illegitimate son who needed money for food and medicine. (The embarrassed order voluntarily provided Stephanie with an adequate settlement after the story was published.) They were equally shocked that Cardinal Levada would have his name attached to a legal argument that claimed a woman had been negligent because she had *not* used birth control.

My problem was, it no longer shocked me. For years, I had

seen worse from priests, bishops and cardinals caught up in the church's sex abuse scandal. Even before Father Uribe's hearing began, I knew how it would play out.

As I walked into the long twilight of a Portland summer evening, I felt used up and numb. I wanted to be angry, but I was too depressed to muster the emotion. From a park bench, I called my wife on a cell phone and told her I was putting in for a new job at the paper.

· EIGHTEEN ·

"Welcome to the Edge"

It takes a long while for a naturally trustful person to reconcile himself to the idea that after all God will not help him.
— H. L. MENCKEN, *MINORITY REPORT*

I WAITED MORE than a year to come out of the closet and tell
people I no longer believed in God. I needed to let the ringing in
my ears subside from the pounding I took on the religion beat and
allow my new feelings about faith to solidify. I also wanted time
for my emotions to settle down. I had left the religion beat—and
my faith—with a lot of anger, and I didn't want to come across as
a spurned lover wanting to exact revenge on religion.

It wasn't hard to keep my lost faith a secret because I hadn't
talked openly about my religion, except to close friends. As I began
to confess to them what had happened to me, the typical reaction
was shock. My loss of faith had taken me years to recognize and
then grow used to, but they had to absorb the revelation in a single
conversation. One day I ran into Christopher Goffard, a journalist who had been just hired by *The Times*. I'd worked with him

some years earlier and was always a huge admirer of his work and his character. We had kept in touch over the years and had talked religion on several occasions. During our newsroom reunion, he off-handedly asked me something about my faith.

"Oh," I said, a sheepish smile on my face, "I don't believe in God anymore."

"What?" he said, as if he'd heard me wrong.

"I don't believe in God anymore, Chris."

"But you were so religious. What happened?"

"I lost my faith on the religion beat."

Christopher responded like any good reporter would have: "That's got to be a great story. Let's go have lunch soon and talk about it."

A few days later, over a plate of chicken tacos, rice and beans, I told him my story as best I could. As I fumbled through it, I realized I hadn't dissected exactly how I had arrived at this place. The reasons for my disbelief were all tangled up in a mess of confused feelings and blur of stories. I had always been a strong believer in Socrates's warning that "a life unexamined is not worth living," so I vowed to myself then to figure out a way to better understand my fall from faith.

Fortunately for me, the newspaper provided an opportunity for me to retrace my spiritual journey and publish my findings. *The Times* had recently started producing first-person pieces of journalism that instantly became some of the paper's best reads. One reporter wrote about discovering she had an extraordinarily high risk for cancer and how it affected her decision to marry, to quickly have children and to undergo a life-changing surgery. Another journalist described his quest to track the source of the salmonella poisoning that had left him hospitalized. A foreign correspondent wrote about the professional and personal dilemmas he faced in

Somalia because of a death threat he received shortly after two of his colleagues had been murdered. Each of those accounts was gripping. I wasn't sure whether my story would stack up against them. I knew the stories I reported on were interesting; I had no idea whether my own journey would be. But I decided to float the idea anyway.

I e-mailed the editor who approved these pieces. There were many good editors working at *The Times*, but Roger Smith stood apart. He looked like a distinguished attorney with his close-cropped white beard, neatly combed hair and conservative and tasteful (especially by newsroom standards) wardrobe of suits and slacks and sport jackets. He had an unflappable demeanor and a fairness and kindness that had endeared him to reporters usually not known for their charity toward editors. He also had an eye for a great story and a gift for elevating an average piece into an excellent one. It was always an honor to work with Roger. His stories ran under the front-page banner of "Column One," where, in theory, the paper's best read ran each day.

Roger e-mailed me back and said he loved the premise for the piece, but that I had to be prepared to reveal myself in ways that could be painful. We journalists, by habit, are not good at revealing ourselves. We are voyeurs who live through others. We step momentarily into the lives of people, scribble down what we see and then write about it in the third person. This was one of journalism's most attractive benefits. Each day, I had a free backstage pass to a different world. Among hundreds of experiences, I have interviewed the president of the United States; stood on the infield grass at Angel Stadium and flinched at the crack of the bat as the Los Angeles Angels took batting practice; and tagged along with a paparazzo, hunting celebrities in Beverly Hills, among many other adventures.

"Report the news, don't make it" was drilled into us from the beginning of our careers. Occasionally, when we can't avoid it, we refer awkwardly to ourselves in the third person, as in "the mayor handed *a visitor* in his office a gavel and said . . . ." Like actors who don't break the fourth wall with the audience, we don't break the wall that puts us in the story. But now I wasn't just part of the story, I *was* the story. I had to keep shooing away doubts—why volunteer for this? The backlash might be vicious: I would be seen as a spiritual wimp, or a traitor to Christianity. Maybe even a tool of the devil. I'd be ridiculed. I'd be told I'm going to hell. Even Jesus said the only unforgivable sin is speaking out against Him.

I wondered why exactly I wanted to write this up in the first place. Yes, I wanted to understand my own journey, but I could do that by writing in a private journal. The journalist part of me wanted to do it because I thought it might be a good story. But there were other motivations. I sensed that there were other people wrestling with doubts about God and religion, but who felt alone and forced to stay in the shadows as I had done. I remembered my relief while watching Julia Sweeney's *Letting Go of God*. Maybe my story could help others, too.

The darkest part of my heart wanted to show, in a very public way, how people who identified themselves as Christians had driven me away from a faith I loved. If someone with my desire for God could come away disillusioned by faith, then Christianity in its present form was in trouble, and someone should point that out to believers. I felt a little like the kid who declared that the emperor had no clothes, though I had no illusion that my revelation would open the eyes of others. It would be enough just to speak up for myself.

I printed out hundreds of stories I had written in my eight years on the religion beat and dove back into them. I flipped through

old notes I took from some of the larger stories. I stared at the photographs that appeared with my articles. I sketched out a timeline
containing key moments in my journey. I talked with old friends
and associates to get their recollections. I was researching a eulogy,
and it felt incredibly sad—and surreal. Part of me still couldn't
believe this had happened, especially as I relived the early joys of
the religion beat, now knowing the sorrow of how the story ended.
At times, I viewed my old self with disgust and disdain—at my
naïveté, my blind faith, my seemingly endless attempts to hold
onto my beliefs and the amount of time, measured in years, it took
to admit my religion was lost. I didn't like the portrait it painted of
me, and I was tempted to touch it up so I would look better.

Believe it or not, right then, I found a new savior: Howard
Stern, the radio personality. Howard is often criticized for being
crude and sophomoric, among other things, but his critics over-
look why millions of people love him: Howard Stern is utterly
honest about himself on the air. Few people are candid about their
lives, even in private; Howard tells listeners his most embarrassing
secrets and darkest thoughts each day. His show is often a stream
of consciousness straight from his id. It takes only a little listening
to Howard to learn that his father's constant criticism of him as a
child fuels his desire to succeed and still haunts him each day; that
he hates the diminutive size of his penis, the largeness of his nose
and the gangliness of his body; that going to a psychiatrist up to
four days a week hasn't cured his narcissism but has made him a
better father; that he loves lesbian stories and the sounds of fart-
ing; and that his relationship with his model girlfriend is growing
a little stale because he finds himself wanting to play chess on the
computer at night instead of going to bed with her.

If you listen to Howard for a few weeks, the chances are you are
going to like him—sometimes in spite of yourself. When someone

is so honest about his life, his failings, his fears and his prejudices, there is something very appealing about the openness. It's what makes testimonies in church—or at AA meetings—inspirational, touching and emphatic. As people pour out their hearts during a bout of honesty—sometimes revealing horrendous behavior—they always become more human, sympathetic and lovable. Everyone has messed up and is screwed up; it's the people being honest about it who gain our admiration. But it is a tough discipline to transfer outside the safety of a church sanctuary, an AA meeting hall or a psychiatrist's office.

As I started to write, Howard Stern was my role model. He was far more honest than the average Catholic bishop. I found myself going back and rewriting passages several times, trying to be more honest and penetrate my feelings more deeply with each pass, Howardizing them. I had to omit a few parts of my story because the people involved were unwilling to allow our private conversations into print. That aside, I tried not to flinch in the writing. By the time I was done, I had a 6,000-word essay. Roger Smith wielded his keyboard like a surgeon's knife and rather painlessly cut it down to a more newspaper-manageable 3,800 words. The piece was ready to go.

The worst part of a journalist's job is waiting for a story to be published. There is a terrible gap between the time a story is edited and when it is published. It feels as if you are approaching an uncharted waterfall and have reached the point of no return. My obsessive-compulsive instincts always kick in during these gaps, and at home (or at a restaurant or in a movie theater lobby), with a printout of the story in hand, I continue to recheck facts and torture myself over each sentence, wanting the nuance and flow to be just right. If I catch something before 10:30 p.m., I call the copy desk and beg them to make a last-minute change. After that, the paper is put to bed, though even that fact doesn't stop me from continuing to go over the story.

On the eve of publishing this story, I felt as though I were heading toward Niagara Falls in a tiny kayak. My intestines cramped. Ask reporters on the religion beat and they'll tell you the most vicious e-mails they ever receive as journalists are from people of faith who feel their beliefs have been slighted. The passion behind religion magnifies any perceived mistakes, slights or bias. My ears began to ring, anticipating how my inner thoughts and feelings and failings would be taken by readers who hold their faith sacred. With the echo effect of the Internet, there was no telling the repercussions. In our bedroom, I relayed this to Greer, just before she turned off the light at 11 p.m.

"There's no use worrying about it anymore," she said cheerfully. "There's nothing you can do to stop it now."

Thanks, dear. That was exactly my problem. It was too late, and I was sure that the whole thing was a stupid idea—and I had volunteered to write it! How stupid could I be?

Whenever I got myself in big trouble, my mind flashed back to the eighth grade. My best friend, Jon Schleimer, was spending the night, and I proposed a daring game: see who could come closer to the fuse of an M-80 with a lighted match. I even volunteered to go first. I struck the match and held it perilously close to a fuse that was attached to the equivalent of a quarter stick of dynamite. Suddenly I heard "Hssssssssssssssssssss"— the sickening sound of the fuse alit. My stomach sank, and my world went into slow motion. I pinched my fingers together on the unburned portion of the fuse, hoping to extinguish it. The fuse burned right through my fingers. Now I had only seconds left. The M-80 was about at my eye level, sitting on a windowsill in my bedroom. It was ten o'clock at night, and my parents were asleep in the next bedroom. I grabbed the M-80 to throw it into the corner of the room, thinking very clearly: How dumb could I be?

It exploded in my hand. In shock, with my ears ringing, I opened my hand and counted the fingers. Miraculously, they were all there, the explosion muffled by my closed fist. Smoke rose from my palm. Much of the skin on my hand had been blown away. As the pain arrived, I started to scream over and over and over again, "I'm so stupid! I'm so stupid! I'm so stupid!"

This is roughly how I felt now, waiting for my story to be published. I attempted to go to bed, but I couldn't get close to sleep. At midnight, I got up and decided to check *The Times* website. The page came up instantly at that late hour, and boom, there it was—the most prominent story on the page, along with a photo of me. The headline, which I saw for the first time, read "Religion beat became a test of faith: A reporter's work covering church sex scandals, religious tycoons and healers tests his beliefs—and triggers a revelation." Oddly, seeing it there on the web calmed me down. I had gone over the falls. No more anticipation. The story was out there, for better or worse. I read it from start to finish, though I had gone over it a hundred times before. Reading my stories on the web or in the paper always gave me some psychological distance. Sometimes, it made me sick to my stomach about the lameness of the writing or the holes in the reporting; other times, I was pleasantly surprised. With this piece, I was actually proud— a rare feeling for someone neurotically critical of his own work. I hated only the photo.

With adrenaline pumping through me, I had some time to kill before I'd be able to sleep. I absent-mindedly checked my work e-mail. It was 12:15 a.m., about an hour after the story had been posted on the web. Most of my stories generated no more than a dozen e-mail responses, often split down the middle between those offering praise and criticism. On routine stories, I might get only a stray e-mail or two. On larger stories—such as the Alaska Native story—I might get several hundred.

When I clicked on my in-box, I was stunned to see an entire screen full of e-mails responding to my story. I checked the next screen and the next and the next—all filled, about 100 messages in just one hour. Fear came roaring back, as I imagined the venom my story had unleashed. But then I scanned the subject lines: "Stay on the Beat," "Thanks," "!!!," "Offering Hope," "Congratulations on your hard-won spiritual progress." I opened the first e-mail that had come in:

> Thank you for writing so frankly about your journey. This was a truly beautiful piece and I believe that many of us Catholics who are struggling through understanding our church's horrible decisions to protect itself will be touched.

I opened the next one.

> My prayers are with you and your family! I pray as I write this letter to you that God is again working in your life. For without God in our life, we are nothing.

In the first batch of 100 e-mails, only two were negative. The rest, each in its own way, were positive. Atheists welcomed me to their world. Evangelical Christians tried to woo me back into the fold. Jews and Muslims wondered whether I might find their religion more appealing. The vast majority of the senders simply said they appreciated the honesty about my religious doubts and admitted that they had experienced similar uncertainties. As one Catholic priest wrote: "Welcome to the edge. There are lots of us here."

This kind of response was completely unexpected. It was humbling and comforting. There were people across the spiritual spectrum who had serious doubts. Many said they felt reluctant to express them. Their stories—tender and infused with raw honesty—poured in. More than 2,700 of them, in the end.

I kept trying to go to bed, only to find myself getting up to log in and seeing that scores more had arrived. The e-mails came from everyone: pastors who no longer believed in God but couldn't tell a soul; a priest deep within the Vatican who voiced his support and his own struggles; a theology professor at Fuller Seminary in Pasadena, California, who said his provost was going to make the story required reading for students; television star Kirk "Growing Pains" Cameron, who invited me out for coffee, believing he could bring me back to Christ.

Hundreds of believers put my name on prayer lists. My newsroom desk soon filled with books, pamphlets, workbooks and CDs that promised to get my relationship with God back on track. I received scores of lunch invitations from pastors and other concerned Christians wanting to keep me in the fold. People sent me links and notes showing how my story had become fodder for sermon topics, radio and television shows, bloggers, podcasts and websites, and university and seminary classes. I received requests to speak on radio and television shows, at churches and atheist meetings and at colleges. The tone of response caught me off guard, but it was what Jesus would have expected of his followers: plenty of love, understanding and gentleness. The outpouring of concern didn't rekindle my belief in Christianity, but it strengthened my faith in humanity.

My story provoked many questions, but two were asked again and again: In spiritual terms, what did I call myself—an agnostic, an atheist or something else? What did I tell my children about my loss of faith?

How to label myself was the toughest question. People—especially journalists—love labels. They are a convenient shorthand to put people neatly into a category. But my feelings about God weren't all that tidy. The truth was, I didn't know whether any label fit me. In a couple of interviews, I called myself a reluctant atheist, but that didn't really capture where I was. I disliked the term "agnostic"— it seemed too wimpy, implying I didn't quite have the guts to commit to atheism. I knew that I didn't believe in a God who intervened in earthly matters, but I didn't have a clue whether life here was put into motion by a creator or by cosmic accident. I leaned toward the creator explanation, because it seemed to me life couldn't come from nothing. But if so, who created the creator? This was a question I have yet to figure out. The closest I could get to a label was something along the lines of "skeptical deist," "wavering deist" or "reluctant atheist." My new God is probably close to the God that Thomas Jefferson and Albert Einstein believed in—a deity that can be seen in the miracles of nature, the complexity of DNA or the wonder of physics. But this God—and I'm not sure even He exists—is incompatible with the God of the Bible.

The answer as to what I told my children comes in two parts because of my children's ages. When the story was published, my two oldest boys were 18 and 15 and my two youngest were nine and six. My older sons had gone with us to Sunday school and youth nights at church but stopped attending when we did. We tapered off slowly enough that they didn't question why we no longer went to church, and I didn't offer an explanation. I didn't mind accepting responsibility for my eternal soul—if it turned out I had one—but I didn't want to be on the hook for sending my sons to hell, no matter how remote the possibility. I figured I'd let them decide what to believe. The morning the story came out, I sat down with my two older boys and asked them to read it. I told them I'd answer any questions they had. I was anxious about how they would react and felt guilty that I had avoided the subject until now. But I soon realized that I had once again underestimated how intuitive children are. Even with no words spoken, they had pretty much figured out where I sat with God. They said my story wasn't a surprise, and they had reached the same conclusion independently. It may sound odd, but I was proud of them for taking a critical look at religion. I'm also guessing that as teenagers, their spiritual journey was just beginning. If they do become Christians at a later time, that will be their decision, and I will respect it—though we'll have some lively debates during Thanksgiving dinner.

My two younger boys were a different story. Matthew, the nine-year-old, had only vague memories of church from long ago. Oliver was too young to remember anything. I'd been careful not to reveal my disbelief to them—it just didn't seem right. With the two little guys, we treat God a little like Santa Claus. They think he's real, and often ask questions about him that all kids ask; for instance, how does God see everyone at once? We answer as best we can. Yes, it's inconsistent with my new beliefs, but there will be time when they are older to fill them in about my thoughts on God and religion. I'm not ready to tell a six-year-old that there's no God and no heaven—or no Santa Claus.

I think many people responded to the story in part because I was not part of the new atheist movement that uses evangelical zeal to warn people about the stupidity and evils of religion. The best-selling trio of Christopher Hitchens, Richard Dawkins and Sam Harris are engaging polemists and, especially in Hitchens's case, dazzling writers. But I am not as confident in my disbelief as they are. Their disbelief has a religious quality to it that I'm not ready to take on. I look at my Christian, Jewish and Muslim friends—many of them intellectuals—and it stops me from insisting that only I know the truth. I know only what is true for me. There are times when I feel confident in my new position of disbelief and catch myself looking down my nose at the faithful who worship a God whom I believe doesn't exist. Is there much difference between the absurdity of Scientologists and their sacred E-Meters that allegedly trace the emotions of adherents, the Mormons and their belief that the Garden of Eden was in Missouri, and the Jews and Christians and their belief that the sound of trumpets caused the fortified walls of Jericho to come tumbling down?

Religious ceremonies I once thought were exquisitely beautiful—the ordination of a priest, for instance—now seem almost comical to me, what with the incense, the holy water, the costumes and the freshly minted priest prostrate on the floor. But then I remember where I was a short time ago, viewing nonbelievers with sadness because they didn't know the Lord. With all that has happened to me, I don't feel qualified to judge anyone else.

My piece did receive criticism, the most consistent being that I had witnessed the sinfulness of man and mistakenly mixed that up with a perfect God. I understand the argument but I don't buy it. If the Lord is real, it would make sense for the people of God, on average, to be superior morally and ethically to the rest of society. Statistically, they aren't. I also believe that God's institutions, on average, should function on a higher moral plain than governments or corporations. I don't see any evidence of this. It's hard to believe in God when it's impossible to tell the difference between His people and atheists.

In some conservative corners, the front-page play of the story was viewed with suspicion. The critics wondered whether the essay would have gotten the same exposure if I had had the reverse experience—moving from atheist to enthusiastic evangelical. Because it would have been equally interesting, I think the editors would have played it the same. There's plenty of bias in the newsroom, but usually a good story trumps it.

The harshest criticism came nearer to home. One close friend, an evangelical, said the story was irresponsible, damaging the Body of Christ and possibly causing people to turn away from God, forcing them to spend eternity separated from Him. This angers me because it reflects a double standard. People of faith naturally demand the right to express themselves and to be granted tolerance by those who disagree. Someone without faith should receive the same treatment. A Catholic neighbor bitterly accused me of going through a midlife crisis and wondered why I couldn't keep my doubts to myself. I argued that if I was experiencing a midlife crisis, I was cheating myself. I didn't have a Porsche or a mistress; I had just stopped believing in God. My first wife—whom I hadn't spoken with in years—called me at work and asked me what it felt like to have wasted most of my adult life believing in something that didn't exist.

My mother-in-law, a regular at Sunday Mass, simply chose to avoid the subject. Another relative on Greer's side of the family, however, decided to attack my disbelief head-on. He left a long message for me on my work voice mail, informing me that the reason I wasn't rich (like him) and the reason our boy Tristan had gotten Type 1 diabetes the year before was because I had turned my back on God and allowed Satan into my family. (He added that the devil also was to be credited with bringing on another of my boy's chronic ear infections.) If I were still talking to him, I'd love to ask why his loving God would allow an innocent child to be inflicted with a life-threatening illness—or even earaches—because of the sins of his father. Why wouldn't God protect the children and allow the devil to strike me? What kind of sadistic God did he worship? One e-mail I received from a church-going mother put it better than I could have. She had watched helplessly as two of her young children succumbed to a terrible disease.

> Your column . . . resonated with me because I find myself at the same spiritual crossroad. Having been raised to believe in a just God, my faith was shaken when my husband and I lost our ten-year-old child to Cystic Fibrosis, a congenital disease for which there is no cure.
>
> We felt betrayed that a loving God could bring such pain to parents who lived by the Golden Rule and followed the Ten Commandments. As we coped with our grief, we couldn't help but wonder why our love for our child wasn't enough to keep her alive and why our faith wasn't bringing us any comfort.
>
> After losing another child to the same illness, we came to the conclusion that we were naïve to believe in the Sunday School version of a deity that sits in a place called heaven and doles out rewards for good behavior and punishment for bad. We have only to look at world events and know this isn't true.
>
> So, who to pray to? An impersonal deity who lets bad things happen to good people? We still haven't figured that out. But it is difficult to abandon a life-long belief. As spiritual beings our souls cry out for something to fill the vacuum. I've even considered going back to church in the

hope of recapturing that leap of faith, but, as you so elo-
quently stated, "there's no faking your faith if you're honest
about the state of your soul."

Though I'm usually hypersensitive to criticism, this time none of it bothered me. I had detailed, as honestly as I could, my spiritual journey. The story was true. I knew this because it happened to me. No criticism would change that. I also felt deeply that I gave Christianity my best shot. Some people argued that I had never been saved (probably true) or that my faith was too shallow to withstand the rigors of the religion beat (probably not true; I'd argue my faith had been deeper than many). Several evangelicals said I lost my way when I headed down the path to the Vatican. Many Catholics believe I quit too soon. But I walked away from Christianity with no regrets, knowing I tried my best to get my faith back.

Epilogue

If the man doesn't believe as we do, we say he is a crank, and that settles it. I mean, it does nowadays, because now we can't burn him.

— MARK TWAIN, *FOLLOWING THE EQUATOR*

I RECENTLY SPOKE about my de-conversion to a group of students at Biola University, a Christian college in Southern California. At the end of my talk, one student asked what had taken the place of God in my life. The question caught me off-guard because I'd felt no vacuum created by God's exit. I didn't have a good answer for her at the time, but it's a good question and it deserves a serious answer.

It is easier to begin by explaining what else departed along with my belief, rather than what replaced it. Frustrating, endless confusion about the way the world worked disappeared. My life makes better sense now, without a personal God in the equation. My mind isn't troubled by the unsolvable mysteries that plagued me as a believer. C. S. Lewis wrote that "God whispers to us in our pleasures, speaks to us in our conscience, but shouts in our pains: It is His megaphone to rouse a deaf world." It is one of the many inspiring things said by apologists that makes absolutely no sense to me anymore. Why would God whisper to us in our pleasures but use pain as His megaphone? That sounds sick.

It can be lonely having no one in the universe as your protector. I now experience this most in the smallest of ways. For instance, I recently caught a particularly nasty strain of the stomach flu. It caused me to spend hours in the bathroom, even forcing me to lie down on the tile floor because I was too weak to return to my bed between bouts of vomiting. Shaking, sweating and in tremendous stomach pain, I became scared that I was profoundly—maybe terminally—ill. I found myself praying, just in case I had been wrong about this whole God thing.

"God, if you are real, please make me better," I pleaded. "I know I've turned away from you, but I could use a little help here. Please, God, I'm sorry." I didn't receive an instant healing, but I did get some insight into the saying that there are no atheists in foxholes. I wonder what would happen to my spirituality if I became terminally ill.

The laws of nature, circumstance and coincidence make more sense than the divine. A friend of mine reached the same conclusion as I did, but said the knowledge was a "major psychological catastrophe." It nearly drove him insane that no loving God was protecting his children. I had the advantage of seeing too much on the religion beat. I knew of many times when faithful Christian parents lost their children. I hadn't seen any evidence, anecdotal or otherwise, that children were safer with God watching over them. It reminds me of a bumper sticker peddled by atheists that makes the point rather bluntly: "20,000 children died of hunger today. Why should God answer YOUR prayers?"

At least now when I see injustice and suffering—my guitar teacher's beautiful boy, all of three years old, died of a brain tumor the day I'm writing this—the randomness is just that. A God in heaven didn't sit by while the little boy died. To simply know that tragic stuff just happens is a much more satisfying and realistic answer.

What the Bible promises—peace and serenity—I've found in larger measures as a nonbeliever. My morals and values haven't changed. I used to see my innate beliefs about right and wrong as something God-given. I now see them as a product of tens of thousands of years of evolution, encoded in my DNA to best insure the survival of my family and myself. A sociopath, not an atheist, has no conscience and no ability to tell right from wrong.

As a believer, I tried to live up to the standards for living outlined in the Bible. (That is, the generous and loving parts of the Scripture.) Nothing has changed since my loss of faith. I still try to follow the same general ideals—morals and values that I'd argue are inherent to each human being. I still find myself stumbling, but now I don't blame Satan. Usually when I do wrong, it's due to selfishness and poor judgment overcoming common sense, self-restraint and experience. Truth be told, my actions aren't much different from when I was a Christian. Many of my basic life struggles are the same. I still worry too much. Hold grudges for too long. Lie, usually in small ways, too easily. Drink more than I should. Am too impatient with the kids. Et cetera, et cetera, et cetera.

What's gone is the placebo of faith that was supposed to transform me into a better person, to protect me, to guide me and eventually to usher me into heaven. The placebo had stopped working long ago. And when I admitted that I had been taking the sugar pill of faith, relief swept over me. My increasing doubts about Christianity hadn't been a sign of weakness or lack of faith or a skirmish with the devil. I had only been slowly, even unconsciously, heading for the truth.

So what *has* taken the place of God in my life? A tremendous sense of gratitude. I sense how fortunate I am to be alive in this thin sliver of time in the history of the universe. This gives me a renewed sense of urgency to live this short life well. I don't have eternity to fall back on, so my focus on the present has sharpened.

I find myself being more grateful for each day and more quickly making corrections in my life to avoid wasted time. I've tightened my circle of friends, wanting to maximize time with the people I love and enjoy the most. I've become more true to myself because I'm not as worried about what others think of me. This may be due in part to maturity, but it also has to do with knowing what's of real importance in my one and only life. The sound of a ticking clock, counting down the minutes of my life, is now nearly impossible to get out of my head. This isn't a bad thing; it's the background beat to a well-lived life.

My teenage son Tristan and I watched *Fight Club* on television the other night. One of its themes is that when people have a brush with death, their lives become richer because they appreciate them more. In one scene, after nearly killing a mini-mart attendant for no reason, the film's antagonist, Tyler Durden, is asked, "What the fuck was the point of that?"

He answers, "Tomorrow will be the most beautiful day of Raymond K. Hessel's life. His breakfast will taste better than any meal you and I have ever tasted."

That's what losing God has done for me. Permanent death—I don't think I have the escape hatch to heaven anymore—now sits squarely in front of me, unmoving as I rapidly approach. And you know what? My breakfast *does* taste better. I feel the love of my family and friends more deeply. And my dreams for my life have an urgency to them that won't allow me to put them off any longer. I can no longer slog through each day, knowing that if my time on Earth isn't used to its fullest potential, it's no big thing, that I have eternity with God ahead of me.

I do miss my faith, as I'd miss any longtime love, and have a deep appreciation for how it helped me mature over 25 years. Even though I've come to believe my religion is based on a myth, its benefits are tangible and haven't evaporated along with my faith. But when believers try to bring me back to the fold, I want to tell them they are wasting their time. It's hard to describe my utter lack of belief; there's just nothing there—there's no smoldering ember that can be coaxed back into a flame.

To borrow Buddha's analogy, I've just spent eight years crossing a river in a raft of my own construction, and I'm now standing on a new shore. My raft was not made of dharma, like Buddhism's, but of things I gathered along the way: knowledge, maturity, humility, critical thinking and the willingness to face my world as it is, and not how I wish it to be. I don't know what the future holds in this new land. I don't see myself crossing the river back to Christianity, as many of my former brothers and sisters in Christ predict and pray for. I don't see myself adopting a new religion. My disbelief in a personal God now seems cemented to my soul. Other kinds of spirituality seem equally improbable.

Besides, I like my life on this unexplored shore. It's new, exciting and full of possibilities. I wouldn't have predicted it as a Christian, but I now feel wonderfully free—not to go on a binge of debauchery like the Prodigal Son, but to stop wrestling with the mysteries of Christianity. I can stop dreaming up excuses for the shortcomings of my faith. I felt relief when I put down what had become the heavy mantle of Christianity. In my case Jesus was wrong when he said, "Come to me, all you who are weary and burdened, and I will give you rest. Take my yoke upon you and learn from me, for I am gentle and humble in heart, and you will find rest for your souls. For my yoke is easy and my burden is light." (Matthew 11:28–30)

I do know one thing for sure: I will never cling to my disbelief as I did to my Christianity. I long ignored the heaviness of Jesus' yoke and the burden of faith because those facts would have put my beliefs in jeopardy.

My last major story on the religion beat detailed how DNA tests—which revealed descendants of American Indians came from Asia, not the Middle East—had undercut the traditional reading of the Book of Mormon and the words of their prophets. Soon after my story appeared, a Mormon organization called the Sunstone Education Foundation invited me to be part of a panel discussion on "The Book of Mormon in Light of DNA Studies: Where Are We Now?" When I arrived at Claremont Graduate University's School of Religion for the symposium, I wondered what I had gotten myself into. The lecture hall was filled with devout Mormons, and I was the only non-Latter-day Saint on the panel. I felt as though I had entered the lions' den—though the lions were remarkably tame.

Despite the odds against me, the evening was going along pleasantly enough, with some interesting discussion from scholars and church historians. When it was my turn, the audience politely listened. I thought I would escape the harsh criticism I had anticipated would come my way. But then the last panelist, Clifton Jolley, spoke.

I didn't know Jolley, but within Mormon circles, he had gained some fame as an entertaining speaker, poet and columnist. With his gray goatee, glasses and narrow face, he looked like a harmless artist of some sort. But then he launched into a bizarre, occasionally funny, often angry 45-minute tirade directed mostly at me.

Early on, he bellowed, "Shame on the *Los Angeles Times* for frightening us. Shame on the *Los Angeles Times* for pretending that it has discovered something that really matters. [That Native Americans] are not Hebrews."

He took offense that the newspaper would even wade into Mormon matters.

"This isn't your story, it's our story, and we'll tell it any damn way we please," he said. "And if you think the story we have to tell isn't a good story, then screw the *Los Angeles Times!*"

He went on to say that Native Americans shouldn't worry about the DNA evidence because "being Chinese isn't half bad. . . ." He next lashed out against science: "If you're a good scientist, a world-class physicist, you're out to murder God . . .

"Screw you, *Los Angeles Times!*" he shouted. "They thought our stories could be proven true or false using the false tools of the apostate priesthood of science."

He wrapped up by suggesting (I think) that the stories in the Book of Mormon didn't have to be accurate for the faith to be real.

"After we have been defeated and all our stories proven untrue, we will perhaps come to know the more important reason and the only question that ever is—not whether the stories are true, but whether we are true to our stories," Jolley said.

What did that *mean*—that it's not whether the stories are true, but whether we are true to our stories?

Despite Jolley's attack on me—which included, as I recall, an ample amount of finger pointing—I had an odd sense of serenity that night. I didn't feel my natural urge to fight back. I sensed his out-of-proportion response was the result of someone trying desperately to defend a faith that had one too many fault lines running through it. Facts were stubborn things, so he resorted to a smokescreen of angry rhetoric, biting humor, sarcasm and clever phrases. I suspect Jolley, like most of his Mormon brothers and sisters, believed his religion had a good thing going—the church members loved each other, looked after those who had fallen on hard times, raised good families—and he didn't need outsiders, or science, to cast doubts on the operation. Mormonism worked, so leave it alone. If too many people chipped away at it, if too much truth were revealed, the foundation that Jolley and other Mormons built their life upon might give way. At least that's what happened to me with my religion.

Leaving the Claremont campus, I thought about how I had not been much different from Clifton Jolley most of my adult life. I had defended my faith rather blindly—if only in my own mind—and refused to acknowledge the reality before me. Because I *knew* Jesus was real—I had felt Him entering my heart, after all—attacks on Him and my faith had to be false. I believed any doubts I had were rooted in *my* shortcomings and not in the veracity of Christianity. Also, I found it nearly impossible to walk away from something that promised to provide comfort, guidance, community, protection, a sense of purpose and salvation. Americans spend billions of dollars on products that promise weight loss. Imagine how much more powerful the lure of religion is.

I recently unearthed an essay I wrote in 2003 during a week-long seminar for religion reporters at the Poynter Institute, a journalism training ground in St. Petersburg, Florida. Near the end of the week, we were asked to write something extremely personal about ourselves, an oddly easy task because the dozen reporters from across the country and Europe had gotten remarkably close in a short time and trusted each other with secrets we couldn't tell our newsroom colleagues. I titled my piece "Spiritual Suicide." It read in part:

> *I am on a narrow ledge, far above the ground. The toes of my bare feet are wrapped over the concrete edge. I'm not even leaning against the building anymore. I don't care anymore. After two years of this, jumping would bring me rest.*
>
> *A plunge wouldn't drop me onto unforgiving pavement far below. It's not that kind of act. Instead, my leap would be into the warm, inviting pool of unbelief.*
>
> *I imagine the water would engulf me like a kind of reverse baptism. It would wash away all the doubts I've had about God. Once I step off this last ledge of faith, the answer [to tough questions such as why good people suffer] becomes easy: A loving God doesn't let it happen because He doesn't exist . . .*
>
> *I'm seeing my spiritual life atrophy into skin and bones. God help me.*

Reading this now, I'm amazed that it took another three years to admit to myself that I had lost my faith, and 12 more months to tell my friends and family—a testament to the power of faith and my lack of courage. The essay reminded me of exactly how I was feeling. It was as though I were sitting at a no-limit poker game, knowing that I should push my stacks of chips to the middle of the table and say with confidence, "All in." But I couldn't. I was frozen, too scared to move.

It took me a while, but now I've gone all in.

I guess time will tell whether my decision was foolish or smart. But I have no regrets. For me, it was the move I had to make.

Index

Stern, Howard, 263–64
Story of a Soul (Therese of Lisieux), 199
Strobel, Lee, 14, 197
Sundborg, Father Stephen, 219–20
Sunstone Education Foundation, 280
Supreme Court, California, 111
Supreme Court, U.S., 82–83
Survivors Network for those Abused by
    Priests, 97, 146
Swaggert, Jimmy, 177
Swaim, Will, 2–4, 8
Sweeney, Julia, 247–50, 262
Swinburne, Richard, 208

Tamayo, Father Santiago ("Henry"),
    100–101
TBN. *See* Trinity Broadcasting Network
televangelists, 13, 17, 70, 167, 173–95
    media characterization of, 29
Temple Beth El, 65
Ten Commandments for religion jour-
    nalists, 80–84
Teresa, Mother, 199–200
Theo Lacy Branch Jail, 87–88
Therese of Lisieux, St., 120, 199
This Is Your Day! (TV show), 178
Thomas Aquinas, St., 14, 120
Thompson, Hunter, 58–59
Thousand Pines Christian Camp &
    Conference Center retreat, 16–22,
    203
Tilton, Robert, 175–76
Times Community News, 33, 53, 56–57
tithing, 47, 70, 124–25, 205
transubstantiation, 84

Tribune Company, 56
Trinity Broadcasting Network, 177, 180,
    187, 188–95
Trinity Foundation, 174, 175–77,
    179–80
Twain, Mark, 207, 253, 275

Unitarian Church, 121, 246
United States v. Ballard (1944), 82–83
University of California, Irvine, 58–59,
    64
Urban VI, Pope, 161
Urell, Monsignor John, 110–11, 113–14
Uribe, Father Arturo, 254–58

Vandenkolk, William, 186–87

Wall, Patrick, 216–17, 226
Warren, Kay, 70
Warren, Rick, 68–71, 166–67, 178
Washington Post, 29, 80
Waters, David, 80–84
"Way of St. James" pilgrimage, 203
Weight of Glory, The (Lewis), 76
Whitmore, Kelly, 191
"Why Does God Hate Amputees?"
    (website), 209–10
Winter, Damon, 226, 230
Woodward, Bob, 59
World Vision, 235
worship music, 9–10, 20

Ybarra, Anthony, 87
Young, Brigham, 130
Young, Father Roy, 6, 10

ABOUT THE AUTHOR

William Lobdell, 48, is an award-winning journalist and a visiting faculty member at the University of California, Irvine. He lives in Costa Mesa, California, with his wife, Greer, and four boys. He competes in the sport of triathlon and is an Ironman. www.williamlobdell.com